GROUPS IN
PROCESS

Study Questions

After you have read this chapter, you should be able to answer the following questions completely and accurately:

1. What are nine basic levels of communication?
2. What are three distinctions between small group communication and dyadic communication?
3. What is the definition of a small group?
4. What is the definition of small group communication?
5. What is the relationship of small group performance to individual performance?
6. Are small groups or individuals superior in the amount of time required for completion of the task?
7. What does the term *process* refer to in the study of small groups?

Ken Karp

1   Introduction

As we noted in the Preface to the first edition of *Groups in Process*, this is a book about small group communication written by a small group. Our basic premise in writing the text was that a group should produce a more complete, relevant, and accurate manuscript than any one of us could write alone. Since the publication of the first edition, several significant variables have affected this book as well as the field of small group communication. The untimely death of our friend and colleague, Bob Kibler, was devastating to those of us who worked with him on the first edition of this book. The contributions Bob made to the field of speech communication and the earlier edition of this book, of course, will carry on through this and future editions. However, the absence of Bob's physical presence was deeply felt.

Bob's absence made our "small group" both smaller and different. The interactions in editing and revising were affected by the new group structure and composition. Moreover, the field of small group communication has also changed during the four years since the book was published initially. These changes, particularly with an increased emphasis on applied small group interactions and conflict management and resolution, affected our orientation to the project and our level, quality, and frequency of interactions.

Our text, in some ways, is a bridge between the traditional discussion book and the newer interpersonal and small group communication texts. The second edition, hopefully, maintains those elements and content areas that were useful and relevant in the first edition. This edition strives to maintain the balance between traditional and newer approaches to teaching small group communication. The balance in the text reflects some degree of compromise. This, of course, is one obvious characteristic of a group decision.

Substantial changes were made in this edition on the basis of many solicited and unsolicited reviews. The comments and criticisms from those of you who used the first edition helped "streamline" the book and make it more relevant to the current and future needs of Discussion and Small Group Communication courses. Those of you familiar with the first edition will

Preface

notice that there has been a major reorganization of chapters. One complete chapter was deleted, several sections from previous chapters were combined into new chapters, and a totally new chapter on Conflict Management and Resolution has been added. The new chapter was included at the request of many of you who reviewed the manuscript for this edition. Of course, new and relevant research findings have also been added, when appropriate, throughout the text; new illustrations have been added; and new suggestions for additional reading and discussion have been included.

We have maintained our goal in the first edition of producing a teachable book. This edition contains a variety of teaching aids, including study questions, ideas for discussion, selected projects and activities, and annotated additional suggested readings. We hope that our concern about teachability will help make this edition a *textbook*—not just a book about small group communication. The teacher's manual for the book also has been revised. Our thanks goes to Kittie Watson for preparing the teacher's manual for the first edition of *Groups in Process*, as well as to Debbie Roach for creating the new manual for the second edition.

We would like to thank the following reviewers for their comments, criticisms, and encouragement: Dan Curtis, Central Missouri State University; Franklin Boster, Arizona State University; Lawrence Frey, Wayne State University; and Pat Smith-Pierce, William Rainey Harper College.

We can never satisfactorily acknowledge all of our students, friends, and colleagues who made this book possible, but they know who they are. We do want to acknowledge two people who helped to make this second edition possible—Kittie Watson and Kathy Shumaker. Although Kittie and Kathy both helped in a variety of ways in reviewing and refining the manuscript, they also made substantial revisions to chapters which should be acknowledged. Kittie completely revised the chapter on Listening and Feedback in Small Groups, and Kathy revised the chapter on Nonverbal Communication in the Small Group. Their good energy and willingness to become "temporary" members of our small group are greatly appreciated.

We also would like to thank Joyce Heeke and Irene Touchton for their patience and perseverance in typing portions of the manuscript.

We hope that the second edition will suit your personal and instructional preferences and instructional needs. As before, we welcome any comments, criticisms, or suggestions you might have for future revisions.

PRENTICE-HALL, INC.
Englewood Cliffs, New Jersey 07632

LARRY L. BARKER
Auburn University

KATHY J. WAHLERS
Lake City Community College

DONALD J. CEGALA
Ohio State University

ROBERT J. KIBLER   SECOND EDITION

GROUPS IN PROCESS

An Introduction to Small Group Communication

Library of Congress Cataloging in Publication Data
Main entry under title:

GROUPS IN PROCESS.

Includes bibliographies and index.
1. Small groups. 2. Communication in small groups.
3. Decision-making, Group. I. Barker, Larry L. (date)
HM133.G76 1983   302.3′4   82-9824
ISBN 0-13-365254-8   AACR2

Editorial/production supervision by Marion Osterberg
Cover photo courtesy of Ken Karp
Cover design by 20/20 Services, Inc.
Manufacturing buyer: Ron Chapman

Printed in the United States of America

10   9   8   7   6   5   4   3   2   1

ISBN 0-13-365254-8

Prentice-Hall International, Inc., *London*
Prentice-Hall of Australia Pty. Limited, *Sydney*
Editora Prentice-Hall do Brasil, Ltda., *Rio de Janeiro*
Prentice-Hall Canada Inc., *Toronto*
Prentice-Hall of India Private Limited, *New Delhi*
Prentice-Hall of Japan, Inc., *Tokyo*
Prentice-Hall of Southeast Asia Pte. Ltd., *Singapore*
Whitehall Books Limited, *Wellington, New Zealand*

Contents

Chances are, since you're reading this book, you've already thought about the role small groups play in your daily life. You might even have stopped to think about the number of groups you participate in on a regular basis. If you haven't thought about these things lately (*lately*, literally interpreted, means, "in the last twenty-one years"), stop and do so now. Are you a member of two groups? twenty? two hundred? What kinds of groups are they? When several students took time to list the number of groups in which they participate, most of them found that they were a member of from twenty to thirty small groups. Of course the students noted that not all of the groups were continuing ones. Some existed for only a few minutes or hours (e.g., small group projects in a biology lab). Others were in existence for years and will probably continue indefinitely (e.g., civic, social, or religious organizations). The students also noticed differences in the way they react in different groups, differences in reactions from others in different groups, and the wide variety of decision-making strategies used in different small groups.

We hope this book will help sharpen your personal awareness of communication behavior in small groups and provide principles to improve your ability to contribute in small group interactions. It assumes that you do have and have had experiences in small group communication and that you will have an opportunity to apply some of the principles and concepts presented in this book in real life situations.

Small groups are important to you not only in interpersonal relationships, but also in such areas as education, politics, business, industry, and religion. Although you may not be a direct participant in many such groups, they often have a direct bearing on your future and your happiness. For example, most businesses and government agencies use committees to make recommendations and decisions, and most committees use the principles of group dynamics in their interactions. This text should help you understand some of the ways in which decisions are made in groups and some of the forces which shape and modify small group communication.

The subtitle of this text indicates that two primary concepts will be discussed: small groups and communication. Our view is that, although "communication" may be discussed without reference to a given level (e.g., interpersonal, mass, cultural), and "small group" may be discussed without reference to communication (e.g., primary groups, social reference groups), the combination of the concepts results in a unique interrelationship. Consequently, in this text, communication will be discussed primarily as it relates to small groups, and small groups will be examined from a communication viewpoint, as opposed to a sociological or psychological viewpoint.

By way of definition, a *sociological* approach to small group interaction would emphasize the role of small groups in establishing and maintaining social order. The emphasis would also be on pressures provided by small groups to conform to social norms. A sociologist would also be concerned with the function small groups serve to help link the individual to society as a whole.

The *psychological* approach to small group behavior focuses on the role groups play in helping people adjust to their world and its problems. Group therapy is used by clinical psychologists and psychiatrists to help individual members feel accepted and secure; T-groups and sensitivity groups are also tools of psychologists and social psychologists. Some of these concepts are discussed briefly in this text, but our major concern is with the broader area of small group behavior—that which takes place on a day-by-day basis in education, business, government, civic organizations, and social settings.

Our approach focuses on a *process* or *systems view* of small group communication (see Chapter 2). However, elements from all approaches may be found in the text, and we attempt to provide both traditional and contemporary approaches to the study of small group communication. The following section attempts to identify the interrelationships among levels of communication, with special emphasis on the relative status of small group communication.

LEVELS OF COMMUNICATION

Several communication scholars (Ruesch and Bateson, 1950; Wiseman and Barker, 1974) have attempted to develop a hierarchy of communication levels, proceeding from the simple to the complex. The levels are identified in Figure 1.1.

A description of defining characteristics of different levels of human communication is provided in Ruesch and Bateson (1950, Chapter 11). Our primary concern here is to illustrate the relationship of small group communication to other levels. Note in Figure 1.1 that small group communication is a subclass of interpersonal communication, near the middle hierarchy of levels in terms of perceived complexity. The diagram suggests that intrapersonal communication and dyadic communication skills may precede or be combined with small group communication skills.[1] In essence, small group communication may be viewed as a level of interpersonal communication which incorporates intrapersonal and dyadic (verbal and nonverbal) elements, but which differs as a function of the increased number of potential interactions possible. (For a formula to compute the number of interactions possible in small groups of differing sizes, see Nixon, 1979.)

[1]Of course, the nonverbal (object) level also may interact with small group communication. Examples of such interaction might be the environment in which a small group communicates, the physical arrangement of chairs in the room, or music in the room. (For additional information related to nonverbal communication in small groups, see Chapter 8.)

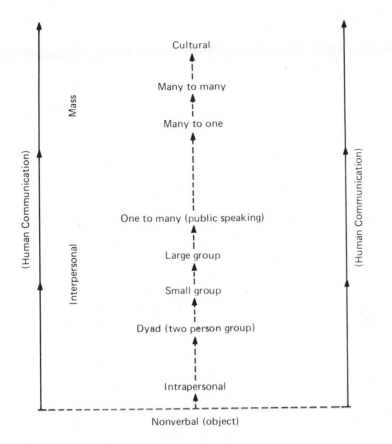

FIGURE 1.1 Levels of Communication

In addition to the increased possibility for interaction inherent in small groups, there are other important distinctions between small group communication and other levels, particularly the dyad. Although some scholars identify dyads (two-person groups) as small groups, we do not because of several important differences between them. Perhaps the most important distinction is in the potential for information sharing and exchange. Figures 1.2 and 1.3 illustrate differences in the number of original combinations of ideas possible between a dyad and a three-person group. The different shadings represent areas in which new combinations of ideas are possible by putting members together with original ideas and allowing them to interact.

What this means in real-life discussion groups is that if member A has an idea which is not fully developed, it is possible that member B might be able to provide some insight on the basis of previous training or experience. However, by adding the background and experience of both member B and

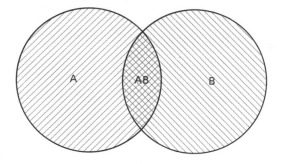

FIGURE 1.2 Dyad (One Combination)

member C, we increase the possibilities of adding valuable information *four* times. As group members are added, the potential for new combinations of ideas among members increases geometrically (i.e., increases several times the actual number of members added). Of course, there is a point of diminishing returns (probably at about fifteen participants) in which adding other members is of little (or negative) value, because possibilities for interaction are limited. It is at this point that the group ceases to have a basic quality of the *small* group: potential for interaction with every member of the group.

Another difference between the small group and the dyad is that there is an observer or "audience" present. In a two-person group there is just a speaker and a listener—no one else. In a small group (three or more), there is always someone else present, usually observing or listening, while the other two people are interacting. This quality of a group is often termed the *quality of co-action*. The presence of the observer does affect group interaction—sometimes positively and sometimes negatively, depending on the topic, the composition of the group, and a host of other factors.

Another critical difference between the dyad and the small group is the potential for a majority (and a consequent minority) to occur in the latter. In the dyad, if there are differing views, no majority can form. If participants disagree on an issue, there is an even split of views. In a small group, a majority coalition can form, creating sensitive or disruptive relationships within the group. Persuasion can be used both in dyads and small groups, but in the dyad it is the only available tool for opinion change (except for physical violence). Voting (by majority rule) is possible in the small group. Consequently, in small groups the number of members present (to outvote the opposition) may be more important than logical arguments or evidence.

Differences between small group communication and higher levels such as public speaking, mass communication, and cultural communication are probably obvious. Perhaps the differences between small group communication and communication in larger groups are not so apparent. The

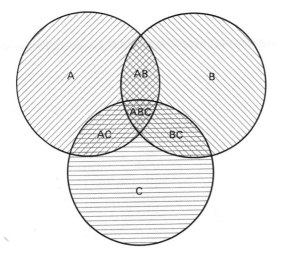

**FIGURE 1.3 Basic Small Group
(Three-Person, Four Combinations)**

following section in which the concepts group and small group are defined should help clarify the differences between these two subclasses of interpersonal communication.

PRINCIPLES

1. There are at least three important distinctions between small group communication and communication in the dyad.
   a. The potential for information sharing is greater in the small group.
   b. There is always an observer or audience present in the small group.
   c. There is a potential for a majority to occur in the small group.

SMALL GROUP COMMUNICATION DEFINED

Before determining the working definitions of small group communication, we should first agree on an acceptable definition of the term *group*. In the broadest sense a group may be defined merely as a collection of individuals. However, this broad definition does not discriminate between random aggregates of individuals and collections of people who meet for a purpose. A definition by an early sociologist, although postulated over a half century ago, adds some important qualifications to the broad definition above:

The term "group" serves as a convenient sociological designation for any number of people, larger or smaller, between whom such relations are discovered that they must be thought of together . . . a number of persons whose relations to each other are sufficiently impressive to demand attention (Small, 1905, p. 495).

Small's definition helps distinguish between a *group* and what some sociologists and communication scholars term an *aggregate* or *class*. The latter terms simply refer to any collection of individuals (i.e., our initial broad definition).

The term *small group* has special meaning to sociologists, social psychologists, and communication scholars. The qualifier *small* refers to more variables than just size. The following definition suggests dimensions of a small group which are generally associated with the term. *A small group is a collection of individuals, from three to fifteen in number, who meet in face-to-face interaction over a period of time, generally with an assigned or assumed leader, who possess at least one common characteristic, and who meet with a purpose in mind.* Let's discuss each of the elements in the definition separately. (For other definitions and discussions, see Nixon, 1979, and DeLamater, 1974.)

Group Size

The absolute size limit of a small group is often debated by small group scholars. The fewest number, three, is generally agreed upon (although some scholars do not distinguish between the dyad, two, and a group of three or more). In this text we differentiate between the dyad and the three-person group because the purposes and interaction patterns of each differ significantly. Our upper limit for a small group (fifteen) is rather arbitrary. The maximum size depends on the maturity of the group, the style of leadership, the personalities of group members, and a variety of other variables. When the potential for face-to-face interaction ceases among all group members, then it has exceeded the upper limit for a "small" group. In most groups the upper limit will be about fifteen, in some groups it may only be seven, while in still others it may exceed twenty.

Face-to-Face Interaction

The face-to-face interaction element in our definition may be questioned by some critics. However, because the focus of our text is on small group communication, groups which do not meet for face-to-face interactions are not our primary concern. In addition, small groups not meeting in face-to-face interaction possess characteristics of larger groups—not those generally associated with the "small" group.

Time Period

Groups which meet over a period of time have somewhat different characteristics from those meeting on a "one-shot" basis. Although this quality of continuation may not apply to all groups who are composed of relatively few individuals, it is usually included in the general connotation of the term small group. Several examples in this text refer to one-shot groups. In addition, much research cited later is based on experiments employing groups formed solely for the purpose of the experiment. Our inclusion of this ongoing quality, in our general definition, is based on the fact that groups which meet over a period of time gain maturity and communication skills difficult to obtain in a temporary group. Thus, from the viewpoint of small group communication framework, this ongoing quality is an important aspect of most small groups.

Leadership

The role of leadership in a small group is discussed widely by writers of discussion and small group textbooks. Many writers insist that a designated leader must be present in order for a group to function effectively. Our view is that whether or not a leader is designated, one or more people in a group generally will assume leadership duties. Thus, our definition acknowledges the potential for leadership, but does not restrict our description of small groups only to those with assigned or elected leaders.

Shared Characteristic

The presence of a common (i.e., shared) characteristic, helps discriminate the small group from the "small aggregate" (see our discussion of this issue with regard to the term "group" above). Shared characteristics may range from having similar religious beliefs to sharing common goals for a class project. Such additional variables as ethnic background, race, geographic location, social class, economic level, life-style, and educational level often create common bonds among people in small groups. The common characteristic may be assigned, assumed, or self-identified, but it must exist.

Common Purpose

Finally, the presence of a common purpose or goal, be it specific or very broad, binds the small group together and gives it a basic level of "cohesiveness" (see Chapter 4). You will find that groups which are formed with no concrete goal in mind generally break up or gradually disintegrate. It is goal-directed behavior which holds group members together, and the more relevant the goal is to the group members, the more motivation group members will have to maintain the group and their identity in it.

This definition of small group provides a basis for defining the phrase *small group communication*. We simply change emphasis from the structure of a group to the communication process involved to form our definition. Thus, our definition of small group communication is: *the process of verbal and nonverbal face-to-face interaction in a small group.*[2]

PRINCIPLES

1. A small group is a collection of individuals from three to fifteen in number, who meet in face-to-face interaction over a period of time, generally with an assigned or assumed leader, who possess at least one common characteristic, and who meet with a purpose in mind.
2. Small group communication may be defined as the process of verbal and nonverbal face-to-face interaction in a small group.

AN OVERVIEW OF EFFICIENCY AND OTHER CONSIDERATIONS IN THE SMALL GROUP

People from other countries often remark that Americans always seem to be in a hurry. As individuals we frequently think that the day is never long enough. Rather than attempting to increase the amount of time to perform our tasks, an alternate solution is to use the time we have more efficiently. Working in small groups may in some cases increase our individual efficiency. Research concerning the efficiency of the group versus the efficiency of the individual has been confined to two areas—performance and use of time—which will be noted here briefly along with other advantages of operating in a group. This section should give you a preliminary overview of some conditions under which groups tend to be more efficient as well as conditions under which groups may be less efficient than individuals.

Performance

A very common finding in the research literature is that differences between groups and individuals are frequently insignificant (Davis, 1969). In fact, there is considerable evidence that group performance is sometimes

[2]This definition reflects an emphasis on private (not public) small group communication. The definition is concerned with intragroup communication, *not* communicating *via* the group to an audience or outside agencies.

inferior to the performance of individuals (Shaw, 1980). However, when achievement is stressed with regard to good, correct, or early responses, the group will probably function better than will individuals (Davis, 1969).

Groups generally are more efficient than individuals in the recall of information (Perlmutter and de Montmillin, 1952; Perlmutter, 1953). If a task concerns naming all of the past presidents of the United States, for example, groups rather than individuals probably could list a greater number of presidents. Presumably the ability of groups to recall more information is due to their greater capacity to store information (e.g., a group of five individuals potentially could store five times more information than one individual). This ability to recall information, however, may be partially dependent on *cues*. As in brainstorming (see Chapter 7), the response of one individual may trigger or cue a response from another individual.

Correct or accurate responses are made more often by groups than by individuals (Shaw, 1980). If you stop and think for a moment, the generalization is very logical. Suppose you were a member of the student government's finance committee and were assigned to formulate a budget for the student senate's consideration. If there were five conscientious members on the committee, do you believe the group or a single individual would produce a budget which most accurately reflected the needs and wishes of the student body?

We would bet our money on the finance committee rather than on the individual. Why? The primary reason is that the combined estimation on the budget of the several members of the finance committee is more likely than a single individual to reflect accurately the needs of students. Several members will be able to research the issue and reach a combined judgment more effectively than could one person.

Fewer errors in judgment will be made by groups than by individuals (Brandstätter, 1978). This generalization is related to the two previous generalizations. It seems reasonable that fewer errors (and, perhaps, greater accuracy) in judgment will be made as a greater variety of alternatives is considered. Consider the potential resources present in the five members of the finance committee mentioned above. The committee is more likely to come up with alternatives than will a single individual. By pooling information, the group provides the potential for solving a problem that an individual may not attack successfully. There is more than one "head" in the group in which information has been stored, and this "stored data" in several "memory banks" is available for the group's use. The net result is more alternatives than those produced by a single person. Consideration of a large number of alternatives in the judgmental process will produce a better decision.

If we continued to add members to the finance committee, would the alternative suggestions increase proportionally to the number added to the committee? Probably not. We would find a point of diminishing return. If we start with a three-person finance committee and continue to add members to it, we would expect a rapid increase in the number of solutions generated, as the first few individuals were added to the committee. After that, the increase in solutions would begin to decline and reach a diminishing point. The point is that there should be enough members in the group to ensure that a variety of alternatives is presented. Equally important is that the group consider the alternatives in an effort to avoid making an erroneous decision. Such consideration is not possible with too many group members.

You should not conclude from these generalizations that groups are always superior to individuals in making accurate, error-free judgments. This is not so. A classic illustration of this is the group of elementary school children who voted on the sex of a rabbit. After much discussion, following all the steps in the problem-solving process, the group unanimously determined that the rabbit was a male—when it was really a female rabbit. If you want other examples that question the infallibility of the group process, think about some high-level decisions made through such deliberations: negotiations in Paris to end the war in Viet Nam, the decision to escalate our involvement in Viet Nam, the decision to support Bangladesh over India, and decisions to continue medièval practices in our penal institutions. The group process is only as sound as those in the group, the conditions under which the group works, the goal it is given or selects, and so on.

To summarize, some implications stand out concerning the probability that fewer errors in judgment will be made by the group than by the individual. Because the group is likely to generate more alternatives than the individual, judicious deliberation on the alternatives probably will yield fewer errors in judgment. So, if it is important to make fewer errors in your judgments, the group's the thing. We would rather have a group than an individual make decisions on whether or not to press the button to start World War III.

If too many members are added to the group, you reach a point of diminishing return in generating alternatives (and, as we shall see later, a possible weakening of interpersonal relationships). So, you may want to keep the group around five to eight for efficiency and productivity.

Finally, a group is not infallible in the judgments it makes, so do not accept group decisions—whether made by your group or another group—without considering the judgments rationally for yourself.

Time

The amount of time used by a group to complete a task is one of the weaknesses of the group process. Your own experience should teach you that working in a group takes a lot of time. Group effort is not the most timesaving way to achieve a goal when a measure of person-minutes (minutes per person) is used as a criterion. There is some evidence that while groups take less time than individuals to achieve learning and make simple decisions, this superiority disappears or is even reversed on problem-solving tasks (Davis, 1969).

An example of how learning occurs in a group will help to clarify the point. Assume that your history teacher has divided the class into small groups, and each group is responsible for completing a specific task related to the assigned reading. Your group is required to list the ten major causes of the United States' entry into World War I. The causes are all listed and discussed in the assigned reading material. Given that all or most of you have read the assignment containing the information, it is a reasonable guess that the group would complete the task in a little less time than it would take an individual. This is true because many of the strengths of group behavior can be utilized efficiently (e.g., information from several people can be pooled, members can check one another for consistency and accuracy, and division of labor is possible). The group's major task is to find or remember the content from the readings. However, on a test over mastery of the content the group might not perform much differently than do students who completed the task on an individual basis. This is the pattern revealed by some of the research on learning groups.

The decision to work as groups or as individuals partially may be the function of the relationship between errors and time. If you have a simple task to perform, on which an early response is required, you should probably use the group rather than an individual to complete it. You will also want to use a group over an individual when an early response is needed on tasks involving learning or simple judgments. If a complex task is demanded, such as problem solving, you should consider using individuals rather than a group when an early response is a priority. The use of individuals over a group, however, will probably decrease the accuracy and increase the errors in judgment. So, if errors are costly relative to success, and the individual's time is cheap, the decision may be to form a group.

Other Considerations

The decision to group or not to group should be based on considerations in addition to efficiency. Working in groups produces at least two additional advantages over working as individuals.

First, the behavior of other persons serves as a source of cues or information about what behavior is permissible or desirable (Back, 1979). You have probably found yourself in social situations in which you were not quite sure what the acceptable mode of behavior was. If you think back to your first formal dinner, you might have had some difficulty figuring out what to do with all those pieces of silver, plates, and glasses. You probably looked around for a clue to identify the behavior that was expected in that particular situation. You might have observed the hostess to determine what object she picked up first, thus gaining information for your own behavior. A similar situation exists with groups. For instance, a new employee in a factory frequently will follow fellow workers in the amount of time they "goof off." In other words, group members may provide a *model* for how one might actually perform and act in a given situation.

Second, working together in a group may represent a source of comfort or support for the group members (Davis, 1969). The old saying that there is comfort in numbers addresses the implication that we find support in large and small groups due to the presence of others. For example, you may recall some instances in which you preferred to do homework with friends rather than by yourself. You also may recall a situation in which the study session became a socializing session and very little was accomplished (see Hill, 1975). In other words, it is easy to replace the task with socializing. If the group remains task oriented, accomplishing the task in a group probably is more pleasurable than working alone.

This section has attempted to provide an overview of some advantages and disadvantages of working in groups versus working as individuals. Groups appear to make fewer errors but require more total hours for their performance. Groups also provide models for individuals and usually offer more pleasure while accomplishing the task. However, these as well as other factors should be considered before reaching a decision on whether the group or the individual would be more efficient in accomplishing the task.

PRINCIPLES

1. Groups generally are more efficient than individuals in recalling information and in accuracy. However, the efficiency advantage may be lost if groups lack the coordination needed for a complex task.
2. Individuals generally are superior to groups in terms of the amount of time required for completion of the task.
3. There are at least two advantages of groups over individuals in addition to the performance advantage.
   a. The behavior of group members serves as a source of information about what behavior is permissible or desirable.
   b. Group members may provide comfort or support for other group members.

GROUPS AS PROCESS

Our definitions of the terms *group, small group,* and *small group communication* might appear to describe an entity (i.e., group) which has a specific location in time and space. Although for purposes of definition this may be theoretically true, in reality groups are dynamic structures and as such are constantly involved in change.

The term *process* is generally used to refer to the dynamics of small group communication. This term suggests the changing nature of the individual and intragroup interactions. It indicates that as individuals modify their own ideas through external stimulation and interaction, they tend to alter ideas and even personalities of those group members with whom they interact. Consequently, to describe a group at one point in time may be misleading because it changes from moment to moment. Chapter 2 describes the process nature of groups more completely. At this point keep in mind that, although we may talk about groups as static entities, you should mentally perceive them as constantly in process.

SUMMARY

This chapter has established a framework for examining and understanding small group communication. Small group communication was identified as a level of interpersonal communication and differentiated from dyadic communication on the basis of (1) greater information sharing, (2) the presence of an audience, and (3) the potential for majorities to form in small groups.

A small group was defined as a collection of individuals, from three to fifteen in number, who meet in face-to-face interaction over a period of time, generally with an assigned or assumed leader, who possess at least one common characteristic, and who meet with a purpose in mind. Small group communication was defined as the process of verbal and nonverbal interaction in a small group.

Groups are formed in order to investigate problems and to devise, propose, and implement solutions. They are more efficient than individuals in the recall of information and in accuracy, but require more time to complete a task. Group members also provide information about what behavior is permissible or desirable and may provide comfort or support for other group members. Groups should be understood and studied as dynamic, constantly changing entities.

IDEAS FOR DISCUSSION

1. What relationships exist among different levels of communication in addition to those mentioned in this chapter? Discuss particularly (1) verbal versus nonverbal differences, (2) formality and informality, (3) purposes and goals, and (4) efficiency of decision making.

2. What would be an example of a situation in which a leaderless group might be more effective than a group in which a leader was appointed? What would be an example of the reverse situation?

3. What role does individual motivation play in group formation?

4. What variables, in addition to those mentioned in this chapter, tend to make groups dissolve quickly? What variables tend to make groups stay together for a long period of time?

SUGGESTED PROJECTS AND ACTIVITIES

1. Make a list of all the small groups to which you belong. Then rank them (1) in order of their importance to you, (2) according to the length of time you have been associated with each, and (3) in terms of the degree of formality and informality of each.

2. Using the reasons for group formation suggested in this chapter as a starting place, select three groups that you currently are a part of and write a brief paragraph about the "history" of the group's formation.

3. Using the other textbooks as your sources of information, locate as many different definitions of group, small group, and small group communication as you can. Then prepare a chart illustrating similarities and differences among the definitions. With which definition(s) do you most agree? Why?

REFERENCES

BACK, K. W. The small group tightrope between sociology and personality. *Journal of applied behavioral science*, 1979, *15*, 283–294.

BRANDSTÄTTER, H., T. H. DAVIS, and H. SCHULER. *Dynamics of group decisions*. Beverly Hills, Calif.: Sage Publications, 1978.

DAVIS, J. H. *Group performance*. Reading, Mass.: Addison-Wesley, 1969.

DELAMATER, JOHN. A definition of "group." *Small group behavior*, 1974, *5*, 30–44.

HILL, RAYMOND E. Interpersonal compatibility and work group performance. *Journal of applied behavioral science*, 1975, *11*, 210–219.

KLUGMAN, S. F. Group judgments for familiar and unfamiliar materials. *Journal of general psychology*, 1945, *32*, 103–110.

NIXON, H. L. III. *The small group*. Englewood Cliffs, N.J.: Prentice-Hall, 1979.

PERLMUTTER, H. V., and G. DEMONTMOLLIN. Group learning of nonsense syllables. *Journal of abnormal and social psychology*, 1952, *47*, 762–769.

PERLMUTTER, H. V. Group memory of meaningful material. *Journal of psychology*, 1953, *35*, 361–370.

REUSCH, J., and G. BATESON. *Communication: the social matrix of psychiatry*. New York: W. W. Norton & Co., 1951.

SHAW, M. E. *Group dynamics: the psychology of small group behavior*, 3rd ed. New York: McGraw-Hill, 1980.

SMALL, A. W. *General sociology*. Chicago: University of Chicago Press, 1905, p. 495.

WISEMAN, G., and L. BARKER. *Speech—interpersonal communication*, 2nd ed. New York: Thomas Y. Crowell, 1974.

SUGGESTED READINGS

BURGOON, M., J. K. HESTON, and J. McCROSKEY. *Small group communication: a functional approach*. New York: Holt, Rinehart & Winston, 1974.

Chapter 1, "The Small Group as a Unique Communication Situation," identifies unique characteristics and functions of small group communications.

GOLDBERG, A. A., and C. E. LARSON. *Group communication*. Englewood Cliffs, N.J.: Prentice-Hall, 1975.

Chapter 1, "The Nature of Group Communication," compares and contrasts group communication to interpersonal, organizational, and laboratory training communication. Chapter 3 provides a section ("Implicit Theory in Speech Communication") which explains the function of communication to the individual and the group.

HARNACK, R. V., T. B. FEST, and B. S. JONES. *Group discussion: theory and technique*. 2nd ed. Englewood Cliffs, N.J.: Prentice-Hall, 1977.

Chapter 3. "Functions of Discussion in Our Society," compares and discusses the many reasons people engage in group discussion.

Chapter 6, "Communication Principles," defines communication, discusses some characteristics of communication, and reviews contributions which are desirable in the communication process.

ROSENFELD, L. B. *Human interaction in the small group setting*. Columbus, Ohio: Chas. E. Merrill, 1973.

Chapter 1 includes definitions, purposes, characteristics, relationships, and interactions of the small group. Chapter 4 includes a comparison of individual and group effectiveness.

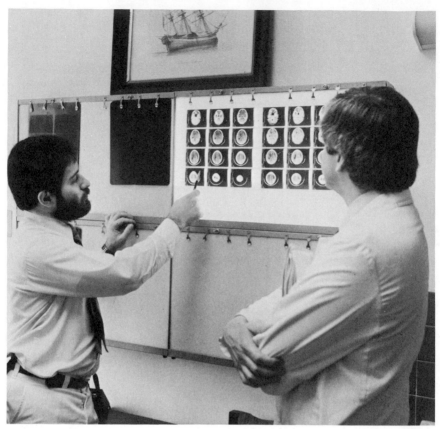

Ken Karp

A Systems Approach to Small Group Communication

2

Study Questions

After you have read this chapter, you should be able to answer the following questions completely and accurately:

1. What is process, and why is a process viewpoint considered valuable in examining communication phenomena?
2. What is meant by the term *system*?
3. What is the difference between an open and a closed system?
4. What are the characteristics of an open system?
5. What are three advantages in analyzing small group communication with a systems approach?
6. In what way(s) can Newcomb's A-B-X Model be considered a system?
7. How can a systems analysis approach be used to predict group interaction and potential success in achieving group goals?

COMMUNICATION AS PROCESS

An ancient Greek philosopher called Heraclitus observed that a person cannot step twice into the same moving river; because of its constant movement, the river is not the same at different points in time. Although Heraclitus did not use the term *process*, his statement reflects a process outlook. *Process* refers to a view of events and relationships between events as dynamic, ongoing, ever-changing, and continuous (Berlo, 1960; Mortensen, 1972; Miller and Nicholson, 1976). A process perspective views events as interrelated, not isolated and discrete.

Consider, for example, a situation where a friend seems irritable and noncommunicative on the way to class one morning. You could view your friend's behavior as a discrete event, unrelated to other events preceding your encounter at a local coffee shop where you meet each morning. Such a viewpoint would reflect a static or nonprocess outlook. On the other hand, you might view your friend's irritability and withdrawal as it relates to other phenomena. For example, your friend may have put in an "all nighter" and is lacking sleep, or he/she may have just received some disturbing news from home or just had a fight with his/her roommate. Notice that a process viewpoint underscores the possibility and probability of change.

Practically speaking, an extreme process viewpoint may not be useful, since we often are forced to examine events by isolating certain elements and their interrelationships. Such is the strategy scholars use in viewing communication in the form of a model (see Smith, 1970). The value of the process outlook is that it serves to remind us that we have isolated only selected elements of the process (e.g., communication) and that other elements may also affect the outcomes we observe. Why is this considered valuable? For one thing, we may be less prone to "jump to conclusions" about assumed relationships between factors affecting communication. Another value of a process perspective is that it prompts communication researchers to examine several possible variables affecting communication simultaneously. A third value is that a process viewpoint gives us a broader perspective with which to examine and understand human communication. Finally, a process viewpoint allows us to examine communication phenomena in a manner consistent with the way events occur in the real world.

The key to a process viewpoint is the *dynamic* relationship among elements. For example, in viewing a motion picture as process we might begin by listing all the elements which comprise the picture. The list may include the actors, camera, lighting, director, producer, setting, and audience. Would we then say that a motion picture is merely the sum total of all of these elements? Probably not. The motion picture is the result of the dynamic interrelationships among all the elements as they affect one another.

In this chapter and throughout the book, we will discuss small group communication from a process viewpoint. In so doing, we will view the small group as a system with all of its elements interacting and affecting one another. The concept of *system*, or *systems analysis*, has been used in a variety of disciplines from investigations of single-cell organisms to entire societal complexes. Obviously, a complete examination of the concept of system is beyond the scope of this chapter; however, additional sources provided at the end of the chapter discuss the concept of system in depth. In this chapter we will consider only a few key concepts relating to systems analysis. The value of the systems approach in analyzing small group communication will be made clear later on in the chapter. For the present, we will focus our attention on a few of the fundamental concepts relating to systems analysis.

THE CONCEPT OF SYSTEM

Definition of System

A system may be defined as a complexity of interacting elements (Bertalanffy, 1968). Although this definition appears relatively simple on the surface, the concept of system is rich in meaning and can be very complex in its implications. A simple illustration may help clarify the difference between a system and a nonsystem approach in viewing a group of people.

In Figure 2.1, A represents a nonsystem. Each numbered circle represents an independent component or element. In this instance, the four circles represent four individuals seated at a table (1 = Tom; 2 = Jane; 3 = Marsha; 4 = Bill). Note that there is no indication of how each person relates to the other persons sitting at the table. We may have considerable information about each person, but we do not know how the individuals relate to each other. However, in B (a system), not only the individual elements but also the interrelationships among the elements are known. For example, assume the arrows in B represent channels of communication between persons sitting at a table. Note that some individuals freely can exchange information with one another (i.e., 1–2, 1–3, and 2–3), while only one-way communication channels exist between other persons (i.e., 2–4, 4–3), and no communication channels exist between others (i.e., 1–4).

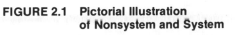

FIGURE 2.1 **Pictorial Illustration**
 of Nonsystem and System

Open Versus Closed Systems

There are basically two types of systems—open and closed. A *closed system* is one which is isolated from its environment (i.e., it does not exchange energy, matter, or information with elements outside the system). Closed systems respond to changes within the system by eventually reaching a state of balance among the elements called "equilibrium" or "homeostasis." For example, a chemical reaction may be considered a closed system. When oxygen and hydrogen (the elements) are combined in a closed vessel, the elements of the system interact and eventually reach a state of equilibrium known as water (H_2O).

On the other hand, *open systems* interact with their environment. As a person, you are an open system. You exchange matter, energy, and information with other people, thus resulting in change (i.e., accommodation or adaptation) and order in your relationships with the environment. For example, your mind increases in complexity when you recognize the difference between "polite lies" and "impolite truth," and that also creates order for you. Small groups are similarly open systems.

There are three important characteristics of open systems. First, open systems are characterized by *circularity*. This means that each element in the system affects all other elements in the system in some way. Consider, for example, the small group depicted in Figure 2.1. The concept of circularity implies that every member of the group affects other members in some way. We know from experience that this is true. Unless we are totally unaware of another's presence, we tend to consider others present before we respond in some overt fashion. Even when we try to ignore a particular person's presence, the fact that we attempt to ignore the person is itself an effect! Again, circularity means that all elements of a system affect all other elements. The concept stresses the dynamic, interactive quality of open systems.

A second characteristic of open systems is *synergy*. This means that the whole is greater than the sum of its parts. In effect, synergy is an extension of the concept of circularity. Not only do the elements of an open system affect one another but the result of this interaction is something unique as well—something that would not exist without the interaction of elements. For example, two people whom you know may both be very nice and seem to be similar in many respects, but they may dislike each other intensely. The interaction involves more than the component parts in isolation.

Consider again Figure 2.1. Even though we may have quite a bit of information about the individual elements in A, since the elements are in isolation (i.e., not interrelated) we do not know how they may change as a result of interaction with other elements. We simply cannot total the separate pieces of information and know how the four individuals will behave together. In B, however, the collective behavior of all elements can be determined.

Suppose, for example, that we know individuals 1 and 2 do not get along (e.g., they hold conflicting values and attitudes), but that individuals 1 and 4 are very similar. The channels of communication indicate that individuals 1 and 2 can communicate with one another, but that 1 and 4 cannot communicate directly. If individual 1 wants to communicate a message to individual 4, the most efficient way of doing so is to transmit the message to individual 2 and ask that person to relay the information to individual 4.

In this instance, 1's behavior may be different within the system than it normally may be outside the system. For example, 1 may modify his or her behavior toward 2 to increase the probability of communicating the message to 4. Though 1's behavior modification may be only temporary, the behavior within the system is nevertheless different from the behavior that might normally occur outside the system or in a system with different communication channels. The point is that because of the interrelationships among the elements in B, each element may behave quite differently within the system than outside the system. In this sense, the whole (i.e., the behavior and interaction of all elements in combination) is greater than the sum of all the individual elements' behavior taken in isolation.

The third characteristic of an open system is *equifinality*. This means that an open system may reach a particular state in time from different initial conditions and in different ways. For example, a group goal (e.g., solution to a problem) may be achieved even though individual elements within the group may change from the initial conditions (e.g., new information may be added, group members may be lost or added, etc.). A group also may achieve its goal in several different ways; it is not restricted to one method or set of procedures for obtaining its goal.

In general, most human phenomena are characteristic of open systems. In this chapter the small group is considered an open system, where the individual group members are treated as elements of the system. Later on in the chapter, we will expand the concept of *element* to include other variables in addition to individual group members. However, at this point in our discussion, the value of a systems analysis approach in examining small group communication may not be clear. There are several advantages in analyzing small group communication with a systems approach. Some of these advantages are listed below.

1. Systems analysis requires us to identify the key variables and interrelationships that may affect the manner in which the system functions. By examining key variables and their interrelationships, we are better able to understand and sometimes control the communication process within the group.

2. Systems analysis can allow us to anticipate possible sources of disruption in the group process. In other words, we can increase the probability

of achieving and maintaining the group goals by successfully predicting factors and events that may interfere with the group process.

3. Systems analysis encourages us to view and examine the group communication process *in toto*, that is, the dynamic relationships as they affect the process as a whole. Such a view broadens our perspective of the small group communication process and provides us with a model for examining the small group process in a manner that is consistent with the way events occur in the real world.

PRINCIPLES

1. A systems analysis requires identification of key internal and external variables and the potential interrelationships among them.
2. Each element in a system affects all other elements in the system.
3. Elements in a system often act differently from the way they do outside the system.
4. Small groups, as open systems, can reach their goal(s) in several different ways and from several different starting points.

The definition of a small group in Chapter 1 did not include the dyad (two-person group) because of its unique characteristics and its limited interaction pattern. However, for clarity and simplicity, we shall use the dyad to illustrate a systems analysis approach to small group communication.

NEWCOMB'S A-B-X MODEL

Several models have been developed to examine social interaction as an open system. One of the most popular models is one developed by Newcomb (1953). Newcomb's model focuses on social interaction specifically as a process of communicative acts. He assumes that "communication among humans performs an essential function of enabling two or more individuals to maintain simultaneous orientation toward one another as communicators and toward objects of communication" (p. 393). What Newcomb means by this statement is that through communication, individuals acquire information about each other and about the things they discuss. For example, as you and a classmate discuss a course that both of you are taking, each of you acquires information about the other as a person in addition to information concerning what each of you thinks about the course. One may view this general process of person A and person B communicating about object X as a system composed of interacting elements. A diagram of Newcomb's model appears below.

It is apparent from the model that there are at least three elements in the system—person A, person B, and object X. However, since Newcomb defines social interaction in terms of communicative acts, we must also consider communicative acts as an element in the system. A *communicative act* is defined as "a transmission of information, consisting of discriminative stimuli, from a source to a recipient" (Newcomb, 1953, p. 393). In its most basic form, a communicative act occurs when person A transmits information to person B about object X. There is at least one additional element in the system: *co-orientation*. Co-orientation refers to the simultaneous orientation (i.e., attraction) of A to B and toward X. Other concepts relevant to co-orientation are discussed more completely in Chapter 4. In essence, the concept of co-orientation suggests that A's attraction to B is dependent upon A's attraction toward X, B's attraction to A, and B's attraction toward X. All of the elements are interdependent.

A number of postulates can be derived from Newcomb's model which serve as a basis for analyzing and predicting events within the social interaction system. The interested student is encouraged to read Newcomb's (1953) original article for several postulates that may be derived from the model.

For purposes of illustration, we will examine only one postulate. It is assumed that there is strain or pressure on the A-B-X system toward preferred states of equilibrium or balance and that the greater the strain on one or more elements in the system the greater the likelihood that equilibrium will result. We might refer to Figure 2.2 to illustrate this postulate. Suppose you (person A) and a classmate (person B) are discussing a course you are both taking (object X). Let us assume that you feel a *strong* positive attraction (i.e., co-orientation) toward person B and that you feel negatively about course X. Let us further assume that person B is positive about course X and positive

FIGURE 2.2   Newcomb's A-B-X Model

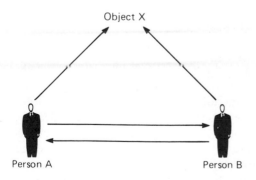

Object X

Person A   Person B

toward you. Newcomb's model suggests that there will be strain or pressure on you to reach symmetry (i.e., balance or agreement) with B's positive views about course X. In addition, it is more likely that symmetry will be reached as you continue to communicate with person B.

Of course, Newcomb is not suggesting that balance will always be reached. We all have disagreements with persons toward whom we have strong co-orientation. However, there does appear to be a general tendency for humans to *prefer* balanced states or agreement with persons we like (see Brickman and Horn, 1973; Tagiuri, 1969) and for that preference to become stronger as co-orientation is increased. Given this general postulate about A-B-X systems, we can often predict and understand the interrelationships of elements in the system. However, it is important to keep in mind that A-B-X systems are open systems. In the above example, emphasis was placed on the interaction of elements within the system, but these elements also interact with the environment. The interaction with the environment often may affect how, or even if, the system will reach a state of balance. For example, contradictions to the prediction above about your tendency to reach agreement with person B may be due to various environmental interactions (e.g., perhaps you are late for your next class and do not have time to talk to B; perhaps a person whom you dislike is in the immediate area and you prefer not to talk with B at that time, etc.).

While useful, Newcomb's model does not allow one to deal easily with complexities of this nature. However, you should begin to see how an examination of the elements in a group system leads to prediction of possible interaction among individuals and the results of such interaction. This information is very important to the maintenance of effective group communication. However, the probability of accurately predicting social interaction events becomes increasingly difficult as more and more elements are added to the system. Just imagine how complex the problem of prediction becomes when you examine a group composed of five or more members in light of all the factors which may affect their interaction! An example of such an analysis is provided in the next section.

Further Application of the Systems Approach

Our initial comments relating the concept of system to small group communication suggested that individual group members were the key elements of a group system. The discussion of Newcomb's A-B-X model broadened the concept of element to include other factors besides individuals (e.g., communicative acts and co-orientation). We now will broaden the concept of element even further. All of the factors which affect group interaction will be viewed as elements in the system. Among the factors affecting group interaction are group norms, group goals and tasks, group cohesiveness, structure, and leadership. Typically these and other factors influencing group interaction are called variables by communication researchers. In the most general sense, a *variable* is anything that may appear in changed amount or quality, such as an attribute or a characteristic (Cook, 1965). For example, researchers often refer to age, attitude, and intelligence as variables.

Considerable research in small group communication has examined numerous variables related to social interaction, and subsequent chapters of this book describe several principles related to key variables which may affect small group communication. Selected group variables are discussed below with a systems analysis perspective. Note, however, that for purposes of illustration only a few variables have been selected for inclusion in the model. They by no means represent all of the variables that may affect group interaction.

A systems model. An illustration of a systems analysis approach to small group communication is difficult to provide without reference to a specific example. Figure 2.3 provides a visual model of the small group variables we will consider.

FIGURE 2.3 A Model of a Small Group

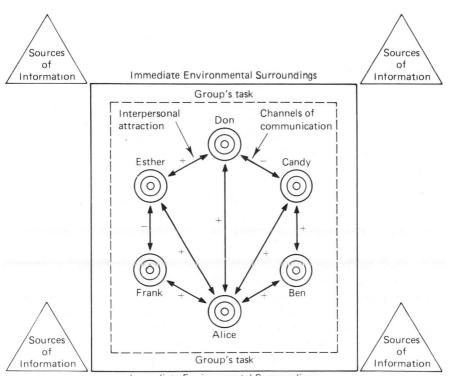

The model in this figure focuses our attention on six variables, three of which are internal group variables and three of which are external to the group. Internal group variables are those factors which specifically relate to the interaction within the group. In our model these variables include individual group members, channels of communication among group members, and the interpersonal attraction (co-orientation in Newcomb's terms) between members of the group. These three variables are represented in the model by the concentric circles next to each participant's name, the arrow drawn between the concentric circles, and the plus or minus sign above each arrow.

Variables that are external to the group include those factors which do not relate directly to the internal functions of the group. This is not to suggest that external variables have no influence on a group's functions, but rather that they operate outside the internal framework of the group itself. In the model in Figure 2.3, external variables include sources of information (represented by triangles), immediate environmental surroundings (represented by solid rectangular lines), and the group task (represented by dotted rectangular lines). Of course, these are only a few of the external variables which can affect a group. University policies, for example, would act as an external variable in a discussion of campus housing.

The distinction between internal and external variables becomes clear when you consider the nature of an open system like the small group. One aspect of open systems seems particularly relevant here: the form and order of open systems are not disrupted seriously by environmental factors (i.e., external variables) outside the system itself. For example, the immediate environmental surroundings in which a group discussion occurs (e.g., the room, temperature, and lighting) can vary without seriously disrupting the internal functions of the group. Of course, extreme changes in the immediate environment obviously would affect the internal group process (Griffit and Veicht, 1971). However, in most normal situations, a group can function smoothly even though external variables may change or vary from time to time. The same generally *cannot* be said for unexpected changes in the *internal* variables of a group. Consider the situation in which two of the most informed members of a group are absent during a crucial stage of the discussion. This may seriously affect the overall function of the group to the point where successful discussion cannot occur.

You might infer from the preceding comments that internal variables are more important to successful group discussion than external variables. This generally is the case *as long as there are no serious problems imposed by external variables*. Remember that an open system characteristically is free to interact with variables outside the system. When this interaction is somehow disrupted, there may be serious consequences for the system. Therefore, when examining small group communication with a systems approach, it is usually a good idea to determine all of the important internal and external variables which affect the relevant functions of the group. As you will soon see, this strategy allows you to "troubleshoot" possible disruptions of the group process and adjust for them in a manner that will help the group achieve and maintain its goals.

Keeping in mind that we have limited the number of variables affecting our system to only six, let us examine how you might employ a systems approach to analyze your own small group. Let us suppose that you are a member of a group whose task is to discuss the legalization of marijuana. The central goal of the group is to gather information about marijuana and prepare guidelines based on the group discussion which either favor or disfavor legalization. The first step in your analysis might be to determine the relevant external variables which may affect the group in achieving its goal. In this case, the checklist might take the form illustrated in Table 2.1 on the next page.

As can be seen in Table 2.1, the standing or rank of most internal and external variables in your imaginary group is favorable. However, there are some potential problems concerning the sources of information, the group task, and the interpersonal attraction among group members. Although the checklist is useful for isolating the key variables affecting the group and the rank of each one, it is important to remember that, as such, the checklist does not indicate clearly the problems that may arise from the interaction among variables. Remember that the key to systems analysis is the examination of the dynamic interrelationships among the elements in the system. Therefore, the second step in your analysis would be to determine what possible effects may result from the interaction of the variables in the system.

There are no universal rules for determining with which variable you should begin the analysis, but it is usually best to examine first the variables that are most important or potentially troublesome to the system. In this particular example, we will examine first the interpersonal relations among group members.

We can see from Figure 2.3 that there is a positive attraction between Ben and Candy and between Esther and Don, whereas there is a negative attraction between Candy and Don and Esther and Frank. It also is interesting to observe that there is a positive attraction between Alice and all other members of the group. Though leadership is not one of the variables we have selected for analysis, it very well could have been. Such a relationship between Alice and the other group members may have important implications for determining who will be the leader of this particular group. (Chapter 9 is devoted specifically to an examination of leadership in small group communication.)

The variable which appears to have the most direct relationship to group members' interpersonal attraction is the channel(s) of communication

TABLE 2.1

Checklist of Internal and External Variables Affecting the Group's Goals

Variables	Rank of Variable	Explanation
EXTERNAL:		
1. Source of Information	fair to good	Considerable information has been published on marijuana, but much of it is biased in one direction or the other. Little experimental data is available, especially concerning long-term physical and social effects.
2. Immediate Environment	excellent	A room very conducive to group discussion is readily available.
3. Group Task	fair to good	The task is clear, but it is extremely complex, due, in part, to the emotionality of the issue. Lack of sufficient time also may be a factor.
INTERNAL:		
4. Group Members	excellent	All the group members are reasonably intelligent and interested in the topic under discussion. There also is a balance among conservative, liberal, and uncommitted factions.
5. Channels of Communication Between Group Members	good	In general, all group members readily can communicate with one another. However, the seating arrangement may cause some difficulties for easy communication among certain individuals.
6. Interpersonal Attraction Between Group Members	excellent to poor	While some members get along very well, interpersonal relations are strained between others.

between group members. As indicated in Table 2.1, the communication channels variable was given a rank of "good." However, when we consider the interaction between interpersonal attraction and communication channels, the rank of the latter variable potentially could be much lower. For example, consider the communication that might transpire between Esther and Frank. Although there is an open communication channel readily available between these individuals, for some reason they are not attracted to one another and perhaps even dislike one another. Are we still justified in assuming that there is an open communication channel between them? Probably not. It is quite feasible that the lack of attraction between Esther and

Frank could serve as a barrier to productive group communication, despite the availability of a seemingly open channel between them.

The solution to the problem is not an easy one. On the surface it would appear that a mere rearrangement of seating order might solve the problem. However, even this strategy probably would not solve all of the problems that could arise. Although an adequate solution to the problem may be difficult to obtain, the analysis still has provided us with useful information. This information is an awareness of the potential for a problem and the probable consequences. Without such information it might be impossible to anticipate potential disruptions in the group process, to say nothing about finding an adequate solution.

Consider the interrelationship between interpersonal attraction, channels of communication, and individual group members. We observed that all of the group members possess a reasonable degree of intelligence, but that there are opposing factions within the group (i.e., conservatives, liberals, and neutrals). Perhaps one of the factors contributing to the negative interpersonal relations among some group members is directly related to differences in basic philosophy. Although it is difficult to overcome differences between individuals' basic philosophies, prior knowledge that such differences exist can help us find a solution to the problem or at least enable us to anticipate it as a possible cause of difficulty for the group.

We might also observe a direct relationship between the external variables and the others we have considered. For example, perhaps if the nature of the task were changed (e.g., from legalization of marijuana to lowering the legal drinking age), many of the potential problems concerning interpersonal relations and channels of communication also would change. However, if deviation from the group task is not possible (i.e., the topic must be considered), we cannot consider changing the task. We already have noted in our consideration of the group task variable that time limitations may be a source of potential difficulty. When we examine the interrelationships between the group task and other variables, time limitations may be an even more important factor for consideration. For example, strained interpersonal relations among group members, closed communication channels, and differing basic philosophies of group members may slow down productive group discussion.

How might the immediate surroundings interact with the other variables? In this particular example there do not appear to be any sources of potential problems for the group. However, until the actual discussion takes place, we cannot be sure that the environmental variables will not somehow interact with other variables in a manner disruptive to the group. For example, the potential of strained relationships between some group members may lead to rather heated arguments at times. If the discussion room were located in close proximity to offices or other rooms where noise would be disruptive to others, there may be adverse effects on the group discussion.

The sources of information would appear to interact with several of the variables we have considered, particularly individual group members' personal philosophy about the topic of discussion and interpersonal attraction among group members. Chapter 6 examines several selectivity and screening devices which individuals use in acquiring, processing, and diffusing information for group discussion. As will be pointed out in that chapter, individuals' values and attitudes often interfere with accurate processing of information. The different philosophies guiding various group members in the present example would suggest that individuals may perceive and interpret information in quite different ways. If this were the case, we might also expect accurate diffusion of information within the group to be affected even if all channels of communication were open.

Although additional statements could be made about the interrelationships among the six variables, the analysis probably is sufficient for you to grasp the essence of a systems analysis approach in examining group discussion. There is, however, one final step in the analysis which we have not mentioned yet. Though the first two steps in the systems analysis approach are important for isolating variables and anticipating potential disruptions in the group process, one must test the validity of the predicted events against the events of the actual discussion.

In the example given earlier, you might notice later that Don and Esther expressed very similar attitudes after they started dating (co-orientation and balance), but that this change in their interpersonal relations did not significantly affect the group—an open system. You might also notice that having group meetings at Frank's apartment was not much different than having them at Ben's, but that meeting in the park significantly affected the discussion (immediate surroundings). These observations can then be compared to the predictions which you made earlier.

It is difficult to predict precisely what events will occur in the discussion, even when the first two steps of the systems analysis are done carefully. We must continually test the validity of our predictions against the events of the real world and modify our analysis accordingly. This is not to suggest that the first two steps of a systems analysis are useless. On the contrary, more often than not we will find that our predictions will allow us to anticipate, and hopefully control, several events which may disrupt the group process. However, things do not always happen the way we expect them to. New situations or variables may arise which were unanticipated or neglected in the initial stages of the analysis. By continually checking our analysis against the events of the real world, we can more effectively cope with new or unanticipated events, and thus achieve and maintain the group's goals.

PRINCIPLES

1. The more elements that are added to a system, the more complex the system becomes and, thus, the more difficult it is to conduct an accurate systems analysis.
2. Generally, form and order of open systems are not disrupted seriously by external variables, unless the changes in the variables are extreme.
3. Unexpected changes in internal variables, especially extreme changes, can have significant effects on the system.
4. It is important to test and monitor predictions derived by a systems analysis against the actual functioning of the system.
5. In conducting a systems analysis for small group communication you are encouraged to use a checklist approach to consolidate relevant information about internal and external variables. You will find the principles listed through this book particularly useful in identifying potentially important variables, hypothesizing their interrelationships, and testing their validity in small group discussions.

SUMMARY

This chapter began with a discussion of the concept of process. The central point of the discussion was that small group communication is a process in which all variables interact with and affect all other variables. The remainder of the chapter focused on the concept of systems analysis and how it may be applied to small group communication. A model was provided illustrating how systems analysis can help predict events that might be disruptive to effective group discussion.

Subsequent chapters of the book examine and discuss numerous small group variables and their related principles. These principles should help you improve and develop your effectiveness in small group communication. However, you need to interrelate the various principles to apply them effectively. We suggest that you use the various principles discussed throughout the book in applying the model of systems analysis presented in this chapter. In other words, use the principles about various small group variables to determine possible interrelationships among the variables of a group system and to predict potential sources of disruption to the group process. In so doing, you may find it useful to include an additional column of information entitled "principles" on the variable checklist used in the first step of a systems analysis. Under this column could be listed the various principles related to each small group variable included on the checklist. This procedure should help you make predictions about the effects of different variables on the group process.

Although it often is difficult to employ a systems analysis perspective to examine small group communication, the benefits are usually worth the effort. A careful systems analysis will help you understand the nature of small group communication and, thus, will help you predict and control events which may help or disrupt your group in achieving its goals.

IDEAS FOR DISCUSSION

1. What implications are there for viewing small group discussion with a process perspective? Is the process perspective consistent with a systems analysis approach? If so, why?

2. Can a process perspective be carried to an extreme when observing events in the real world? How?

3. What are some advantages of a systems analysis approach to small group communication? What are some alternative approaches?

SUGGESTED PROJECTS AND ACTIVITIES

1. Observe a small group discussion in process and attempt to isolate the key variables which appear to affect the nature of the discussion.

2. Ask your classmates if you can sit in on the first few meetings of their small group. As you learn about the group, make a checklist similar to the one presented in this chapter. Give each variable a rank and make some predictions about how the variables might interact and affect the discussion. Be sure to check your predictions against the actual events in the discussion.

3. Each chapter in this book contains principles which, when applied, will help you to perform well in group discussion. As you read subsequent chapters of the book, make a list of these principles. Devise some method of coding the principles so you can refer to them on your checklists as you perform systems analyses on various small groups.

REFERENCES

BERLO, D. K. *The process of communication.* New York: Holt, Rinehart & Winston, 1960.

BERTALANFFY, L. *General system theory.* New York: George Braziller, 1968.

BRICKMAN, PHILIP, and CHARLES HORN. Balance theory and interpersonal coping in triads. *Journal of personality and social psychology,* 1973, *26,* 347–355.

COOK, D. R. *A guide to educational research.* Boston: Allyn & Bacon, 1965.

GRIFFIT, WILLIAM, and RUSSELL VEICHT. Hot and crowded: influence of population density and temperature on interpersonal affective behavior. *Journal of personality and social psychology,* 1971, *17,* 92–98.

HAWES, L. C. *Pragmatics of analoguing: theory and model construction in communication.* Reading, Mass.: Addison-Wesley, 1975.

MILLER, G. R., and H. E. NICHOLSON. *Communication inquiry: a perspective on process.* Reading, Mass.: Addison-Wesley, 1976.

MORTENSEN, C. D. *Communication: the study of human interaction*. New York: McGraw-Hill, 1972.

NEWCOMB, T. M. An approach to the study of communication acts. *Psychological review*, 1953, *60*, 393–404.

SMITH, R. L. Theories and models of communication processes. In L. L. Barker and R. J. Kibler, eds. *Speech communication behavior*. Englewood Cliffs, N.J.: Prentice-Hall, 1971, 16–43.

TAGIURI, R. Person perception. In G. Lindzey and E. Aronson, eds. *The handbook of social psychology*. 2nd ed. Reading, Mass.: Addison-Wesley, 1969.

SUGGESTED READINGS

GRANGER, R. L. *Educational leadership: an interdisciplinary perspective*. Scranton, Pa.: International Textbook Company, 1971.

This introductory text discusses philosophical and theoretical foundations, managerial functions, and applications of social system ideas to organizational groups.

JOHNSON, R. A., F. E. KAST, and J. E. ROSENZWEIG. *The theory and management of systems*, 3rd ed. New York: McGraw-Hill, 1973.

This book presents the systems approach in three levels: systems philosophy, systems design and analysis, and systems management. The text also includes exercise questions and a number of cases to illustrate methods and applications in systems analysis.

JOHNSON, R. A., R. J. MONSEN, H. P. KNOWLES, and B. O. SAXBERG. *Management, systems and society: an introduction*. Santa Monica, Calif.: Goodyear, 1976.

Chapter 4, "The Systems Approach," includes discussion on theory, philosophy, management, analysis, and behavioral subsystems. Other chapters provide information on systems within the group process.

LAWLER, E. E., and J. G. RHODE. *Information and control in organizations*. Santa Monica, Calif.: Goodyear, 1976.

This book discusses how information and control systems affect behavior in organizations. The chapters describe such areas as human and organizational behavior, types of motivation, effects of control systems, and measurement in the organization.

Margot Granitsas

3

Nature of Goals and Their Relevance to Small Group Communication

Study
Questions

After you have read this chapter, you should be able to answer the following questions completely and accurately:

1. What is a general definition of a goal?
2. What is a task as it relates to the goals of the small group?
3. What are the definitions of personal goal, conscious personal goal, and unconscious personal goal?
4. What are the two major types of group goals? How do you define each? What are some examples of each?
5. What do we mean by subgoals, and how do they relate to major achievement goals?
6. What should one expect to happen if the personal goals of members conflict with the goals of the group?
7. What are some problems participants would be expected to encounter when working on achievement goals for the group? What are some functional behaviors that can be employed to reduce the magnitude of these problems?
8. What problems are likely to appear when one is working on the group's maintenance goals, and what selected functional behaviors might be implemented to curtail such problems?
9. How are personal and group goals related, and what are the consequences of various possible relationships between such goals?
10. What is the interrelationship between achievement goals and group maintenance goals? What can members do to help provide the optimal balance between the two types of goals?

Six members of the student-faculty Committee on Problems of Minority Students are sitting around a table in attendance at their first meeting. For over an hour they have floundered aimlessly from topic to topic and all have expressed their personal opinions on the status of various problems of minority groups. At the request of different members, the chairperson has read the committee's charge and statement of responsibilities several times, but there was no response from members. Each person seems to have his or her own expectations, aims, and reason for being there. Each member also appears to have a different concept of what should be expected from others. Individuals are beginning to repeat themselves, and the conversation appears to be going in circles. Finally the members begin to quiet down and everyone seems to have had his or her say. People look at their watches, squirm anxiously in their chairs, and a general climate of restlessness is established. At last, someone says, "I guess we better figure out why we are here and what we intend to get done on this committee." Then the participants begin systematically to list some possible goals.

Does this sound familiar? Most of us have been in a similar situation at one time or another—and have been bored to the point of sleep, frustration, or worse. This example illustrates some of the classic characteristics of a collection of people in search of goals, goals needed to give a group some meaning, direction, and even its very existence in some cases.

This concern about goals for a group serves as the focal point for our discussion here. In this chapter we will examine the nature of goals and their use in small group communication. We hope that you will apply the concepts and principles discussed to those events which you personally encounter in small groups. This is something no textbook can do for you.

We begin the chapter with an overview concerning the general concept of goals and tasks as they relate to small groups. Next, we discuss personal goals and then examine the two principal types of group goals—achievement goals and group maintenance goals—that you are likely to experience in small groups. We conclude with a discussion of the key relationships concerning group goals.

AN OVERVIEW OF THE CONCEPT OF GOALS AND TASKS IN SMALL GROUPS

Suppose you are on a diet and a friend asks you what weight you are aiming for. Or, suppose you are taking your first art course. As you dab paint here and there, your instructor questions, "What effect are you trying to achieve?" Whether you are "aiming" or attempting to achieve an effect, you are setting goals and will have to accomplish certain tasks (e.g., lose pounds) in order to achieve those goals. However, first it is important to understand exactly what a goal is and then to understand how goals differ from tasks.

A General Definition of Goal

To avoid possible confusion as you read other literature on small groups, we still use the unglamorous term *goal* throughout the book to describe the end result sought in small groups. (However, the term *goal* is a bit heavy on the academic side for our personal taste.) *A goal is defined as the objective or end result that a group or an individual seeks to achieve.* As such it refers to the objective, target, or end product which is sought. A goal is also a state of affairs that people value and toward which they work (Johnson and Johnson, 1975). Theoretically, but not always in practice, the goal's achievement by a small group is a major reason for its existence.

If you stop and think for a moment, you can undoubtedly recall several small groups in which you have participated recently. Further reflection on the goals of these groups probably will reveal to you that they varied widely. You may have met with a regularly scheduled small group *to learn to repair motorcycles.* In a sensitivity group you may have attempted *to gain a better understanding of yourself* through your interaction with others. You might have assembled with a small group of close friends for lunch under a tree or in a restaurant *to enjoy the pleasure of one another's company and/or to share experiences.* The italicized portions of the previous examples reveal that groups and individuals usually, but not always, have goals—however vague—and that these goals vary across groups.

Like individuals, groups often have more than one goal. Some goals are considered primary, while others may be of a secondary nature. In addition, group members do not always agree upon which goals are primary and which are secondary. An individual's perception of group goals may be affected by several factors; however, one of the most important appears to be the individual's needs and reasons for joining the group. In general, the interaction among group members causes individual goals to become more and more uniform. Additional research on group goals is needed, but it is fairly safe to state that group goals affect the formation of groups, involvement in groups, and group pressure.

In the final analysis, it may not really matter why a group formed originally, why the members have continued to be involved, or what initial pressures motivated members to be there. What is important is for each individual member of a group to determine why he or she is *currently* present and communicating in that group, what objective(s) he or she desires to achieve, and what end result(s) the group seeks.

Goals may vary considerably, depending on the nature of the group, the physical environment and social climate in which the group functions, the personal needs of individual members, and a multitude of other factors. In this chapter, we will scrutinize some of the salient features of the goal-seeking behavior of small groups and the individuals in them. We will examine such relationships as how different variables influence the nature of goals, how goals affect various matters related to group performance, and how goals and other particular factors interact to influence group performance.

Some words you employ in common usage may have special implications when they are applied to the behavior of small groups. For this reason we next examine briefly the relationship between tasks and goals.

Relationship of Goals and Tasks

A favorite word used to characterize a goal in the small group is *task*. Sometimes the terms *goal* and *task* are used interchangeably and almost synonymously in the literature on small group research. *Task may be defined as an act, or its result, that a small group is required, either by someone or by itself, to perform.* A task is thus viewed as what people do, what they produce, or that on which they work in small groups. Tasks are performed by the group to accomplish goals. Generally we think of members of small groups as working on the task to achieve the goal, but sometimes the goal is to complete the task satisfactorily (in other words, "to get the job done"). When the latter occurs, there is considerable overlap in usage of the two terms. As a general rule, however, the task is usually the work done by the group to achieve the goal.

Suppose a goal for the Women's Liberation Council on your campus was to show a series of movies reflecting alternative life-styles available to women. Among the tasks the group might perform to accomplish this goal are the following: gather information on available films, select in priority those films the group wishes to show, obtain funds for or otherwise determine how the movie rentals will be funded, schedule a place for showing the movies, obtain the equipment and personnel to show the movies, etc. All these and other tasks might be necessary to complete in order to accomplish the group's one goal.

To the extent possible, tasks should be stated in behavioral terms (statements of what people will do when performing the task). For example, send a check to David Brightbill for $20 for his services as a projectionist to show the movie *The Liberated Feminist*, scheduled for Ace Hall on February 10, 1983, from 8:00 to 10:00 p.m. Such specific wording of tasks avoids ambiguity in interpretations and directs the effects of the group in a precise manner. These specific statements of tasks may be viewed as subordinate tasks and by some as enabling objectives for the major goals set for the group. Finally, brief descriptions should be written concerning how each task is to be completed, who is responsible for its completion, the date by which it is to be completed, and how its completion will be evaluated by the group.

Goals or aims may be expressed by individuals or by groups. In the next section we examine both individual personal goals as well as several types of group goals.

PRINCIPLES

1. *Goal* is a term that refers to the objective or end result that a group or an individual seeks to achieve; it is a state of affairs that one or more people value and toward which they work.
2. *Task* is a term that refers to an act, or its result, that a small group is required, either by itself or someone else, to perform; you perform tasks to accomplish goals.
3. Among other factors, the group's goal affects the formation of groups, involvement in groups, and group pressure.
4. You should select the group's tasks with other members after you have selected and placed in priority the goals of that group.
5. You should arrange sequentially, in concert with other group members, the series of tasks required to accomplish a given goal.
6. Where possible, you and other members of the group should state both the goals and, particularly, the tasks for the group in behavioral terms.

PERSONAL GOALS

A personal goal is an objective or end result that an individual attempts to achieve. The emphasis in this definition is on determining and defining the end result that a person seeks as an individual—that objective which he or she desires to achieve. Each of us has our own set of personal goals that we have derived on the basis of our personal experience, or perhaps through a formal needs assessment procedure (see Appendix). Later in the chapter we will discuss the relationship between personal and group goals.

Conscious and Unconscious Personal Goals

Conscious goals. Frequently, personal goals are considered at a *conscious level*, in that there is an awareness of the goal to satisfy a need. We typically have thought about our goals to some extent, are cognizant of them, and have made a deliberate decision about them. Once determined, conscious personal goals are pursued with varying degrees of intensity, depending upon the level of commitment to their achievement. Consider these examples of personal goals that might be determined consciously: to lose ten pounds; to get into good physical shape; to quit smoking marijuana; and to tell Professor Schmuck what I think of his tests. It is unlikely that anyone would pursue such goals without some degree of awareness.

Unconscious goals. Sometimes personal goals are considered at an *unconscious level*. We seemingly just try to achieve such personal goals out of habit, without much awareness that we even seek an objective. While unconscious personal goals may have been pursued consciously at one time, an individual's awareness of them may subside over time. The objectives that can be identified as unconscious personal goals vary from individual to individual, depending on personal needs and circumstances. Possible examples of unconscious personal goals for some individuals include: to smoke a cigarette; to pray; to pretend to listen to a professor's lecture; to avoid walking under a ladder; to open doors and to pull out chairs for women; to avoid burping in public. Behavior related to our unconscious personal goals is frequently the most difficult to control and regulate. Even so, it is important to determine personal unconscious goals and evaluate those which may place constraints on one's effectiveness in group situations.

As group members, we seldom make our goals public. Sometimes we don't announce them because they are unconscious and we don't know what we want. Sometimes we don't speak of them because we fear personal rejection if we make them public. The term *hidden agenda* often is used to refer to these unrevealed goals.

PRINCIPLES

1. A *personal goal* refers to the objective or end result that an individual attempts to achieve.
2. *Conscious personal goal* is a term that refers to an awareness of the goal to satisfy a need:
3. Because conscious personal goals will guide your behavior in a small group and influence the responses of other members to you, you should continually evaluate them and be aware that they may influence the work of the group either negatively or positively.
4. *Unconscious personal goal* is a term that refers to a goal pursued without much awareness.

GROUP GOALS

A group goal is the objective or end result that a group seeks to achieve. It is probably fair to say that groups need goals to survive. At least, logic suggests little reason for groups to exist without goals—however vaguely or specifically defined, apparent or unapparent to members, accepted or unaccepted by members, and so on. Of course, there are rare exceptions when groups seem to survive and perhaps continue to meet over time with little effort devoted to determining or achieving goals. But even in such groups, it is likely that a careful analysis of the needs of individual members might provide insight into some possible goals for these groups. To live on love, hope, and status for very long is not much of a promise for group members.

Two general types of group goals have emerged from the literature on small groups (Cartwright and Zander, 1968). One type of group goal is an *achievement goal*, which usually refers to *the major outcome or product that the group intends to produce.* The second major type of goal for groups is a *group maintenance goal*, which refers to *the maintenance or strengthening of the group itself.* Probably the achievement goal is generally considered at the highest level of priority. But as we shall see, it is easier in theory than in practice to accept the priority levels for the two kinds of goals. Sometimes, the establishment and maintenance of a group's structure may be necessary before any serious consideration of achievement goals is introduced.

Achievement Goals

Suppose you were appointed to the Student-Faculty Advisory Committee on Promotion and Tenure. An achievement goal of the committee might be "to recommend faculty members for promotion and to present the list to the President and Vice-President for Academic Affairs." The terminal product sought by this group is the *list of names of faculty members recommended for promotion.* In all likelihood your committee would be presented with a list of faculty members recommended for promotion by each college, school, institute, and other academic unit on the campus. Members of the committee would probably seek to achieve this goal by engaging in decision-making and/or problem-solving activities to derive their final list of names from among all the names submitted and others considered through individual appeals or related means.

However, the above achievement goal has another end result specified in it which is related to its implementation. Once the committee has completed its list of faculty members recommended by the group for promotion, it must then *present the list to the President and Vice-President for Academic Affairs* in order to achieve the end result specified in the original goal. You might choose to view the goal stated for this committee as two separate goals or as one goal composed of two separate parts or phases: (1) the production of the final list of names of faculty recommended for promotion and (2) the presentation of the list to the president and vice-president. Frankly, it does not make much difference to which viewpoint you subscribe. But it is important to recognize that both end results specified in the goal must be achieved in order to accomplish the goal satisfactorily.

At times there may be additional goals that are implied, hidden, or buried in the one end result stated in the main goal. These implied goals are *subgoals,* or *subordinate goals.* We refer to them as subgoals if they are implied in the main goal or if they are explicitly stated as subordinate goals by the group after the formulation of the main achievement goal. The point is that those types of goals that are *subordinate* to the main achievement goal are subgoals—whether they are implied in the main goal or explicitly stated as a related goal by the group.

Some literature on small group communication does not distinguish between tasks and what we have called subgoals or subordinate goals here. As we stated earlier in this chapter, *task* may be conceptualized most accurately as that which the group does or performs to accomplish a goal. A statement of what the group values, intends to do, and the end result it seeks are the task(s). Accordingly, just as there are tasks specified for achievement goals (or maintenance goals, for that matter), so are there tasks specified to accomplish the subgoals or subordinate goals derived from or related to those primary achievement goals.

Functional behaviors employed to accomplish achievement goals. There are a number of functional behaviors that you can employ, along with other group members, to improve the efficiency with which achievement goals are accomplished (Cartwright and Zander, 1968). No effort has been made here to include all such relevant behaviors of members. Rather, we present some examples of members' behavior that serve the function of attaining achievement goals.

Group members frequently have a difficult time keeping their thoughts and interactions focused on their goal and its achievement. Should you find yourself in such a group, you might direct the attention of other members to the goal. You could do this by reminding members what the goal is, asking them how the discussion is relevant to their objective, or pointing out that the group has strayed from its target. Sometimes you will encounter a group situation in which the members appear unclear about an issue. When this occurs, you might restate the salient points concerning the issue in a summary, or state the points that seemed to be understood and develop those which were not clear to members. Other times, members may not understand how a topic is related to the accomplishment of an achievement goal. You can help overcome such circumstances by enumerating the ways and reasons that the topic is relevant to the goal's achievement, or by developing one or more brief examples that illustrate the topic's relevance to the goal.

Another way of helping to attain an achievement goal is to contribute a procedural plan to achieve the goal. You might do this in combination with other members, or you might present the entire plan to the other members for their reactions. Similarly, you might initiate action by making concrete suggestions to the group on how to implement their ideas to effect the achievement goal.

Other functional behaviors of members may help group members reach their achievement goals. Some of these behaviors are getting and giving information, and evaluating the group's ideas and progress toward the goal.

When you possess information needed or that could be used by the group, you have an obligation to contribute it. This is particularly so if you have some personal expertise on the problem or have collected pertinent information from experts. There are other times when you will need to get or elicit information from individuals in the group, perhaps by asking either open or direct questions of specific members. Evaluation of the quality of the ideas and of progress toward the goal is another set of functional behaviors that you might employ to attain achievement goals.

The extent to which members attain their achievement goals for the group will depend substantially on their ability to pool their ideas freely, make significant contributions willingly, reconstruct and summarize their ideas effectively, and accept compromise objectively. These and other functional behaviors that lead groups toward the accomplishment of achievement goals will be discussed in greater depth in Chapter 9 on leadership in groups.

Group Maintenance Goals

When you work alone on a task, almost your entire attention can be directed toward achieving the goal. This is not the case when you work in groups. Working on an achievement goal in the presence of other people requires attention to interpersonal obstacles which are a function of both the goal and the presence of others also working on the achievement of that goal. So, it is not enough simply to focus only on the task. To accomplish an achievement goal of an interacting group, you must also attend to maintaining the group at a satisfactory level of operation.

Maintenance goals have been related to the "climate" of the group (Harnack, Fest, and Jones, 1977), and refer to the kind of relationships existing among the various members of the group. These goals dealing with the social climate of groups are of primary importance to continuing groups; but, at the same time, their relevance for one-time groups cannot be ignored.

The most common kind of group maintenance goal is *to keep the group together*. In fact, some group experts do not even bother to identify other kinds of maintenance goals. When you are in a group that does not achieve this goal to a minimal degree, you can expect your group to experience difficulties, if not failure, in its efforts to master the achievement goal.

Another kind of maintenance goal is *to ensure the continued existence of the group itself*. Just as your group must maintain itself to function effectively and efficiently, so must the group continue its existence if it is to function at all. This goal is closely related to the first, and the functional behaviors required of you and other members to achieve both of them are almost identical.

The third and final kind of common maintenance goal is *to strengthen the group*. The emphasis in this goal is on *upgrading* the current level of the group's *existing state*. All of the considerations discussed under the goal "to maintain the group" also apply to this goal, except that the major focus with this goal is on the *improvement* of the group maintenance behaviors. With this goal, we seek to achieve, over present operating conditions, more effective interpersonal relations, greater cooperation, and a higher level of cohesiveness (Johnson and Johnson, 1975).

Functional behaviors employed to achieve group maintenance goals. What types of behaviors should you execute in groups to attain these group maintenance goals? As we emphasized previously, the behaviors required of participants to achieve one of these kinds of group maintenance goals are the same as or similar to those required to achieve the other two types of goals. Therefore, we will identify here some examples of the functional behaviors (Cartwright and Zander, 1968) of members that contribute to the achievement of the three kinds of group maintenance goals described above.

1. You might spend more time in the group encouraging or reinforcing the behavior of other members. Particularly, you could reward the contributions of any participant who gets involved in the group's activity, but had not been involved previously. Compliment the idea presented and make a reference to it the next time you speak.

2. You similarly might work to establish more pleasant interpersonal relations among members of the group by limiting the number of critical comments made about other members' ideas and by avoiding direct personal criticism of fellow participants. This can also be accomplished by directing more positive comments to other members. Any behaviors that can increase interpersonal attraction, the perceived task success, and improved communication among members will probably facilitate more effective interpersonal relations within the group (McGrath and Altman, 1966). Of course, it is also quite possible that the presence of too much or too little of any of the "facilitators" of group maintenance behavior will interfere with performance. It seems likely there is some optimal balance point between too much and too little of these characteristics in group behavior (McGrath and Altman, 1966). A sensitive group member can learn to recognize when other members want to return to the task or continue "socializing" by observing nonverbal behavior.

3. You might even find it useful to help arbitrate disputes. This could be done by first trying to find common points of agreement and then moving the discussion progressively toward points on which there is greater disagreement. Of course, if you really care about the total involvement and participation of your fellow members, you should be sure that the minority is given a chance to be heard. It is difficult to keep people involved in a group if they feel that what they say has no possibility of influencing the group.

4. A final example of members' functional behaviors that contribute to the achievement of group maintenance goals is an effort to increase the interdependence among you and your fellow members. Such behaviors reinforce the common fate of the group, the feelings of "we," and the commitment to "together as a group." When group members are involved in a common cause and feel they are working together in a cooperative movement toward an agreed upon achievement objective, their group maintenance goals usually are also being achieved satisfactorily. However, a word of caution is in order as we leave this section. Even though social-personal variables may serve to improve group performance, the limits of such enhancement will probably be set by the abilities, training, and experience of group members (McGrath and Altman, 1966). We will discuss more of these functional behaviors of members that lead toward the achievement of group maintenance goals in later chapters dealing with feedback, leadership, nonverbal communication, and conflict in groups.

As a result of completing this section on group goals, you should now be able to define group goals. You should also be capable of defining two general types of group goals—achievement goals and group maintenance goals—distinguishing among three types of group maintenance goals. In addition, you should be able to identify some particular functional behaviors used to accomplish achievement goals and group maintenance goals.

PRINCIPLES

1. Because you must rely upon the group to satisfy some of your personal goals, you must accept that an interdependent purpose with other members exists where group goals are concerned.
2. If the personal goals of the individual members in the group conflict with the goal of the group, you should expect members to be dissatisfied, to reject the group goal or personal goals, or to realign personal and group goals into a harmonious relationship.
3. *Achievement goal* is a term that refers to the major outcome or product that the group intends to produce or seeks to achieve.
4. If a goal is the *principal* end result or product the group seeks to achieve, then you should probably classify it as an achievement goal.
5. *Group maintenance goal* is a term that refers to a goal designed to maintain, strengthen, or ensure the continued existence of the group itself.
6. Hidden, buried, or implied goals in the stated outcome of an achievement goal are *subgoals*, since they are subordinate to the main achievement goal.

7. When members of the group are having difficulty focusing thoughts or interactions on their goal, you should direct the attention of the members back to the goal or to tasks related to the achievement of the goal.

8. Giving and seeking information, evaluating members' ideas, accepting compromise objectively, making contributions willingly, pooling members' ideas freely, and assessing the group's progress toward the goal are among the important functional behaviors you should employ to facilitate the group's accomplishment of achievement goals.

9. Since a group's cohesiveness, morale, unity, solidarity, and cooperation among its members contribute to or at least mobilize the potential of the group's productivity, you should be aware of problems in the group relevant to these factors and establish through consensus the necessary goals to maintain the group when appropriate.

KEY RELATIONSHIPS
CONCERNING GROUP GOALS

With some background concerning the nature of personal goals and group goals, we are now ready to examine some of the key relationships relevant to the goals of groups. First we will consider the relationship between personal goals and group goals. Then we will discuss the important relationship and interaction between achievement goals and group maintenance goals.

Relationship Between Personal Goals
and Group Goals

We have already indicated that each of us has personal goals and that there are goals for groups. The pursuit of these personal goals is compelling and occupies much of our attention and energy. When you enter a group you are asked to determine, accept, and/or agree upon a group's goals. Can you do it? Most of us cannot without some degree of difficulty. What we have is a person out "doing his or her thing" and pursuing his or her own interests; then, that person is confronted with whether or not he or she can accept the goals of a group of other people who have been pursuing their "things" and their interests. Is it any wonder so many of us find it difficult to join and participate in groups? How do we cope with this dilemma, and what procedures are involved?

We acknowledge throughout this text that groups may be capable of performing functions and achieving goals to which individuals can only aspire. So, one of the first assumptions you, as an individual, must accept is that a group may be able to produce results that you are unlikely to achieve as a single individual. (We discussed these advantages of groups over individuals in Chapter 1.) There is a price to pay for these results that groups are capable of achieving. You might be required to compromise or modify your commitment to your individual goals. That is, if you are to function effectively within the group, you must be willing to reassess your personal goals in terms of those goals which the members of the group can accept as relevant and significant to their individual and collective purposes.

At this point you still have considerable choice, and no one is forcing you to conform against your will. You might decide that the group holds limited potential for you to effect the ends which you hold in high priority, or you might determine that the members of the group share objectives that are compatible with your own. Still, the choice is yours, and you must make the determination. No one forces you to compromise concerning your personal commitments and goals, even though there may be some social pressure exerted by the group. But if you elect to join the group and to pursue the goals determined, accepted, or assigned by or to the group, then you must agree to play by the rules agreed upon by the group.

While we have been saying that groups have goals, we have also emphasized that a group is composed of individuals, each possessing personal goals. So the observation that a group has a goal carries with it the understanding that a group's goal refers to some degree of consensus reached by individual members of the group on the end result sought by that particular group. This is so whether the goal is assigned to or selected by the group. Generally, the desired outcome of this struggle between personal goals and group goals is the individual members' agreement on a common set of objectives to be pursued by the group.

Relationship Between Achievement Goals and Group Maintenance Goals

Our mechanistic discussion of goals thus far may have given you the false impression that you simply give a group a goal, plug the group into an energy source, turn on the switch, and wait for the desired outcome. Here we will try to correct any such possible misconception by suggesting some of the important relationships between achievement goals and group maintenance goals. Additional attention also will be devoted to the relationship between these kinds of goals in later chapters.

Previous comments have emphasized that when a group attempts to accomplish achievement goals, its members must cope with two basic problems almost at the same time: the attainment of the achievement goal and the maintenance and continuance of the group itself. Of course, we approach ideal conditions in groups when achievement goals are accomplished effectively, and, simultaneously, the goals of group maintenance are achieved satisfactorily. Unfortunately, the nature of human behavior in groups seldom permits such ideal relationships to emerge smoothly. Either obstacles to the attainment of achievement goals or obstacles to satisfactory interpersonal relations among the group's members may result in the failure of the group.

The most realistic perspective concerning the emphasis to be placed on the attainment of achievement goals and group maintenance goals we can recommend is probably a balance between the two kinds of goals. You should probably shift or fluctuate the weight placed on the achievement of each kind of goal depending on the conditions of the group. When the group is moving smoothly toward its achievement goal and interpersonal relations are favorable, primary attention may be devoted to the achievement goal. This is so because you can use interpersonal rewards among members to support the attainment of the achievement goal. Similarly, rewards for the group related to the accomplishment of an achievement goal may serve to maintain and strengthen interpersonal relations among members. Either or both classes of the group's activities can be supported by both types of rewards (Collins and Guetzkow, 1964).

Under other circumstances, as when the group's structure is deteriorating but reasonable progress is being made toward the achievement goal, it may be necessary to shift the emphasis of the group to the attainment of group maintenance goals. Sometimes you might envision these two kinds of goals as competing against one another for members' time. Other times the two goals may be worked on harmoniously and simultaneously by members. The point is that there is usually a continual fluctuation of the priority of weight assigned to each kind of goal. Your responsibility as a member of a group is to determine when to weigh the priorities in favor of one kind of goal over the other and then to shift the attention of your fellow members to the appropriate kind of goal. The consequences of being unable to make such determinations may mean temporary disaster, if not the finish, for your group.

PRINCIPLES

1. A group's goals are almost never 100 percent compatible with the personal goals of the individuals composing the group. Accordingly, you should be prepared to compromise and/or modify your commitment to individual goals and to help other participants make a similar adjustment, *if* you decide to participate in the group.

2. Since members' commitment to the group's goals increases the probability that desirable interpersonal relations will evolve and be maintained in the group, you should recognize that the initial time spent developing this commitment may actually save the group time in latter stages of discussion.

3. Knowledge about the relationship between members' personal goals and the group's goals is necessary but not sufficient information for you to

predict the group's performance. You must also know the extent to which the group demonstrates cooperative or competitive behavior as this variable interacts with the relationship between participants' personal goals and the group's goals.

SUMMARY

The nature of goals and their relevance to small group communication has been examined in this chapter. The chapter started by providing an overview of the general concepts of goals and tasks in small groups. Goal was defined as the end result that a group or an individual seeks to achieve. Task was defined as an act, or its result, that a small group is required to perform.

The second major section of this chapter dealt with personal goals and their consequences for the goals of the small group. Personal goals were defined as the objective that an individual seeks to achieve. Conscious and unconscious personal goals were discussed with regard to their influence on the members' acceptance of the group's goals and the productivity of the group. The degree of awareness of one's personal goals was considered a basis for distinguishing between conscious and unconscious personal goals.

Group goals were analyzed as the third major topic in the chapter. A group goal was defined as the end result that a group seeks to achieve. Two principal types of goals pertinent to the small group were discussed: achievement goals and group maintenance goals. The former refers to the major outcome or product that the group intends to produce, while the latter refers to those goals designed to maintain, strengthen, and/or ensure the continued existence of the group. In addition, subgoals were identified as those implied in the main goal or those goals explicitly stated as subordinate to and formulated after the main goal. Functional behaviors employed to accomplish achievement goals and maintenance goals in small groups were reviewed independently, with the caution that the functional behaviors required for these two types of goals frequently overlap.

The fourth and final section of this chapter focused on key relationships concerning group goals. The relationship between personal goals and group goals was reviewed and implications and consequences of trying to make personal goals compatible with the group's goals was stressed. Finally, the relationship between achievement goals and maintenance goals was examined.

IDEAS FOR DISCUSSION

1. What are the really important distinctions and relationships between goals and tasks? Why is it important to make them?

2. What are some of the most important implications relevant to the role of

perception in small groups that you have experienced, and what can or should you do about them?

3. What are some of the implications of conscious and unconscious personal goals for small group behavior? How do such goals influence you and others in the small group?

4. How can you maintain a balance between the group's need to accomplish achievement goals and maintenance goals?

5. How would you attempt to deal with the following situations in a group: members seem unclear about an issue; participants are not focusing on the goal; the topic is not related to the goal; and the group is bogged down and not moving toward achievement of the goal?

6. What are some personal goals you have that would not permit you to accept conflicting group goals *under any* circumstances?

SUGGESTED PROJECTS AND ACTIVITIES

1. List three groups to which you belong. Identify the goals of the three groups, listing achievement and maintenance goals separately. Finally, determine which tasks are used to accomplish those goals.

2. Using the same three groups, list your personal goals for the group. In a brief essay discuss how your personal goals are or are not satisfied by your group membership.

REFERENCES

CARTWRIGHT, D., and A. ZANDER, eds. *Group dynamics*, 3rd ed. New York: Harper & Row, Pub., 1968.

CHAPLIN, J. P. *Dictionary of psychology*. New York: Dell Pub. Co., Inc., 1968.

COLLINS, B. E., and H. GUETZKOW. *A social psychology of group processes for decision-making*. New York: John Wiley, 1964.

HARE, A. P. *Handbook of small group research*, 2nd ed. New York: Free Press, 1976.

HARNACK, R. V., T. B. FEST, and B. S. JONES. *Group discussion theory and technique*, 2nd ed. Englewood Cliffs, N.J.: Prentice-Hall, 1977.

JOHNSON, D. W., and F. P. JOHNSON. *Joining together: group theory and group skills*. Englewood Cliffs, N.J.: Prentice-Hall, 1975.

McGRATH, J. E., and I. ALTMAN. *Small group research: a synthesis and critique of the field*. New York: Holt, Rinehart & Winston, 1966.

MILLS, T. M. *The sociology of small groups*. Englewood Cliffs, N.J.: Prentice-Hall, 1967.

SHEPHERD, C. R. *Small groups: some sociological perspectives*. New York: Harper & Row, Pub., 1964.

SUGGESTED READINGS

GOLDHABER, G. M. *Organizational communication*, 2nd ed. Dubuque, Iowa: Wm. C. Brown, 1979.

Chapter 7, "Small Group Organizational Communication," defines group and small group in terms of social systems. The chapter identifies and describes types of small groups found in organizations, discusses group variables, and illustrates the assessment of group effectiveness.

JOHNSON, D. W., and F. P. JOHNSON. *Joining together: group theory and group skills.* Englewood Cliffs, N.J.: Prentice-Hall, 1975.

Chapter 4, "Group Goals," includes discussion and exercises to increase understanding of the definitions, skills, structure, and types of goals.

KHANDWALLA, P. N. *The design of organizations.* New York: Harcourt Brace Jovanovich, Inc., 1977.

Chapter 10, "The Goals of Organizations," discusses several types of operating goals in organizations as well as individual personal goals.

KIBLER, R. J., D. J. CEGALA, K. W. WATSON, L. L. BARKER, and D. T. MILES. *Objectives for instruction and evaluation,* 2nd ed. Boston: Allyn & Bacon, 1981.

Chapter 1 provides a rationale for instructional objectives (goals) and their use. Chapter 2, "Application of Instructional Objectives to Specified Educational Levels," explains the values, applications, and difficulties of designing objectives for differing educational levels.

4

Variables
Affecting
Small Group
Behavior

Study
Questions

After you have read this chapter, you should be able to answer the following questions completely and accurately:

1. What does the term *communication net* mean?
2. What are communication channels?
3. How does a central position in a communication network differ from a less central position?
4. What are three reasons that groups exhibit different communication structures?
5. What are three consequences of the group structure for the individual group member?
6. How does the communication structure affect the performance of the group?
7. What does the term *role* mean as it is applied to group structure?
8. What are the three broad sets of roles?
9. What are two types of role conflict that may arise?
10. What are three ways that one person can influence another person?
11. What does the term *group cohesiveness* mean?
12. How does group cohesiveness relate to responsible activity?
13. How does group cohesiveness relate to communication?
14. How does group cohesiveness relate to interpersonal influence?
15. How does group cohesiveness relate to task performance?
16. Is it possible for a large group to be cohesive?
17. What are the effects of group size on the group member?
18. What are the effects of group size on the group?
19. How may the large group disadvantage of less available interaction time per member be eliminated?
20. What is the principle of least group size?

Considerable research has been conducted in the area of small groups.[1] Most of the research on which this chapter is based was conducted in the laboratory rather than in natural settings. Before you read the discussion and application of the findings of laboratory studies in this chapter, we would like to draw your attention to several differences between laboratory groups and natural groups. Individuals in laboratory studies are brought together, usually for the first time, to function as a group; frequently they never see one another again. The researcher has control over most of the variables in the situation and systematically can manipulate the variables and observe the effects. For example, the researcher may vary group size and observe the effects on cohesiveness. One major advantage of laboratory groups is control.

The advantage of control in laboratory studies is somewhat costly because natural groups often cannot be studied in the laboratory context. Natural groups, as contrasted with groups formed in the laboratory, are ongoing groups. Without experimental control, all of the variables interact and make accurate predictions difficult. The lack of experimental control in natural groups should not prohibit the application of these research findings to the small groups in which you participate, however. The research should help you to understand what takes place in a small group by enhancing your perceptiveness and sensitivity.

This chapter focuses on four areas of research: *group structure, roles, group cohesiveness,* and *group size.* When analyzing your group as a system, you should examine these four variables closely. They affect communication, friendship formation, information availability, and many other dimensions of your group. Including them in your systems analysis can help you better understand and perhaps improve your group.

GROUP STRUCTURE

Communication interactions in a small group may take many different forms. One form of interaction is who talks to whom, or the *communication structure,* a concept that was introduced in Chapter 2. The simplest communication pattern exists in a two-person group, or dyad, where Ann and Bob are interacting. Ann may send a message to Bob and/or Bob may send a message to Ann. The communication pattern in a triad, or three-person group, becomes more complex with the possibilities listed below. The system changes with just one new element.

Ann to Bob	Bob to Ann	Charlie to Bob
Ann to Charlie	Bob to Charlie	Charlie to Ann
Ann to Bob and Charlie	Charlie to Ann and Bob	Bob to Ann and Charlie

[1]See Cartwright and Zander, 1968; Hare, 1962; Hare, Borghatta, and Bales, 1965; Hoffman, 1979; McGrath and Altman, 1966; Shaw, 1980.

The communication pattern in a group, such as in the above illustration, sometimes is termed *communication net*.

Social scientists have focused on communication in a considerable number of laboratory studies. The research primarily has been concerned with the various *types of communication networks, the reasons groups become structured*, and *the effects of group structure*.

Types of Communication Networks

Scientists who study communication structure usually specify communication channels. Between any two positions (individuals), there may be a two-way channel, a one-way channel, or no channel at all. In a two-way channel, Ann may send a message to Bob and Bob may send a message to Ann. However, in a one-way channel, Ann may send a message to Bob but Bob may not send a message to Ann (or vice versa). In the *wheel network* (see Figure 4.1), Bob, Charlie, Diane, and Ed may send and receive messages from Ann, although they may neither send nor receive messages from each other. The *circle network* allows sending and receiving of messages from the positions to either the right or left; for example, Bob may send messages to Ann and Charlie but not to Diane or Ed. The *chain network* is similar to the circle network, except that two of the positions may send and receive messages from only one position; for example, Ann only may send a message to Bob and Ed may only send a message to Diane. In the *all-channel network*, all positions may send and receive messages from all other positions; Ann, Bob, Charlie, Diane, and Ed may interact freely with each other. Thus, the type of network restricts the communication interaction.

Scientists frequently refer to *centrality of position* in communication networks. Individuals who interact with only one or two other participants

FIGURE 4.1 Communication Networks Frequently Employed in Experimental Studies

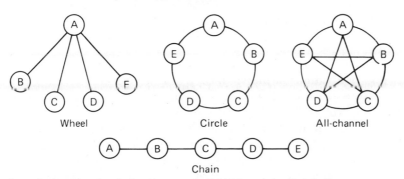

In each structure the circles represent individuals and the lines indicate communication channels.

(e.g., Bob in the chain network) occupy a restricted or less central position, while individuals who interact with all or most all of the group members (e.g., Ann in the wheel network) occupy a less restricted or more central position. Several experimental studies (Shaw, 1954a, 1954b; Gilchrest, Shaw, and Walker, 1954) have indicated that individuals who occupy a more central position have higher individual morale and have a greater probability of being chosen group leader. Further research findings concerning the effects of group structure will be presented later in the chapter.

Reasons Groups Become Structured

Research in the area of group structure has produced several possible reasons that groups form differing communication patterns and, therefore, exhibit differing structures. Three of several possible reasons that groups exhibit differing structures are noted by Shaw (1980): (1) requirements for efficient group performance, (2) different abilities and motivations of different individuals, and (3) physical and social characteristics of the group's environment.

Efficient group performance.   You may recall being in a small group which was organizing a party or some other similar social function. The group probably agreed to divide the responsibility for entertainment, decorations, refreshments, admissions, etc., among the individuals in the group. The decision to divide the responsibility probably was reached with little disagreement; most individuals who participate in a group task find that a group is more efficient if it specializes the tasks (e.g., responsibility for entertainment). Suppose, for example, that Ann is responsible for entertainment for a social function. For the sake of efficiency, she assigns to each member of her subgroup a different band and asks them to determine the cost of having that group entertain at their social function. Each individual (Bob, Charlie, Diane, and Ed) reports back to Ann and does not find it necessary to communicate with the other members of the subgroup. Thus, the group exhibited the characteristics of the wheel network (Figure 4.1) because the members determined that an efficient way to complete the group task was to assign each member a part of the task and to have each member report directly to the leader.

Abilities and motivations of individuals.   If you have been a member of a group which organized and divided responsibility for various tasks (as in the above example), you probably had a preference concerning the nature of the task to which you were assigned. For example, you may be interested in music and prefer to find a band for entertainment rather than push a grocery cart and purchase refreshments. The task you select generally will determine with whom you must communicate and therefore will determine the communication pattern or structure. Preference for such tasks is common in most groups, as individual differences in ability and personality lead people to prefer to do certain types of tasks.

Individual preferences usually are healthy for the group because group members generally are motivated to do tasks they enjoy. A systems analysis may help you allocate specific tasks to specific group members. However, sometimes there is a task that no one is motivated to perform. In such cases it may be necessary to place the group goal above individual preference. If the unpleasant task is ongoing, the group members may elect to take turns at performing the task.

Environment of the group. You may recall the times in elementary school when you had recess or recreation. As you may recall (or observe in young children) the same group of children playing outside on a playground may seem to be totally different when having recess inside on a rainy day. The environment (an external variable discussed in Chapter 2) of a classroom usually restrains both the activities (kickball is not permitted, for example) and the communication pattern (shouting to a friend across the room probably will result in a reprimand from the teacher). For example, Charlie may talk to every group member when the group is outside (all-channel network, Figure 4.1), but he may talk only to Bob and Diane, who sit on either side of him, when the group is inside (circle network). Although the environment of the group will be discussed in Chapter 8, variables such as the space available to the group and the arrangement of the group members may influence the group structure.

Effects of Structure

In addition to studying communication networks and discovering reasons that groups become structured, researchers in the area of group structure have studied the effects of group structure. Two of the effects of group structure (Cartwright and Zander, 1968) which will be discussed are: (1) the consequences of structure for the individual group member and (2) the effects of structure on group performance.

Consequences of individual location in group structure. The position occupied in a communication structure produces several consequences for the individual. Morale, leadership, and friendship are three of the possible consequences.

Research (see Berkowitz, 1978) has indicated that members in the more central positions in a group's communication structure show a higher degree of satisfaction (presumably because they send a greater number of messages) and are more frequently nominated as leaders. For example, antagonism is likely to result in a situation in which Ann is allowed to send a message to Bob but Bob is not allowed to send a message to Ann (see Pool, 1976).

This type of situation frequently occurs in hierarchical organizations when one individual is subordinate to another. Although the "superior" individual ("leader" or "president" of a company) may feel a high degree of satisfaction, the "subordinate" individual may feel minimal satisfaction. This especially may be apparent when a male is subordinate to a female in our society (although change is in progress). Individual morale would generally be the highest in the all-channel network (Figure 4.1) where each individual may send and receive messages and where each individual has a relatively equal chance of being chosen as the leader. This may be the reason that individual morale and satisfaction generally are higher in a sorority or fraternity group, for example, than in the army with its hierarchical structure and its primarily one-way channel of communication.

Leadership is an important variable in communication networks. As suggested, research in the past has shown that member satisfaction is generally lower in centralized networks such as the wheel. Snadowsky (1974), however, found that democratic leadership produced satisfied group members in spite of centralized communication. Chapter 9 provides more information about leadership so that you can investigate it in your systems analysis, along with group structure.

In addition to affecting morale and leadership, group structure also affects friendship formation. An experimental study conducted by Byrne and Bouehler (1955) found that students in neighboring seats are more likely to become acquainted than are classmates in general. For example, Charlie would be more likely to become acquainted with Bob and Diane in the chain network (Figure 4.1) than with Ann and Ed. There seems to be little probability that individuals will become friends if they do not interact with each other. Friendship formation also is related to group cohesion, which is discussed later in this chapter.

Effects of structure on group performance.   The experimental studies in the area of communication structure have shown that the performance of a group is affected by the communication structure imposed on the group. Research (see Shaw, 1980) has indicated in general that some structures solve problems faster, make fewer errors, and send fewer messages. Frequently, the wheel network has been found to promote performance superior to that of the other networks.

Consider, for example, a situation in which each group member has part of the information needed to solve an arithmetic problem. Because only Ann (the individual in position A) can communicate with each of the remaining positions, the information is sent to her, and she solves the problem. The wheel network usually solves problems faster and makes fewer errors than the remaining networks (e.g., circle) that have no established leader or organizational pattern.[2] Thus, although morale appears to be lowest in centralized structures such as the wheel, they may be superior to less centralized structures where performance is concerned. This information may be valuable to you when you join either social or task-oriented groups.

Communication networks, the reasons groups become structured, and the effects of structure on group performance have been discussed in this section. Small group discussions in which you participate more than likely will not be typical of any specific communication structure. However, during the interaction that occurs while the discussion itself is in progress, you may recognize the group's tendency to conform to a particular structural pattern.

PRINCIPLES

1. The communication pattern in a group sometimes is termed a *communication net*.
2. The communication channels between the positions in the network (or who talks to whom) determine the type of communication network (and vice versa).
3. Individuals who interact with all or most of the group members occupy a less restricted or more central position.
4. Three of several possible reasons that groups exhibit differing communication structures are: group efficiency, individual abilities, and group environment.
5. The position an individual occupies in a communication structure affects morale, probability of being chosen leader, and friendship formation.
6. Centralized structures (e.g., wheel) appear to be more efficient, although morale tends to be lower.

In addition to the principles listed in this chapter, here are some guidelines for you to follow in your group performance.

1. Every time you add a new element to your group, either in the form of a new group member or situation, you should analyze its effects on the system.
2. Put group members who seem to be left out in more central positions. This will give them a greater opportunity to interact without forcing them.

---

[2]It should be noted that the research in this area is not conclusive. Berkowitz (1978) notes that the effect a structure has on the performance of a group may depend in part on the nature of the task (i.e., whether or not the task requires considerable organizational behavior).

3. Analyze why your group became structured and the usefulness of the structure.

4. When dividing responsibilities in a group, have each member construct a list of the tasks in his or her order of preference. Then give each member a task which is one of the top three choices and take turns doing those listed at the bottom.

5. To allow maximum interaction, provide for maximum eye contact when arranging the seating for your group.

ROLES

To many people the term *role* means behaving in an artificial manner. Frequently we make statements such as, "He was acting like a child," or "She was putting on a big show." However, when applied to group structure, the concept of role in the theatrical sense is not intended. As related to groups, a role is a set of behaviors that is expected of and/or displayed by the individual who occupies a particular position in a group's structure.

Perhaps the concept of role may be understood best through the example of the structure of a university. President, dean, professor, and student are positions in the university structure. In each of these positions there is a specialization of behavior; rarely does the president of a large university attend classes! Similarly, there is a tendency for various degrees of specialization to occur among members of discussion groups. For example, you may prefer to gather information about the group problem or task while another member may prefer to promote group harmony by telling funny stories at particularly tense moments. When you are more likely to perform some types of behaviors (e.g., going to classes or giving information) than other behaviors (e.g., teaching classes or promoting harmony), you have assumed a role.

Several individuals may perform the same role in different ways. One of the variables influencing an individual's performance of a role is role skill. *Role skills* refer to the characteristics an individual possesses which enable him or her to effectively enact a role. Role skills include variables such as aptitude, appropriate experience, and specific training. For example, you may recall a group member (perhaps yourself) who was especially skilled in leadership. This individual probably was influential in the group and may have had considerable experience as a leader. In addition, he or she may have "done his or her homework" by reading about leadership (see Chapter 9) prior to leading the discussion. As you know, not everyone is a good leader. In a similar manner, not every individual possesses the same skills to enact a role with equal effectiveness.

This section of the chapter first will present the *general roles* that individuals enact during a discussion. The enactment of each role will affect the group as a system. Sometimes problems arise when individuals enact roles; these problems frequently result from *role conflict*. In addition, *role influence*, or specific persuasive roles, will be discussed.

General Roles

Earlier (see pp. 58–59) we pointed out that groups become structured and divisions of responsibility come about whenever a group divides responsibilities to accomplish its goals. As the group members assume responsibility, roles tend to develop. Individual group members may assume several types of roles.[3] One of the oldest but more useful classification of role types was developed by Benne and Sheats (1948), who divided roles into three broad sets: group task roles, group building and maintenance roles, and self-centered roles. In your systems analysis, you should identify the roles played by different members of your group and analyze how they affect the interaction.

Group task roles are related to the accomplishment of the group's task or achievement goal (see Chapter 3). Frequently an individual who enacts group task roles is referred to as a *task specialist*. Group task roles include:

Initiator-Contributor—offering new ideas to be considered by the group or stating old ideas in a novel fashion. ("Let's consider the financial aspect of this problem.")

Information Seeker—asking for clarification of ideas or requesting evidence and facts. ("Does anyone have information regarding the cost of this survey?")

Opinion Seeker—asking for agreement or disagreement with ideas/ proposals under consideration. ("I would like to know how the rest of the group members feel about conducting a survey.")

Information Giver—contributing relevant information. ("Dan can have the survey duplicated for two cents per page.")

Opinion Giver—offering own opinion. ("I'm in favor of a fund-raising project.")

Elaborator—clarifying and further explaining another member's ideas. ("Perhaps Cindy is thinking that having the bake sale downtown would provide an unsaturated market.")

Coordinator—showing relationships among statements of fact or opinion from group members. ("The statistics from the Registrar's Office certainly seem to support the dean's opinion.")

---

[3]It should be remembered that one individual frequently exhibits the characteristics of several different roles throughout the discussion.

Orienter—guiding the discussion by keeping the group on track and moving the discussion along. ("Let's get back to our criteria.")

Evaluator-Critic—evaluating the adequacy of the group's information and accomplishments according to some set of standards. ("That would be a good suggestion if we had enough money in our budget, but it doesn't seem to be feasible with our limited finances.")

Energizer—prodding the members to action. ("Who would like to help me with the computer analysis?")

Procedural Technician—handling routine tasks such as seating arrangements, handouts, etc. ("I've placed a packet of information for each of you on the table.")

Recorder—keeping track of the group's progress, or taking minutes. ("According to my notes, we agreed to limit this meeting to one hour.")

Group building and maintenance roles are behaviors which contribute to the functioning of the group by striving to maintain constructive interpersonal relations (see Chapter 3). An individual who enacts group building and maintenance roles frequently is referred to as the social-emotional leader. Group building and maintenance roles include:

Encourager—providing support or showing acceptance of another member's idea or statement. ("That's a good idea, Michael. I'll help.")

Harmonizer—resolving conflict and reducing tension, frequently with humor. ("Since we're all friends again, let's agree to bring squirt guns to our meetings so we can have *real* battles.")

Compromiser—attempting to come up with an idea that will please everyone. ("Even though I'd rather have the bake sale on campus, maybe we would have time to do both—we could have the bake sale in town this Friday and on campus the following Friday.")

Gatekeeper—opening the channels of communication and promoting evenness of participation. ("Just a minute, Sam. Sue, what were you starting to say?")

Standard Setter—expressing standards for the group to achieve or applying standards in evaluating the group's progress. ("Why don't we try to reach a workable decision in forty-five minutes? Then this will be our shortest meeting!")

Group Observer—evaluating the mood of the group. ("It seems as though group consensus has been reached.")

Follower—accepting ideas of others and going along with the group trends. ("If everyone is going this Saturday, I'll go, too.")

Self-centered roles are behaviors that satisfy personal needs rather than group goals (see Chapter 3). These behaviors tend to be either unrelated or

negative related to group goals and may operate at the conscious or unconscious level. Self-centered roles include:

Aggressor—attacking other members in an effort to promote own
status. ("Bake sales are immature and a pretty dumb idea. My suggestion has class.")

Blocker—opposing all ideas and refusing to cooperate. ("I don't think a
good idea has been suggested by this group yet!")

Recognition Seeker—boasting about past accomplishments (frequently irrelevant) usually in an attempt to gain sympathy. ("Last
year's fund-raising project was my idea and it was successful, too. I
think the group should reconsider their thoughts about my idea for
having a carnival this year.")

Self-Confessor—engaging in irrelevant discussion to work out personal
mistakes and feelings. ("Last night I had this sudden insight into why I
can't study. It all goes back to my fourth-grade teacher . . . .")

Playboy—displaying a lack of involvement in the group through in-
appropriate humor or horseplay. ("Let's go shoot some pool instead.")

Dominator—embarking on long monologues and trying to monopolize the group's time. ("I guess what I've been trying to say for the past
ten minutes is . . . etc., etc., etc.")

Help Seeker—attempting to gain sympathy from other group members
through expressions of insecurity or inadequacy. ("I really don't think I
should be responsible for the computer analysis. I've never been very
good in math and I'd probably lose the computer program, too.")

Special-Interest Pleader—bringing in irrelevant information and arguing incessantly from own point of view. ("Tuesday is still a better day
for a bake sale because it's the day after a 'blue Monday.' ")[4]

Experimental studies (see Slater, 1955; Bales, 1958) generally have indicated that different individuals, rather than the same person, perform group
task roles and group building and maintenance roles. For example, to
perform both roles an individual must strive toward the performance of the
task and at the same time be concerned with interpersonal relationships.
These inconsistent obligations may result in role conflict.

Role Conflict

You probably remember the biblical story of Abraham and his son
Isaac. When God told Abraham to sacrifice Isaac, Abraham found himself in
two positions which required contradictory behaviors. In his role as a servant

[4]Based in part on Benne and Sheats (1948) with permission.

of God, he was to sacrifice Isaac, yet in his role as father he could n kill his only son. This condition may be termed *role conflict*. Role con exists when an individual is expected to simultaneously meet role expecta s that are inconsistent or contradictory. The conflict results from the pr re to behave in opposing ways at the same time.

Sarbin and Allen (1969) identify two types of role conflict: ole conflict and intrarole conflict. *Interrole conflict* results when an in al simultaneously occupies two roles which have incompatible role e tions. This type of role conflict may be experienced when a teache student to proctor an exam, for example. If the student observes a cheating on the test, he or she faces conflict between the role of friend a role of proctor. Similarly, a group member of a zoning board may expe role conflict when he or she simultaneously must assume the some inconsistent roles of promoter of new industry and preserver of ecolog one role the board member might zone an area for a paper mill, but in an role that same person might zone the area as a recreational park.

Intrarole conflict exists when one or more relevant others hold cor dictory expectations for the same role. For example, a married woman experience conflict when her husband expects her to be "liberated" a independent, but at the same time he places on her the sole responsibility raising the children and maintaining the home. In a similar manner, a grou leader may experience role conflict. For example, some group members m expect the leader to be task oriented while other members may expect th leader to be concerned with interpersonal relations (see Chapter 9). Thus, group member may experience role conflict when he or she simultaneously enacts two roles which have incompatible expectations, or when one or more relevant others hold contradictory expectations for the role he or she is enacting.

Sometimes individuals who are experiencing conflict behave differently than they ordinarily behave. For example, imagine a liberally dressed boyfriend who meets his girlfriend's conservative parents. Pressure is placed on the boyfriend because the girlfriend's parents want their daughter's boyfriend to enact a different (i.e., conservative) role. Ordinarily the boyfriend is friendly and outgoing, but in the presence of the parents he becomes defensive and belligerent. Role conflict may create similar effects in group members. A group member who is experiencing role conflict may become overinvolved or monopolize the discussion. Or, on the other hand, the member may withdraw from interaction with the group and be silent. Techniques for stimulating an uninvolved group member and for regulating the participation of an overinvolved group member are given in Chapter 9. However, it should be remembered that if an individual is experiencing role conflict, these techniques treat only the symptoms and do not resolve the conflict itself.

Role Influence

One person may influence another person by means of power, authority, or persuasion (Blau and Scott, 1962). The individual roles of the group leader and group members usually determine the type of influence that is exerted over the other members of the group.

Influence based on *power* may occur when the relationship between the individuals (or groups) is such that the individual holding power is in a position to carry out his or her will despite resistance. The firing squad is an example of a general's power to enforce his will. Influence based on power will occur rarely in your small groups.

On the other hand, influence based on *authority* may occur in your small groups. Such influence depends on voluntary obedience. An individual who responds to authority often considers it legitimate (sometimes even rewarding) for another individual to control his or her behavior in particular cases. Influence through authority usually occurs in the teacher-student relationship. For example, a student usually responds to the teacher's request to be quiet, and a teacher usually complies to the student's request for a conference after class. Similarly, most of you will consider it legitimate for a democratic leader to influence your behavior. For example, the leader may have the authority to ask you to be quiet or to perform a certain task. Since you are responding to another individual's role (rather than to the message alone), persuasion has not occurred even though there has been voluntary compliance.

In both the power and authority relationships, *persuasion* is helpful but not necessary to control the behavior of others. Persuasion, like authority, depends upon the voluntary acceptance of another's ideas, but, unlike the power or authority relationships, persuasion arouses the perception and exercise of choice among the various alternatives. Suppose, for example, that a group member asks you to move your chair a little so that he also can sit at the table. Unless the individual is the world's heavy weight or an individual who has legitimate power over you, persuasion most likely will operate. The effect (whether or not you move your chair) will be due to the message, rather than to the force or superiority of one individual over another.

A particular danger in small groups composed of individuals with varying degrees of status (prestige) is that persuasion will not be the primary mode of influence. Individuals with high status tend to ignore or reject ideas from persons of lower status. On the other hand, low status persons tend to accept without logical criticism the ideas of higher status persons. The result frequently is a one-way channel of communication from superior to subordinate with power or authority the chief means of influence. A systems analysis should help you determine the type(s) of influence exercised in your group.

The manner in which a group reaches a decision (power, authority, or persuasion) often is a key indicator of interpersonal attraction. When the group members reach a decision by acquiescence to the leader, attraction to the group is probably low. On the other hand, attraction is probably high in groups where all members have had their say, and even though some members still may have reservations, they are personally willing to express agreement with the decision.

PRINCIPLES

1. A role is a set of behaviors that are expected of and/or displayed by the individual who occupies a particular position in a group's structure.
2. Role skills are the characteristics an individual possesses which enable him or her to effectively enact a role.
3. The three broad sets of roles that a group member may enact are: group task roles, group building and maintenance roles, and self-centered roles.
4. Two types of role conflict are interrole conflict and intrarole conflict.
5. Role influence (influence of one person over another) may be based on power, authority, or persuasion.

The following guidelines should help you improve the interaction in your group:

1. Identify the various roles you play in your group and determine whether or not they facilitate the group process.
2. The leader should take responsibility for meeting privately with group members who play self-centered roles. Their behavior should be discussed with them in a nonthreatening way.
3. Role playing (see Chapter 11) might help group members alter their behavior.
4. Determine the types of influence used in your group and whether or not they promote interaction. Try to change the situation if power and authority are used to restrict other group members unreasonably.

GROUP COHESIVENESS

One of the major difficulties facing individuals who want to understand groups is how to explain differences in "groupness." Why do individuals in some groups have warmer interpersonal relationships than individuals in other groups? Why are individuals in some groups more involved with the group than individuals in other groups? Many researchers in small group communication say that the answers to these questions lie with a concept called *group cohesiveness.* Although variously defined over the years, cohesiveness generally is regarded as the complex of forces which bind members of a group to each other and to the group as a whole. *Complex of forces* may be thought of as the things or people that keep us functioning as members of the group. To many of us a cohesive group represents the "perfect" group composed of happy group members.

Considerable research[5] has been conducted in the area of group cohesiveness. Cohesiveness primarily has been measured by interpersonal congeniality (e.g., friendliness, acceptance of each other's ideas, etc.) and the desire to remain a member of the group. You can evaluate these dimensions of your group by including them in your systems analysis. Researchers have related cohesiveness to variables such as a sense of responsibility, communication among group members, and readiness of group members to be influenced by the group. Task effectiveness and cohesiveness also have been positively correlated when the group values accomplishment of the task over sociability. We shall examine these variables in greater detail below.[6]

Responsible Activity

Individuals who are highly attracted to a group more often take on responsibilities, participate more readily in meetings, persist longer in working toward difficult goals, attend meetings more faithfully, and remain members longer (Brilhart, 1974). Conversely, if an individual participates in a group and the group's efforts are a success, his or her participation in the group is a reinforcing experience and personal attraction to the group is increased (Silver, 1974). For example, an individual is highly attracted to a group aimed at gaining equal employment benefits for women. The individual attends meetings faithfully and accepts responsibility for the distribution of leaflets which present the group's position on the equal employment issue. If the group is successful in raising the salary of women in a neighboring business, the group member probably will find the experience rewarding and will be willing to accept even greater responsibility for future tasks.

You may want to remember and apply this principle to small groups that have only a few of the "old faithfuls" attending and participating in the meetings. One method of increasing cohesiveness or reviving the group would be to structure tasks that would provide success to the group. The tasks initially may or may not be directly related to the group goal. For example, suppose you are a member of a group which is assigned the task of formulat-

---

[5]See Hoffman (1979), Blakeman and Helmreich (1975), and McGrath and Altman (1966).
[6]The discussion is based on Collins and Raven (1969).

ing an acceptable proposal for raising money to build an addition to the pediatrics wing of the hospital. All of the group proposals have been vetoed by the board of directors and the group members are losing interest. You analyze this situation and arrange for the group to put on a free puppet show for the children in the hospital and their families. The show is entertaining to the audience and provides sufficient success for the group that the members are motivated to formulate another money-raising proposal and submit it to the board of directors. Thus, even limited success may increase attraction to the group with the result that the members may be more willing to engage in responsible activity.

Communication

Communication and group cohesiveness also are related. "If the frequency of interaction between two or more persons increases, the degree of their liking for one another will increase and vice versa" (Homans, 1950, p. 112). In other words, the more times that Ann and Bob communicate or interact, the greater will be their liking for one another. For example, integration of the schools may illustrate this principle; if black children and white children interact more often, perhaps their liking for one another will increase.

Similarly, it seems logical that the frequency and length of conversations will be greater when two individuals share a close interpersonal relationship. Try to recall various groups to which you have belonged, some highly cohesive groups and some groups low in cohesiveness. If you could remember a large enough number of such groups, you probably would recall that the members of some groups were sociable and interacted while the members in other groups mostly sat and looked at each other. Most likely the groups with considerable interaction among the members were highly cohesive groups.

Interpersonal Influence

The tendency of individual group members to influence (persuade) and be influenced (persuaded) is greater in highly cohesive groups. This tendency may occur because generally individuals who are highly attracted to a group are more willing to listen to others and are more accepting of the opinions of others.

For example, imagine two groups. You have been elected to the first group, which is trying to improve the food in the student union cafeteria of a large state university. You don't agree with a solution proposed by one of the group members which was that the group should plan the menus. You listen and finally suggest that the school really needs a new company to provide the food service. A vote is taken and the majority of the members are in favor of planning menus. Although your solution was rejected, you agree to help plan menus for the cafeteria.

A second group in a nearby private school for boys shares a similar problem. One member from each of seven cabins was assigned to the group. One member proposes the menu solution that was proposed in your group. Another group member remarks that the supervisor won't read the menus anyway and walks out of the meeting. The six remaining members sit for a while and wait for someone to say something. Finally two more members leave, followed by the rest of the group. Thus, members of highly cohesive groups are more likely to listen and be more acceptant of the opinions of others than are members of groups that are low in cohesiveness.

Task Performance

Results of experimental studies investigating the relationship between cohesiveness and productivity are inconclusive. There are studies which show that groups formed to include friends show higher productivity as well as studies which fail to demonstrate a positive relationship between cohesiveness and productivity (see Porter, Lawler, and Hackman, 1975). It would seem possible that the accepted ways of behaving in a group would interact with the productivity factor. For example, two highly cohesive groups meet each week for the stated purpose of improving conditions at the local animal shelter. One group appears to have an implied purpose of reinforcing group friendship. The accepted ways of behaving at the group meetings include drinking coffee and sharing the past week's experiences and rumors. The other group also values friendship. However, those group members who are task oriented are closer friends with each other than with the other members of the group. They stop for coffee after the meetings to socialize as friends, but the conversation always seems to drift back to improving conditions at the animal shelter. Thus, it would seem that a highly cohesive group would be productive only if group value was placed on accomplishing the group task (see Hill, 1975).

Sometimes group value is placed on bolstering group morale rather than on accomplishing the task. Reaching agreement becomes dominant and tends to override critical analysis of alternative courses of action. Group members are amiable and avoid conflict even if that means failing to carefully scrutinize the advantages and disadvantages of various alternatives. In other words, loyalty to the group becomes more important than critical thinking or task orientation (see pp. 199–200). This type of group situation is termed "groupthink" by Janis (1971; 1972). It is difficult to estimate the number of highly cohesive groups that fall into Janis' groupthink category.[7] However,

[7]In his 1971 article, Janis provides examples of government groups which have become victims of groupthink; he also describes symptoms of groupthink and remedies to the problem.

highly cohesive groups should be sensitive to the possible development of norms which place group loyalty above task orientation. Groups are encouraged to become cohesive primarily because of the advantages of cohesiveness for group process and task performance.

Group Size

Cohesiveness also is related to group size. The topic of group size is discussed further in the next section. Imagine, if you will, two musical groups. The first is a rock group composed of a drummer, a bass player, an organist, and a couple of guitar players. The group is highly cohesive, well organized, and individually motivated to play. They have experienced an increase in job offers. The second musical group is much larger and is composed of several flutists and clarinetists in addition to trumpet and trombone players. Although the second group is considerably larger than the first, the larger band can also experience a high degree of cohesiveness because of the cohesiveness of small subgroups which form.

Small subgroups (e.g., flutists, clarinetists) within a large group generally do not affect the cohesiveness of the group if they are committed to the performance of the group's task. However, the cohesiveness of the larger group would be reduced if some subgroups protested the rules and regulations or norms and standards of the group (e.g., if the trombone players objected to band practice on Sunday afternoons). Thus, even though individuals in large groups may develop close interpersonal relationships with members of their subgroup, the large group still may be considered cohesive.

PRINCIPLES

1. Group cohesiveness generally is regarded as the complex of forces binding group members to each other and to the group as a whole.
2. Individuals who are attracted to a group usually engage in responsible activity (e.g., participate more readily, attend meetings more regularly). Conversely, if a member's participation is a reinforcing experience, his or her attraction to the group increases.
3. Interpersonal attraction usually increases as the frequency of interaction between two or more persons increases. Conversely, if two members share a close interpersonal relationship, most often their communication will increase.
4. Individuals who are highly attracted to a group tend to be more willing to listen to others and be more accepting of the opinion of others.
5. Cohesive groups appear to be more productive than other groups when group value is placed on accomplishing the task.

large group disadvantage of less
y be obtained with the orderly
ke use of the potential resources
interaction in smaller groups.
ups, or if the goals of the sub-
arger group, the advantages are
ffer a valuable alternative to the

throughout this discussion of
g just what is the optimum size
re is no clear agreement about
Guyer, and Fox, 1975). Many
bers is the optimum size for
ly would not be the optimum
Therefore, it would seem that
m number of group members

given problem, Thelen (1949)
he group should be just large
vant skills necessary to solve
pportunities for individual

each member to participate

information-giving phase of
when consensus must be

the large group disadvan-
ber.

that is just large enou
cessary to solve t
es for individua
p size."

ion of
es, the
y have
on in a
l group
t group
related to
members
resigning

p size. For exam-
the potential for
the group problem.
reater variety of opin-
sensus or agreement on
y in reaching consensus
s clear objective criteria for
Chapter 7), may lessen this
r that large groups are at an advantage in the
blem solving but at a potential disadvantage

The resource advantage without the
available interaction time per member m
formation of subgroups. The subgroups m
in the larger group, yet allow for greate
However, if there is rivalry between subg
groups are inconsistent with the goals of the
lost. Thus, when structured, subgroups may
disadvantages of large groups.

The term *small group* has been used
group size. At this point you may be wonderi
for a small group. As we suggested earlier, th
this issue (see Benjamin, 1978; Hamburger,
authorities think that around five or six me
small groups. However, a group of five proba
size for a class in small group communication
the group task and goals may affect the optim
in a small group.

To select the appropriate size group for a
suggested the "principle of least group size." T
enough to include individuals with all the rel
the problem, yet small enough to provide
participation.

PRINCIPLES

1. As group size increases, the time available fo
   orally decreases.
2. Large groups usually are an advantage in the
   problem solving but a potential disadvantag
   reached.
3. The use of structured subgroups may elimina
   tage of less available interaction time per men
4. The optimum size for a small group is a group
   include individuals with all the relevant skills n
   lem and yet small enough to provide opportuni
   tion. This is known as the "principle of least g

You may wish to apply the following gui
in your group.

1. Develop tasks which can be accomplis
   member involvement in your group.
   task into several smaller, more mana

2. Give the ideas of other group members a fair hearing before rejecting them.

3. Analyze the balance in your group between productivity and cohesiveness to determine whether you are emphasizing one at the expense of the other.

4. If your group size restricts the participation of group members, schedule regular buzz sessions (see Chapter 11) to maximize interaction. Switch members around so that they do not always form subgroups with the same members.

SUMMARY

This chapter has focused on four areas of research: group structure, roles, group cohesiveness, and group size. In the section dealing with group structure, we discussed the various types of communication networks, the reasons groups become structured, and the effects of group structure on the individual and the group. Although your small groups most likely will not follow the same pattern throughout the "life" of the group, you should be able to recognize the group's tendency to conform to a particular structural pattern at various points in the discussion.

We also discussed roles. Most likely you will be able to recognize the various roles that group members enact during a discussion and will be sensitive to role conflict and the pressures it places on group members. When one group member influences another member, you should be able to determine whether the influence is based on power, authority, or persuasion.

In addition, we presented several variables which relate to group cohesiveness. You should be aware of the effects of cohesiveness on responsible activity, communication, interpersonal influence, and task performance.

Finally, we suggested several effects of group size on the group member and on the group. Keeping these effects in mind, you should try to conform to the "principle of least group size" when you structure the size of your group.

We have not intended this chapter to be a summary of the research related to small group communication. Such summaries can be found elsewhere. The intention of this chapter has been to sensitize you to several important variables which might affect your behavior in small groups.

IDEAS FOR DISCUSSION

1. Which communication structures are more likely to emerge in authoritarian groups? democratic groups? Does group size affect the communication structure?

2. How might persons with differing personality variables (e.g., self-confidence, aggressiveness) affect the enactment of the same role in a group structure?

3. What are specific games that are played by people enacting different roles? What are specific games that are played by people who are experiencing role conflict?

4. How is the type of role influence one person exerts over another group member(s) affected by the communication structure? role enactment? group size?

5. What are the effects of disagreement on group cohesiveness? Is it possible for a group to experience hostility and be cohesive at the same time?

6. What are the effects of group size on creativity? on conformity?

SUGGESTED PROJECTS AND ACTIVITIES

1. Attend meetings of three different small groups (e.g., classes, religious groups, fraternities, clubs, etc.) and attempt to diagram the type of communication network employed in each. Compare and contrast each network discovered in terms of group efficiency and effectiveness.

2. Over the period of two weeks, observe your own roles in three groups you participate in. Write a paragraph describing your assumed role in each group. Discuss briefly the reasons that your roles differ across different groups.

3. Observe a small group at least twice. Record the amount of time each member speaks during the meetings. Then rank order the group members according to the amount of time they spoke in the group. Did the amount of speaking time relate to (1) contribution of the individual to the group, (2) credibility of the individual, or (3) attractiveness of the individual to other group members?

REFERENCES

BALES, R. F. Task roles and social roles in problem-solving groups. In E. E. MACCOBY, T. M. NEWCOMB, and E. L. HARTLEY, eds. *Readings in social psychology*, 3rd ed. New York: Holt, Rinehart & Winston, 1958.

BENJAMIN, A. *Behavior in small groups*. Boston: Houghton Mifflin Co., 1978.

BENNE, K. D., and P. SHEATS. Functional roles of group members. *Journal of social issues*, 1948, *4*, 41–49.

BERKOWITZ, L., ed. *Group processes*. New York: Academic Press, 1978.

BLAKEMAN, R., and R. HELMREICH. Cohesiveness and performance: covariation and causality in an undersea environment. *Journal of experimental social psychology*, 1975, *11*, 478–489.

BLAU, P. M., and W. R. SCOTT. *Formal organizations*. New York: Harper & Row, Pub., 1962.

BRILHART, J. K. *Effective group discussion*, 2nd ed. Dubuque, Iowa: Wm. C. Brown, 1974.

BYRNE, D., and J. A. BOUEHLER. A note of the influence of propinquity upon acquaintanceships. *Journal of abnormal and social psychology*, 1955, *51*, 147–148.

CARTWRIGHT, D., and A. ZANDER, eds. *Group dynamics: research and theory*, 3rd ed. New York: Harper & Row, Pub., 1968.

COLLINS, B. E., and B. H. RAVEN. Group structure: attraction, coalitions, communication and power. In G. Lindzey and E. Aronson, eds. *The handbook of social psychology*, 2nd ed. Reading, Mass.: Addison-Wesley, 1969.

GILCHRIST, J. C., M. E. SHAW, and L. C. WALKER. Some effects of unequal distribution of information in a wheel group structure. *Journal of abnormal and social psychology*, 1954, *49*, 554–556.

HAMBURGER, H., M. GUYER, and J. Fox. Group size and cooperation. *Journal of conflict resolution*, 1975, *19*, 503–531.

HARE, A. P. *Handbook of small group research*, 2nd ed. New York: Free Press, 1976.

HARE, A. P., E. F. BORGATTA, and R. F. BALES. *Small groups: studies in social interaction*. New York: Knopf, 1965.

HILL, R. Interpersonal compatibility and workgroup performance. *Journal of applied behavioral science*, 1975, *11*, 210–219.

HOFFMAN, L. R. *The group problem solving process: studies of a valence model*. New York: Holt, Rinehart & Winston, 1979.

HOMANS, G. *The human group*. New York: Harcourt Brace Jovanovich, 1950.

JANIS, I. L. *Victims of groupthink: a psychological study of foreign-policy decisions and fiascoes*. Boston: Houghton Mifflin Co., 1972.

MCGRATH, J. E., and I. ALTMAN. *Small group research: a synthesis and critique of the field*. New York: Holt, Rinehart & Winston, 1966.

PORTER, L. W., E. E. LAWLER III, and J. R. HACKMAN. *Behavior in organizations*. New York: McGraw-Hill, 1975.

POOL, J. Coalition formation in small groups with incomplete communication networks. *Journal of personality and social psychology*, 1976, *34*, 82–91.

SARBIN, T. R., and V. L. ALLEN. Role theory. In G. Lindzey and E. ARONSON, eds. *The handbook of social psychology*, 2nd ed. Reading, Mass.: Addison-Wesley, 1969.

SHAW, M. E. Group structure and the behavior of individuals in small groups. *Journal of psychology*, 1954a, *38*, 139–149.

——— . Some effects of problem complexity upon problem solution efficiency in different communication nets. *Journal of experimental psychology*, 1954b, *48*, 211–217.

——— . *Group dynamics: the psychology of small group behavior*, 3rd ed. New York: McGraw-Hill, 1980.

SILVER, B. Group success and personal commitment in game simulations. *Simulation and games*, 1974, *5*, 415–424.

SLATER, P. E. Role differentiation in small groups. *American sociological review*, 1955, *20*, 300–310.

SNADOWSKY, A. Member satisfaction in stable communication networks. *Sociometry*, 1974, *37*, 38–53.

THELEN, H. A. Group dynamics in instruction: principle of least group size. *School review*, 1949, *57*, 139–148.

SUGGESTED READINGS

BERKOWITZ, L., ed. *Group processes*. New York: Academic Press, 1978.

Part 6, "Communication Networks," consists of two articles by Marvin Shaw on recent research on communication networks. Included is a description of group network research methodology.

BORMANN, E. G. *Discussion and group methods: theory and practice*, 2nd ed. New York: Harper & Row, Pub., 1975.

Chapter 7, "Cohesiveness and the Task-Oriented Group" discusses group cohesiveness and its relationship to member characteristics, member needs, and group processes. Chapter 9, "Roles," reviews the concept of role and discusses the mechanics of roles and role status.

HOFFMAN, L. R. *The group problem solving process: studies of a valence model*. New York: Holt, Rinehart & Winston, 1979.

Chapter 10 investigates the effects of cohesiveness and attraction to the group on commitment to the group decision.

JANIS, I. L. Groupthink. *Psychology Today*, 1971, *5*, 43ff.

This article traces foreign-policy disasters to group dynamics in high places. The article presents information to suggest that the Viet Nam, Bay of Pigs, Korea, and Pearl Harbor disasters were caused by group conformity that diminished critical thinking.

Ken Karp

5

Listening and Feedback in Small Groups

Study
Questions

After you have read this chapter, you should be able to answer the following questions completely and accurately:

1. What is the definition of listening?
2. How does listening differ from hearing?
3. What are three differences in listening in small groups and other levels of communication?
4. What responsibilities do listeners have during communication?
5. How do group members listen intrapersonally?
6. What is the major difference between active listening and passive listening?
7. What is social listening?
8. What is serious listening?
9. What are five listening pitfalls to avoid in the small group?
10. What are five suggestions for effective listening in the small group?
11. What is the definition of feedback?
12. What are three different types of feedback which indicate levels of comprehension on the part of the listener?
13. What are four classes of feedback response?
14. What are two specific response patterns?
15. What are two sources of misunderstanding due to unintentional feedback effects?
16. What are four causes of distracting or undesirable feedback sent by the participant-listener?
17. What are two causes of incorrect interpretation of feedback in the observer-speaker?

You probably have been told to "listen" many times in your life. The first time probably occurred when your parents were talking to you as a child while you were busy playing with a favorite toy. Occasionally, you still may be reminded to listen to someone while you are occupied with your thoughts or another project. Yet, although most of us are aware of the need to listen, few of us have made concerted attempts to improve our listening behavior.

Recently, a study examining communication activities of college students found that 53 percent of their communication time was spent listening (Barker, et al., 1980). This percentage rises in the small group setting. Because of the amount of time you spend listening, it is important for you to become aware of the role listening plays in the small group situation. This chapter is designed to help you understand the responsibilities of listeners, to identify some common listening pitfalls, to provide suggestions for improving listening behavior, and to discuss the importance and types of feedback necessary for effective small group communication.

Listening has been defined as "the selective process of attending to, hearing, understanding, and remembering aural (and at times visual) symbols" (Barker, 1971, p. 17). Note that hearing is a *part* of listening, but is not the same as listening. Hearing only implies that sound waves have been received, or are capable of being received. Before you hear a message, you first have to attend. If you are not mentally prepared to listen, sound waves may reach your eardrums (i.e., you may hear), but you will not attach meaning to them consciously. Total listening adds to hearing the dimension of "meaning" or understanding. Only if you understand the verbal and nonverbal messages will you be able to remember the messages accurately.

In addition to attending, hearing, understanding, and remembering, listening also involves evaluating and responding to what has been communicated. Listening is not complete until there is a response or feedback. (Chapters 4 and 7 discuss the importance of evaluator roles and of evaluating evidence.)

Most of the principles and ideas in the other chapters of this text refer to the speaking (verbal or nonverbal) dimensions of small group communication. However, in most instances, individual participants will be listening more than they will be speaking. For example, in a three-person group in which each member participates (speaks) the same amount of time, each individual member will be listening approximately 65 percent of the time. In a ten-person group, each person will listen about 90 percent of the time, and so on. Thus, since as a group member you spend considerably more time listening than speaking, it is essential for you to understand the need to sharpen your listening skills.

Kittie W. Watson of Tulane University provided revisions to this chapter as it appears in the second edition.

LISTENING AND THE SMALL GROUP

Listening Differences Between Small Groups and Other Levels of Communication

The small group places demands on the listener which differ from other levels of communication. In the dyad, participants switch from speaker to listener and back to speaker again. The social pressure to listen to the other person in a dyad is great because the listener knows that he or she will have to respond. The pressure to listen is also great in a small group because listeners must shift to speaking roles periodically during a discussion.

Yet even in a small group, there is less social pressure to listen constantly, because others in the group are expected to respond if one particular individual fails to do so. Thus, some listeners in small groups may tend to become *passive* and let the other person do it. The small group requires all participants to be *active* listeners in order for group efficiency and effectiveness to be maintained.

In the *public speaking* setting, there is somewhat less social pressure to listen, especially if you are a member of a large audience. However, unless the speaker is boring or the topic is uninteresting, you probably will listen actively in order to comprehend the message. Motivation to participate in a small group should be sufficient to generate a desire for members to listen carefully. Unfortunately, after several hours of discussion, or if one or two people dominate the conversation, it is easy to slip into the role of a passive listener and, at best, simply fake attention. The fact that listeners do occasionally become speakers in groups is the primary difference between the small group and the public speaking event.

Listener Responsibilities

It may be difficult for you to believe that your personal listening habits cause major problems in the groups in which you participate. Yet, each time you daydream or pay attention to a side conversation, you are jeopardizing the final group outcome. Repeating instructions, policy issues, or solutions to a problem because of poor listening is a waste of time. In fact, in a five-member group, repeating a two-minute dialogue wastes at least twenty group-member minutes. Poor listening habits cause some organizations to issue follow-up memorandums after meetings and others to appoint phone reminder committees. In addition to wasting group member time and money, poor listening also increases tension among group members. Try to remember the frustration you have felt when other group members failed to pay attention, interrupted others while speaking, or showed up unprepared because they did not *hear* the instructions.

It is important for us to develop our listening skills. Effective listening helps to shorten meetings, creates less paperwork, increases group member morale, improves accuracy, and raises productivity.

In the small group setting, group members alternate between speaker and listener roles. At one moment as a speaker, you may give information, offer an opinion, or ask for clarification. Later, you may evaluate what others contribute, think about what you need to do later, or internally summarize the group solutions as a listener. Both roles are important, and effective group communication is dependent on responsible listeners and speakers, no matter which role they assume. At times we believe that it will not matter if we take a break from concentrated listening, but this just is not the case. You never know when you might miss critical information. Remember, poor listening risks unsatisfactory final outcomes.

Listening Intrapersonally

Individuals are constantly involved in intrapersonal communication during group meetings. Reviewing the day's agenda, controlling tempers, making decisions, evaluating alternatives, and noticing hunger pangs are all forms of intrapersonal listening. Many people are relatively unaware of how their intrapersonal processes can be used to improve communication among members in the small group. By listening to the messages you are sending verbally and nonverbally, you will be in a better position to evaluate your communication effectiveness.

Think for a moment about communication behaviors in others that have a tendency to bother you while working in a small group. Behaviors which often cause breakdowns and frustration in groups include: incessant talking, giving lots of advice, asking loaded questions, interrupting others, talking in generalities, and fabricating, misquoting or identifying incorrectly (Geeting and Geeting, 1976). Through intrapersonal listening, you can check your own communication to see if you are also guilty of these or similar behaviors. If you have a tendency to want to express your ideas, make sure that you are giving others a chance to express their ideas, too. Other methods of listening intrapersonally will be discussed later with the discussion of giving and receiving feedback.

Types of Listening

Listening scholars have found it desirable to classify listening behaviors in several different ways. Many of these classes refer to a specific listening purpose or occasion, such as in the classroom or at a cocktail party. The classes noted below refer primarily to types of listening needed or used in the small group setting.

Active listening implies that the person listens with the total self—

including attitudes, beliefs, feelings, and intuitions. In the small group setting, active listening is essential. The opposite of active listening is *passive listening,* in which the listener simply absorbs messages without critically evaluating them or taking the effort to understand or remember them. Although it is easy to fall into a pattern of passive listening, especially in small groups when the discussion gets dull or one-sided, group members should always attempt to stay alert and active.

Some writers have differentiated between social and serious listening (Barker, 1971). The type of listening used during small group communication should be matched to the group's purposes and goals.

Social listening is the type of listening most often employed in informal small group settings. Social listening is often used during the preliminary stages of both social and task groups. It is often associated with interpersonal conversations or entertainment. One subtype of social listening is *conversational listening,* which demands that the participant switch from the role of speaker back to the role of listener, and so on. The listening which occurs serves as a framework for a response to the speaker.

Courteous listening is another form of social listening used in many small group settings. This type of listening may occur in interpersonal conversations, but generally occurs in settings in which you are primarily the listener—not the speaker. Courteous listening is difficult because you may not be deeply interested in the subject matter under discussion, but you tend to demonstrate concern in order to reinforce others in the group and/or not offend them. Giving feedback (see last section of this chapter) is an essential behavior of a successful courteous listener.

In addition to social listening, participants in small groups also may engage in serious listening. While some social groups use serious listening, it is most often observed in task groups. Serious listening is subdivided into *critical* and *discriminative listening.*

Critical listening involves listening to analyze the evidence or ideas of others in the group and making critical judgments about the validity and/or quality of materials presented. *Discriminative listening* involves listening for the purpose of remembering or understanding. It indicates a serious intent on the part of the listener, but does not imply that he or she is making a critical judgment of the material presented. Both subtypes of serious listening occur in small group settings. You should determine your purpose in listening before engaging in small group interactions, and then listen in the manner dictated by the listening setting.

Listening Pitfalls

Most listening experts agree that the first step in improving your listening behavior is to identify bad habits which you have fallen into in the past. This section lists five listening problems which you might recognize in

3. *Tolerating or failing to adjust to distractions.* Environmental distractions can create good rationalizations for not listening carefully. Such things as noise in the hall, music on the radio playing outside the room, paintings within the room, or furniture can cause distractions which make it difficult to listen with total efficiency. Failure to adjust to or compensate for such distractions is a common listening problem. If you cannot modify the environment in which you are communicating, then you must modify your internal listening behavior in order to assimilate fully the messages being transmitted within the group. In other words, you have to work harder at listening when distractions are present.

Establish a listening environment which is conducive to listening. Some specific suggestions for establishing an ideal environment for listening are:

    a. Establish a comfortable, quiet, relaxed atmosphere in the room.

    b. Make sure the audience senses a clear purpose for listening.

    c. Prepare listeners for what they are about to hear.

    d. Break up long periods of listening with other activities.

4. *Allowing emotionally laden words to interfere with listening.* This habit is similar in part to the first problem noted above. However, in this particular instance, group members react to specific words rather than to the general idea expressed in the message. Such words as *pig, Fascist, Communist,* and the like tend to have emotional connotations associated with them. Regardless of their context, such words often trigger what are called "signal reactions," in which people react to the words and not their intended meanings.

Compensate for emotion-arousing words. Many words evoke reactions which are a function of habit or conditioning as opposed to cognitive deliberation. We must become aware of the particular words which affect us emotionally and try to compensate at the cognitive level for them. Some specific suggestions to help compensate for emotion rousing words are:

    a. Identify, prior to listening, those words that affect you emotionally.

    b. Attempt to analyze why the words affect you as they do.

    c. Try to reduce their impact upon you by using a defense mechanism.

Examples of defense mechanisms are rationalization (i.e., attempting to convince yourself that the word really is not such a bad word) and repression (e.g., trying to relegate to your subconscious those meanings of words which are offensive to you). In other words, try to eliminate a conditioned or signal reaction to words, and determine objectively what meaning the word holds for the speaker.

5. *Permitting personal prejudices or deep-seated convictions to impair comprehension and understanding.* This habit is related to the concept of close-mindedness. It tends to exist when listeners hold positions that are strong and other members of the group threaten them by questioning or challenging those positions. This is a difficult listening problem to overcome since it is a deep-seated (fully conditioned) one, and it is often a function of one's personality structure. However, if you are aware that you have certain deep biases or compunctions, you can at least sensitize yourself to them and learn to moderate your reactions if such topics are discussed.

Be flexible in your views. Try not to be close-minded. Examine the basis for your views and try to ensure that the views you hold, if they are inflexible, are held strongly for a good reason. Try to acknowledge that other views contradictory to your own may be possible, and even have some merit, although you cannot give them total acceptance. If you approach situations with an open mind, you will not only be a better listener but you may help move the group more efficiently as well.

These listening problems are only a few of the variety which may affect your listening in a negative way. Remember that you as an individual are an open system and can conduct a personal systems analysis of your own listening behavior. If you note problems similar to these in your own behavior, begin changing them by recognizing them every time that they occur. By doing so, you will be in a position to eliminate them systematically.

The suggestions, in part, were derived from research in listening. However, many of them could be classified as pure common sense. They are ideas about which you probably said, "Everyone knows that!" and you are right. The key to improving listening behavior primarily is to be sensitive to what you are doing while listening. By so doing you will begin to increase your comprehension skills and your general listening ability. So, view the suggestions as common sense, but examine them carefully, one by one, to ensure that they are things which you are doing to improve your listening behavior. An occasional reviewing of the list may help remind you of things you need to do to increase your effectiveness as a listener, particularly in the small group.

Additional Suggestions
for Effective Listening in the Small Group

Professionals in business, education, government, and industry have utilized the following principles effectively. By identifying specific listening weaknesses and implementing plans of action you, too, can become a successful listener (Steil, et al., 1983).

1. *Prepare and commit yourself to active listening.* Effective listening requires you to "psych" yourself up to listen during small group interactions.

2. *Think about the topic and situation in advance.* Find ways to make the information useful to you. Thinking about the topic in advance increases learning and retention.

3. *Concentrate.* If you let your thoughts wander or take "mental trips" while listening, you will probably miss valuable information.

4. *Plan to report.* Commit yourself to repeat what you have heard to someone else later. A decision to be responsible for a message will change your listening behavior.

5. *Exhibit behaviors which are characteristic of good listeners.* Some behaviors which you should try to exhibit at all times include:

   a. Concentrate your mental and physical energy on listening for a long period of time.

   b. Avoid interrupting the speaker when possible.

   c. Demonstrate to the speaker that you have both interest and alertness.

   d. Seek areas of agreement with the person speaking.

   e. Search for meanings and avoid arguing about words in particular.

   f. Demonstrate patience by understanding that you can listen faster than the speaker can speak.

   g. Provide clear and unambiguous feedback to the speaker.

   h. Repress the tendency to respond emotionally to what is said.

   i. Ask questions when you do not understand something.

   j. Withhold evaluation of the message until the speaker is finished and you are sure you understand it.

By trying to imitate these behaviors which are characteristic of effective listeners, you can improve your listening significantly. In this particular instance, imitation may not only be a sincere form of flattery; it also may help you become a better listener.

PRINCIPLES

1. Listening has been defined as "the selective process of attending to, hearing, understanding, and remembering aural symbols." Listening also includes evaluating and responding to messages.

2. Hearing only implies that sound waves have been received, while listening includes understanding.

3. There are at least three differences between listening in small groups and other levels of communication.

   a. The listener experiences social pressure to listen in the dyad because the listener knows he or she will have to respond.

    b. There is less social pressure to listen in the small group because others can be expected to respond if one particular individual fails to do so.

    c. There is little social pressure to listen in the public speaking setting because the listener usually does not have the opportunity to become a speaker (as he or she occasionally does in the small group).

  4. Poor listening increases the strain among group members while wasting valuable time and money.

  5. Effective listening helps to shorten meetings, create less paperwork, increase group member morale, improve accuracy, and raise productivity.

  6. Group members must assume responsibility for effective communication both in speaking and listening roles.

  7. Active listening is listening with your attitudes, beliefs, feelings, and intuitions. Passive listening is absorbing messages without critically evaluating them or making the effort to understand or remember them.

  8. Social listening is often associated with interpersonal conversations or entertainment. Social listening may be divided into conversational and courteous listening.

    a. Conversational listening demands that the participants switch from the role of speaker back to the role of listener, and so on.

    b. Courteous listening generally occurs when you are primarily the listener rather than the speaker.

  9. Serious listening may be divided into critical and discriminative listening.

    a. Critical listening involves making critical judgments about the validity and/or quality of the evidence or ideas of others in the group.

    b. Discriminative listening involves listening for the purpose of remembering or understanding, without a critical judgment of the material presented.

10. Five listening pitfalls to avoid in the small group are:

    a. Getting overstimulated or emotionally involved.

    b. Preparing to answer questions before fully understanding them.

    c. Tolerating or failing to adjust to distractions.

    d. Allowing emotionally laden words to interfere with listening.

    e. Permitting personal prejudices or deep-seated convictions to impair comprehension or understanding.

11. Five suggestions for effective listening in the small group are:

    a. Compensate for main ideas to which you react emotionally.

    b. Hold your fire.

    c. Establish a listening environment which is conducive to listening.

    d. Compensate for emotion-rousing words.

    e. Be flexible in your views.

12. Principles of effective listening need to be incorporated into all types of listening situations.

    a. Prepare and commit yourself to active listening.

b. Think about the topic and situation in advance.

c. Concentrate.

d. Plan to report.

e. Exhibit behaviors which are characteristic of good listeners.

FEEDBACK AND RESPONSE IN THE SMALL GROUP

Imagine that you are watching a television suspense thriller. The leading character is about to be murdered. Just as the villain raises his weapon, you scream, "Look out!" As if the hero doesn't hear you, he blunders into the villain's trap. It takes a full sixty minutes for him to escape because he didn't respond to your warning. You remind yourself that it is not "real life," and continue to watch the program.

However, what if in real life you were forced to observe group discussions in the same way that you watch television? What if you could observe other members but not respond to them? You probably would miss much of what others said because you could not question messages you did not understand. Undoubtedly, you would feel frustrated and perhaps aggressive.

The previous example illustrates the principle of *feedback*—a perceived message transmitted to indicate some level of understanding and/or agreement or disagreement to a stimulus or verbal message from another. As mentioned earlier, the listening process is not complete until there is a response. There are three classes of feedback: positive, negative, and ambiguous feedback.

Positive feedback is feedback which demonstrates that a message has been received and understood. However, it does not necessarily mean that the responder (i.e., giver of feedback) agrees with the point of view of the speaker. From a communication framework, the term *positive feedback* means that the process of communication has been completed and that a potential for continued interaction exists. In small groups, members often send positive feedback nonverbally through a nod of the head, a smile, frown, hand gesture, or other similar cue.

Negative feedback, conversely, suggests that the message was not received or understood. It does not necessarily mean that the responder disagrees, merely that the message didn't get through, at least in the form intended by the speaker. In small groups, negative feedback often results when members do not listen carefully or when there are distractions in the group or environment. When a speaker notes that the message is not received or understood via negative feedback, the speaker usually will send it again, either in different words or in a different way (e.g., shout the message instead of speak it in a normal voice).

A third type of feedback is *ambiguous* in that the speaker is not certain whether or not you correctly understood the message. Just looking at a person and not verbally responding to his or her request for a ride home is ambiguous feedback; the group member is not sure that you even heard the request.

These three types of feedback are sent in response patterns discussed in the next two sections: *classes of feedback response* and *specific response patterns*. Problems in interpreting these types of feedback are discussed in *interpreting the feedback message.*

Classes of Feedback Response

Try to recall the feedback that you have sent in group discussions in which you have participated. You probably recall using words and gestures. Most likely you will not remember the times that you were silent, but silence may be a meaningful response to a speaker's message. The four classes of feedback response discussed in this section are: verbal feedback, nonverbal feedback, a combination of verbal and nonverbal feedback, and silence (absence of verbal and nonverbal feedback).

Verbal feedback. It is obvious that verbal feedback assumes an important role in group discussion. Verbal feedback may be analyzed both qualitatively and quantitatively.[1] In *qualitative* analysis, the speaker determines the presence or absence of a particular feedback message (what the listener did or did not say). For example, in response to a group member's question on the solution, a participant states that he or she objects to higher parking fines as a solution to the parking problem on campus.

Quantitative analysis of verbal feedback counts the frequency of the particular feedback message (e.g., how many times the listener said certain words). For example, while responding to the question, a group member mentions three times that he or she objects. Frequently, a quantitative analysis yields an indication of the intensity of feeling. If a group member states his or her objections to the solution a fourth time, for example, that person will probably vote against it.

Nonverbal feedback.[2] As a group member, you receive nonverbal feedback from the other group members (listeners). For example, a group member may infer that enough has been said about a topic from bored facial expressions and lack of eye contact, while prolonged eye contact and forward-leaning posture indicates interest, which may prompt a group member to contribute more to the discussion.

---

[1] For more information on qualitative and quantitative analysis, see Holsti (1969).
[2] Although most of the chapter on nonverbal communication focuses on speaker-initiated messages, it also may be applied to feedback responses.

Nonverbal responses are sent continuously during small group discussions. Paying attention to group participants' nonverbal feedback messages is a method of dealing with "overloading" of verbal messages, especially when more than one person is speaking.

Verbal and nonverbal feedback combined. As in most face-to-face interaction, the majority of group members respond to a speaker's message both verbally and nonverbally. Usually you are unaware of sending verbal and nonverbal feedback simultaneously unless someone calls your attention to your gestures. However, you probably would experience difficulty in explaining the directions to the campus administration building with words only. You most likely would use gestures to accompany each verbal "left" and "right."

Silence. Silence may mean more than just the absence of verbal feedback. It also may signify the lack of nonverbal feedback. In the context of disagreement, silence may be an indication of restrained hostility (as contrasted to shouting). In other contexts, however, silence may communicate sympathy or warmth.

Earlier it was stated that one of the risks involved in responding with ambiguous feedback is that a speaker is not certain whether or not the listener understood the message. On occasion a speaker may interpret silence as ambiguous feedback. Suppose, for example, that a group member were asked if he or she would be willing to accept responsibilities to find out the cost of newspaper advertising in surrounding localities. If the group member failed to respond either verbally (e.g., "yes" or "no") or nonverbally (e.g., nodding or shaking his or her head), the silence might be misunderstood. For example, the other group members might interpret silence as inattention, not hearing the question, indecisiveness concerning acceptance of the task, and/or not wanting to accept responsibility of the task.

The example above illustrates the risk involved in responding to a speaker's message with silence. Verbal and nonverbal messages that are easily interpreted help to improve accuracy in communication. Ambiguous feedback may be transmitted if the speaker is not sure of the meaning of silence. In more extreme cases, a communication breakdown may result if the speaker misinterprets the silence (e.g., the group members believe that he or she does not want to accept responsibility for the task). Silence should be distinct in meaning because it places a greater interpretive burden on the speaker.

Specific Response Patterns

Suppose that a group member proposes that someone interview the president of the university to learn his or her views on exchange programs with foreign students. One group member responds, "That's a fantastic idea!" Another group member responds, "Um, I'd like to hear more about this." By agreeing with the speaker, the first group member hopes that the group will accept the proposal. The response of the second group member (neither agreement nor disagreement) is designed to get the speaker to explain the proposal further. This example illustrates the specific response patterns of *rewarding or punishing feedback* and *directive or nondirective feedback*. The specific patterns may employ silence, verbal, and/or nonverbal patterns of response.

Rewarding versus punishing feedback. Learning theorists generally would agree that reward and punishment change behavior and feedback in groups (Mortensen, 1972). For example, you may recall a situation in which you were especially good and your parents gave you a treat in the hope that it would maintain your new behavior. On the other hand, you probably can recall a situation in which you were punished (e.g., given a spanking) to change your existing behavior. In this chapter, "punishment" will be used to denote words or actions suggesting either disagreement with the speaker or misunderstanding of the speaker's message.

In some instances, punishment (disagreement) may hinder encoding. A study by Amato and Ostermeier (1967)[3] investigated the effects of punishment (disagreement) on encoding. The results indicated that punishment or disagreement prompted deterioration in delivery (eye contact, nervousness, body movement, and fluency) for the beginning public speaker. The length of the speeches given by the speakers who received punishment also were shorter than were the speeches of the speakers who did not receive punishment.

Punishment such as disagreement may have a similar effect in group discussion. A group member who is continually disagreed with (or "punished" in other ways) probably will decrease the frequency of his or her contributions. (In the case of an overtalkative group member this may be desirable.) Generally, disagreement should be worded tactfully so that group members still will contribute to the discussion.

Reward (agreement) appears to have the opposite effect; that is, reward tends to increase the frequency of contributions. Collectively, reward and punishment may be effective tools for stimulating involvement in the discussion and regulating the participation of overtalkative group members. A systems analysis will help you decide when to use rewarding or punishing feedback with specific members. You should also examine who should give the feedback. John may accept punishing feedback from Mary, but not from Steve, even though there is good communication among all of them.

---

[3]It should be noted that some scholars have questioned the results of this study on methodological grounds. For example, see Combs and Miller (1968).

Nondirective versus directive feedback. The terms *nondirective* and *directive* are borrowed from counseling theory.[4] *Nondirective feedback* essentially is an attempt by the listener to replicate the message. The purpose of nondirective feedback is to encourage the speaker to further explain the message (ideas and/or feelings). *Verbal nondirective feedback* includes a questioning repetition of the last few words spoken by the speaker and other feedback such as: "Would you explain a little more?" "Really?" "Oh?" The tone in which verbal nondirective feedback is uttered is important; an unsympathetic tone may cause the speaker to withhold or distort information.

Similar to verbal nondirective feedback, *nonverbal nondirective feedback* expresses an interest in the speaker's message. This includes nodding the head, leaning toward the speaker, and maintaining eye contact.

Directive feedback involves a value judgment of the speaker's message. The listener either rewards or punishes the speaker for the message.

To be an effective listener, a group member should not rely totally on either directive or nondirective feedback. Suppose, for example, that the group members continued to send nondirective nonverbal feedback to a speaker for a considerable length of time. The speaker probably would feel that he or she should continue talking even after the message had been communicated. Distortion, repetition, and irrelevant responses likely would result. Alternating between nondirective and directive feedback is much like driving a car on slippery pavement; as the car skids, you adjust your steering to compensate for the skid. Similarly, you will need to alternate between directive and nondirective feedback as you determine which you need to keep the discussion flowing smoothly among all participants.

Interpreting the Feedback Message

Suppose that a male member of your group leans over and ties his shoe while you are talking. You think to yourself, "He's not interested in what I'm saying." If, in fact, the member was trying to communicate lack of interest, the feedback had planned (or intentional) effects. If, on the other hand, the group member just noticed his untied shoelace and leaned over to tie it, the feedback had unintentional effects. Breakdowns in communication occur when there are problems with *participant-listener* and *observer-speaker* feedback.

Problems in the participant-listener. You may recall instances when you raised your hand to respond to a teacher's question. However, you might have raised your hand only a little, because you were nervous about being

---

[4]Both Carl Rogers' and B. F. Skinner's positions have been simplified in this section to the point that they represent only portions of their total contributions to counseling theory.

called on to give the answer. Although you did send feedback, it may not have been observed. This example illustrates the idea that to be effective, your feedback should be observable.

Feedback may be observable and still be ineffective. There are at least four reasons that individuals send distracting or undesirable feedback.

1. *Social conditioning.* You probably would agree that it is socially unacceptable to talk or tie a shoelace while someone else is talking; however, frequently such distracting feedback is tolerated in group discussions, as it is elsewhere in society.
2. *Attention seeking.* You probably can recall a loud and boisterous group member who you felt was trying to gain the group's attention.
3. *Nervous tension.* Feedback such as tapping a pencil on the desk can distract the attention of one or more group members.
4. *Organic defect.* You may recall participating in a discussion with a group member who had a speech impediment. It may have made your interpretation of his or her feedback more difficult.

Sending feedback is a learned set of behaviors. You can learn to become a more effective responder if you can avoid sending feedback that is not perceivable or that is undesirable when perceived.

Problems in the observer-speaker. At times listeners send feedback correctly, but speakers interpret it incorrectly. Misinterpretation of the feedback message may result from *prior experiences and distortion.* Messages (whether feedback messages or speaker-initiated messages) are interpreted in light of prior experiences. Misunderstanding of feedback will occur to the extent that experiences of the speaker and listener differ. For example, if one group member has been taught to show respect by lack of eye contact and another group member has been taught that lack of eye contact shows inattention to the message, the feedback will not have the same meaning for both of the participants. The meaning of verbal language differs between people just as the meaning of nonverbal language differs; word meanings differ from individual to individual and from group to group.

Methods of Improving
Feedback Effectiveness

Feedback given and received during small group interaction influences the effectiveness of group outcomes. The following guidelines should help small group participants (adapted from Johnson, 1972).

Giving
1. Give feedback in a form that group members can understand.

2. Quality feedback is more important than quantity; try not to overload the system.
3. Give feedback to help the other members, not for your own satisfaction.
4. Ask questions and make statements that are important.

Getting
1. Listen carefully to the feedback messages and understand the response before you defend your position.
2. Remember that suppressing, avoiding, and denying are methods of not letting feedback through to you.
3. Use feedback to learn about your own communication behavior and its influences on others.
4. Adjust your communication behavior based on the feedback you receive.

PRINCIPLES

1. Feedback may be defined as a perceived message transmitted to indicate some level of understanding and/or agreement to a stimulus or verbal message from another.
2. The three different classes of feedback include positive, negative, and ambiguous feedback.
   a. Positive feedback demonstrates that a stimulus or message has been received or understood. It does not imply agreement with the speaker.
   b. Negative feedback suggests that the message was not received or understood.
   c. Ambiguous feedback suggests that the speaker is not certain whether you correctly understood the message.
3. The four classes of feedback response are: verbal feedback, nonverbal feedback, a combination of verbal and nonverbal feedback, and silence.
4. Two specific response patterns are rewarding versus punishing feedback and directive or nondirective feedback.
   a. Punishment (e.g., disagreement) probably will decrease the frequency of a group member's contributions. Reward (agreement) tends to increase the frequency of a group member's contributions.
   b. Nondirective feedback (an attempt by the listener to replicate the message) tends to encourage a group member to further explain the message. Directive feedback (placing a value judgment on the speaker's message) has the same effect as rewarding and punishing feedback.
5. Misunderstanding due to unintentional feedback effects may occur from the incorrect sending of the feedback by the participant-listener, or it may result from the incorrect interpretation of the feedback in the observer-speaker.

2. Tape record a fifteen- to thirty-minute small group discussion in which you participate. Two weeks later ask all group members to recall the ideas that were presented in the discussion (record them on paper if possible). Next, play back the tape and see how much information was remembered accurately, how much information was remembered inaccurately, what ideas were identified as having been presented that were not presented at all, and how much information was not remembered at all. Discuss the possible reasons for the discrepancies.

3. During a fifteen-minute period of a small group discussion, blindfold all group members so that no visual feedback may be received. After the time period is up, discuss the feelings of group members concerning not being able to receive visual feedback and their perception of its importance.

4. In a group of from four to six members, conduct a five-minute brainstorming session (see Chapter 7) to find as many ways as possible to improve listening in a group. (Use the suggestions in this chapter to get started.)

5. Have each member of your class make a list of irritating listening habits during small group communication. Compile and number the different habits and ask each member to evaluate one other small group member. Finally, ask class members to identify their own irritating listening habits.

REFERENCES

AMATO, P., and T. OSTERMEIER. The effect of audience feedback on the beginning public speaker. *Speech teacher*, 1967, *16*, 56–60.

BARKER, L. *Listening behavior*. Englewood Cliffs, N.J.: Prentice-Hall, 1971.

BARKER, L. L., R. EDWARDS, C. GAINES, K. GLADNEY, and F. HOLLEY. An investigation of proportional time spent in various communication activities by college students. *Journal of Applied Communications Research*, 1980, *8*, 101–110.

COMBS, W., and G. MILLER. The effect of audience feedback on the beginning public speaker—a counter view. *Speech teacher*, 1968, *17*, 229–31.

GEETING, B., and C. GEETING. *How to listen assertively*. New York: Monarch Press, 1976.

HOLSTI, O. *Content analysis for the social sciences and humanities*. Reading, Mass.: Addison-Wesley, 1969.

JOHNSON, D. *Reaching out: interpersonal effectiveness and self-actualization*. Englewood Cliffs, N.J.: Prentice-Hall, 1972.

MORTENSEN, C. *Communication: the study of human interaction*. New York: McGraw-Hill, 1972.

STEIL, L. K., L. L. BARKER, and K. W. WATSON. *Effective listening: key to your success*. Reading, Mass.: Addison-Wesley, 1983.

SUGGESTED READINGS

BARKER, L. L. *Listening behavior*. Englewood Cliffs, N.J.: Prentice-Hall, 1971.

This book was designed to provide a foundation for effective listening. To provide methods to improve listening behaviors, the book discusses the importance of the listener, the listening process, variables influencing listening, listening problems, methods to improve listening, biased listening, and listener feedback and response.

STEIL, L. K., L. L. BARKER, and K. W. WATSON. *Effective listening: key to your success*. Reading, Mass.: Addison-Wesley, 1983.

This book is used to improve listening effectiveness in educational and organizational settings. Through the use of a variety of exercises and examples, the book discusses the neglect of listener training, costs of poor listening, benefits of effective listening, listening Ear-Q, individual listening strengths and weaknesses, and tips and techniques for improving listening behavior.

STEWART, J. *Bridges not walls*, 3rd ed. Reading, Mass.: Addison-Wesley, 1982.

Chapter 9, "Empathic Listening," includes four articles discussing variables, guidelines, and obstacles of empathic listening.

STEWART, J., and G. D'ANGELO. *Together: communicating interpersonally*. Reading, Mass.: Addison-Wesley, 1975.

Chapter 6, "Being Aware of the Other: Responsive Listening," presents listener attitudes, types of listening, and exercises designed to improve listening skills.

WEAVER, C. H. *Human listening processes and behavior*. Indianapolis: Bobbs-Merrill, 1972.

This book presents a theory of listening behavior based on research. The book, designed for teaching and learning, includes definitions of listening, cognitive processes involved in listening, cognitive structuring in listening, and methods to improve listening behavior.

Ken Karp

6

Information
Acquisition,
Processing,
and Diffusion

Study
Questions

After you have read this chapter, you should be able to answer the following questions completely and accurately:

1. What is at least one definition of the term *information*?
2. What are four selectivity/screening devices that individuals may employ when acquiring, processing, and/or diffusing information?
3. What are some useful sources of information one may employ in acquiring information for group discussion?
4. What is meant by the term *diffusion*?
5. How can we apply the four selectivity/screening devices when diffusing information to an audience?
6. What is the division of labor, and how can it be applied in diffusing information within a group?
7. What is an information intermix, and how can it be applied when diffusing information within a group?
8. What is the most important aspect of public discussion concerning the diffusion of information?
9. What is meant by the terms *homophily* and *heterophily*?
10. What are some guidelines to follow for presenting information from a group to an audience?
11. What are the major steps in conducting an audience analysis?
12. What are some salient principles of attitude change?

One reason people form groups to solve problems is that it is generally assumed that "two (or more) heads are better than one." However, the success of a collective problem-solving effort is dependent upon the amount of relevant information that each member of the group possesses. We would not expect a group of five idiots to arrive at a brilliant solution to a problem. Similarly, a group of expert historians probably would not find an adequate solution to a problem in physical chemistry. The success of any group effort is dependent upon the worth of each individual member's contribution to the solution of the problem, and the worth of an individual's contribution to the group usually is directly related to the amount and type of information that person possesses.

As was noted in Chapter 2 on systems analysis, the quality and quantity of available information act as important variables in the group process. Good information is essential for a good decision. In this chapter we will examine the nature of information acquisition, processing, and diffusion in small group communication.

INFORMATION ACQUISITION AND PROCESSING

Definition of Information

Information is a common term. We are bombarded daily with "information" from various media and in our relations with persons, objects, and events. For our purposes, we may define *information* as "knowledge about objects and events and about the relationships between objects and events" (McCroskey, 1970). It is important to note that our definition suggests that information is not a physical entity such as a chair or desk. Knowledge "exists" only in the minds of persons; as such, it cannot be equated with reality. If a person perceives an object or event incorrectly, the knowledge he or she acquires is still information, although it may be incorrect. For example, if you tell your film club that a particular movie is worth seeing, but you unintentionally frown while doing so, they may misperceive your message. Even so, your group has acquired information and may behave in a manner consistent with it (e.g., question you further about the film, not bother seeing it, etc.).

Communication of information is the process whereby knowledge about objects and events or relationships between objects and events is transmitted from one person or persons to others. We are all too familiar with terms such as *miscommunication* and *communication gap*. The occurrence of such phenomena has prompted speech communication scholars to write textbooks and develop courses designed to help us become "better communicators." However, people also acquire information by means other than direct interaction with others. We acquire considerable information from personal observation, reading, and exposure to numerous messages through the mass media. Various sources of information will be discussed later on in the chapter; at present, however, we will focus our attention on selectivity and screening in the processing of information.

Selectivity and Screening in the Processing of Information

Regardless of how humans acquire information, there is a tendency for people to select and/or screen out certain information. Sometimes we find it necessary to select or screen stimuli to avoid an "information overload." Even groups can become so bombarded with information of various sorts that they cannot attend to all of it simultaneously. For example, a national commission on violence could easily be overloaded with information. In such instances we are forced to focus our attention only on the most relevant information inputs.

People may select and screen information, however, even when there is little chance of information overload. Considerable research has investigated human selectivity and screening processes in the acquisition of information. Space does not permit an extensive discussion of this research, but the next few sections briefly examine four basic selectivity and screening devices that have been found to affect the manner in which information is acquired and processed. These four screening devices are *selective exposure, attention, perception,* and *retention.* Though research suggests that these four devices often are employed by people in responding to information, it should be stressed that these are tendencies and not universal responses. In other words, there is yet insufficient data to indicate precisely when people employ selectivity and screening devices in processing information.

Two theories have provided the basis for most of the research on selectivity and screening. One theory is concerned with the concept of reinforcement. Simply stated, the theory suggests that people process information that potentially is rewarding and avoid information that potentially is not rewarding (Janis and Mann, 1968). The other theory contends that people respond to and process information that is consistent with their existing cognitions (e.g., attitudes) and avoid information that will produce or increase inconsistency (Festinger, 1957). Sources in the suggested reading list at the end of the chapter contain additional information on the nature of these theories and their relationships to selectivity/screening of information.

Selective exposure. How often have you consciously or unconsciously avoided exposure to information which was potentially nonrewarding and/or inconsistent with your intended attitudes? Consider the following communication between Fran and Mike, a member of her group who smokes.

> FRAN: *The American Cancer Society is presenting a TV special tonight on smoking and lung cancer. You really ought to watch it; maybe you'll be convinced to quit smoking.*
>
> MIKE: *Baloney! I've heard all that junk before, and it only makes me feel uncomfortable. Besides, CBS has a great movie on tonight.*

Sound familiar? Perhaps the specific situation may have been different, but we all have responded as Mike on occasion. The tendency for people to avoid information which they feel potentially is nonrewarding and/or inconsistency producing is referred to as *selective exposure.*

The phenomenon of selective exposure has important implications for you when you begin to acquire information in preparation for (i.e., prior to) a group discussion. You may want to avoid "extra work," avoid possibly contradicting previous research on a topic, or avoid sources which contain information that does not support the group's goal. Remember that selection of the best solution to a problem depends on knowing all relevant information concerning the problem. You cannot expect to obtain an adequate solution to a problem with information relating to only one side of an issue. More will be said later about selective exposure as a potential barrier to effective group discussion. For the moment, consider another type of selectivity/screening device.

Selective attention. Though people may want to avoid certain information, it is not always possible to avoid exposure to undesirable information. In instances where it is impossible to avoid exposure to nonrewarding or inconsistent information, people will often focus their attention only on information that is consistent with their attitudes, beliefs, and values. This type of selectivity/screening device is called *selective attention.*

If you examine your own behavior for a moment, you probably will find an illustration of selective attention. For example, it is not uncommon for an owner of a new car suddenly to notice how many autos of similar make and style are on the highways, because the new car owner selectively attends to stimuli that were not attended to previously. The result is that there appear to be more autos on the highway of a particular make and style similar to the newly purchased one.

A similar phenomenon may occur with respect to the processing of information for group discussion. It is possible that the group's goal or an individual's attitudes about the discussion topic may cause a group member to look for only certain kinds of information when researching the discussion topic. For example, if a person proposes putting more money into cancer research, that person may ignore information which claims that a doctor shortage is the major barrier in cancer research.

There often is confusion regarding the distinction between selective exposure and selective attention. Remember that selective attention will tend to occur when it is difficult to avoid exposure to nonrewarding or inconsistent information. In other words, people tend to demonstrate selective attention once they are exposed to information. In these instances, people tend to focus their attention on only those parts of the information that they perceive desirable in some way and avoid information that is undesirable.

The distinction between selective exposure and selective attention is perhaps made clearer when you examine the communication occurring during a group discussion. We are exposed to all sorts of information during a group discussion. Often not all of the information transmitted in a discussion is consistent with other information group members possess. While this state of affairs often leads to disagreement among group members, it may also lead some group members to attend only to information that is consistent with information they already possess and to avoid inconsistent information. The situation is not unlike the one in which a student attends only to information in a lecture which is new, interesting, or consistent with initial beliefs. The unfortunate student may find that such a strategy often results in misconceptions and misunderstanding, particularly on examinations. It should be clear that selective attention can pose a barrier to effective group discussion. Later on in the chapter, principles are provided to help you avoid selective attention. Below we will consider another common selectivity/ screening device which potentially can interfere with effective group discussion.

Selective perception. Experience tells us that it is often impossible to avoid paying attention to undesirable information. In such instances, people may perceive what they want or expect to perceive and interpret the information in a manner consistent with their expectations. This device is called *selective perception.*

Students often become confused about the distinction between selective attention and selective perception. The distinction between these processes will be clear if you remember that selective perception occurs after a person somehow has made a commitment to attend to a given stimulus. For example, the owner of a new car demonstrates selective attention when he or she begins to notice how many similar autos are on the highway. However, if after reading an ad that an alternative, nearly identical model is significantly cheaper in price than the one just purchased, a new car owner may demonstrate selective perception by seeing the more expensive model as more stylish and desirable. In other words, selective perception is related to the manner in which people interpret information once they are exposed to it and attend to it.

The research on selective perception suggests that people often perceive what they want or expect to perceive whether or not such perceptions are in accord with other people's perception of reality. The classic research example often used to illustrate selective perception phenomenon is taken from Asch's (1948) study on suggestion. Asch attributed various statements to well-known sources and presented these statements to different people. Each group of people was presented with the same statements, but they were attributed to a different source. Examples are:

> Those who hold and those who are without property have ever formed two distinct classes.
>> Karl Marx
>> John Adams (correct)

> I hold it that a little rebellion, now and then, is a good thing, and as necessary in the political world as storms are in the physical.
>> Jefferson (correct)
>> Lenin

The results suggested that people tend to approve the statements more when they are attributed to a source they perceive in a positive way.

It is not difficult to see how the phenomenon of selective perception potentially can affect the manner in which information is acquired and transmitted in group discussion. The mere exposure, and even attention, to information which is inconsistent with the group's goal will not necessarily ensure unbiased assessment and evaluation of the information.

Selective retention. It is not uncommon for us to "process" potentially nonrewarding or inconsistent information. However, if the information "survives" the other selectivity/screening processes we have discussed, there is a good chance that the undesirable information will be quickly forgotten. The tendency for people to forget information that is nonrewarding or inconsistent is called *selective retention*.

All of us at some time probably have demonstrated selective retention. We may tend to forget that we owe money to a roommate or that we have an assignment due for a class we dislike. On the other hand, we do tend to remember best the information that we view positively. Considerable evidence from research on learning and memory suggests that information which coincides with our values and attitudes is learned more quickly and forgotten more slowly than information which is inconsistent with our initial values and attitudes.

Since all phases of group communication involve the transmission of information from one source to another, selective retention potentially is a serious barrier to effective group discussion. You may be puzzled as to what you can do to prevent selective retention from occurring, since most of us have enough difficulty in remembering information we want to retain, let alone information that we would just as soon forget! Similarly, you may be equally puzzled about what you can do to prevent other selectivity/screening devices from interfering with effective preparation for participation in group communication. Some researchers have suggested that several key factors such as the usefulness of the information and educational level of the individual partially will determine whether or not nonrewarding or inconsistent information will be processed (Sears and Freedman, 1967).

These researchers have suggested that information which is perceived as highly useful may be processed even though it is nonrewarding or inconsistent. Similarly, more educated persons have been found to seek and process information that is not rewarding or consistent with other information they possess. However, while these and other factors probably do relate to the frequency and extent to which people employ selectivity/screening devices, we should not be misled into thinking that we are free to ignore them as potential barriers to group discussion. All of us maintain certain values and attitudes that can bias our perceptions and interpretations of information.

Gathering Information

Perhaps the most effective strategy to employ in guarding against selectivity/screening processes is to be aware of them. You also may find the following guidelines useful in avoiding the four selectivity/screening processes when gathering information for discussion and engaging in group communication:

1. To the greatest extent possible, keep an open mind regarding the discussion topic and specific topic about which you are seeking information. Try not to allow your initial attitudes about the topic to interfere with the manner in which you acquire and interpret information.

2. Seek several credible sources of information pertaining to all sides of the topic you are investigating and attempt to evaluate the information obtained as objectively as possible.

3. Consider your possible initial biases regarding the topic about which you seek information. If necessary, make a list of these biases and determine at what points in your search for information they might influence the manner in which you process information.

4. When in doubt, check your interpretations of information with others, particularly those individuals whom you know to think differently about the issues than you do.

5. If possible, obtain photocopies of the relevant information you gather. This will prevent miscopying of information and will serve as a permanent reference source for rechecking information.

Engaging in Group Discussion

The following additional guidelines should prove useful when you begin to use your information in a group discussion.

1. Organize the material you intend to present to the group in an orderly fashion. An outline of main ideas may be very useful for this purpose; you can then check your outline against the information you have obtained to ensure that no inaccuracies will be transmitted to the group.

2. If possible, duplicate your outline of main ideas and the most relevant information and disseminate the materials to group members before discussion begins. This will allow the other members of the group to examine your outline and information before you make a presentation to the group. Such a procedure will increase the redundancy of your message and, thus, increase the probability of accurate transmission of information.

3. Avoid the use of emotional language when transmitting information to the group. Emotionally laden language may cause other group members to misinterpret your intended message and/or to focus on their own reactions to your language rather than to pay attention to the relevant information being presented.

4. Provide opportunity for group members to ask questions about your information while it is being presented. This will provide continuous feedback in the discussion and will tend to increase the probability of accurate transmission of information.

5. Employ the suggested guidelines for effective listening (Chapter 5) during group discussion to enhance the accuracy of your own perceptions of information that is transmitted by others.

Sources of Information

We have briefly examined four devices which people may employ in selecting and screening information. While it is important for you to consider these devices when engaging in group communication, it is equally important to realize that each one of us may be affected by various selectivity and screening devices during the research phase prior to group discussion. In this section we will examine various sources of information which you may find useful when acquiring information in preparation for group discussion. You should consider possible effects of various selectivity and screening devices when using any of these sources for acquiring information.

Personal knowledge. All of us have some amount of relevant information on hand which might be employed in a group discussion. Generally the task is to recall accurately the information so that it may be applied in solving a problem or whatever the group's task is. From what we have learned about various selectivity and screening devices, it is probably wise to prepare written, well-thought-out statements of your personal knowledge before presenting ideas to the group. However, often it is difficult if not impossible to prepare a well-thought-out, written statement before the discussion. In these instances you must gather your thoughts quickly and present them to the group while the information is relevant. Even in these instances there often is enough time to consider carefully your statements before presenting them to the group. For example, you at least should consider how the information was obtained, where it was obtained, and what its source was.

Observation. Although personal observation is a valuable way of obtaining information for a group discussion, it is limited to certain kinds of problems (i.e., those to which group members have immediate access). If extensive personal observation of a problem is feasible and/or required, it is perhaps more efficient for the group to interview experts who have dealt with or observed the problem for an extended period of time. For example, a mayor or municipal treasurer may be a good person to interview for information about the federal revenue sharing program.

Three criteria are essential when personal observation is employed for gathering information. These criteria are that persons, objects, and/or events must be: (1) viewed accurately without bias, (2) reported accurately without overgeneralization, and (3) reported fairly. It should be obvious that personal observation potentially can be affected by any one or all of the selectivity/ screening devices. Therefore, you should exert a fair amount of caution in using personal observation when gathering information for group discussion.

Interview. Considerable information may be obtained by interviewing persons who are in the position to know relevant facts. However, the success of an interview is dependent upon a number of factors. The interviewee should be a person who is considered an expert, or at least very knowledgeable, in information relevant to the group. It often is difficult to determine a person's expertise solely on the basis of a title or status. For example, a physician may have a high standing in the community and may be considered knowledgeable about the functions of the human body, but that person may not be an expert in ecology, super highways, or a number of other topics with which a group must deal. Therefore, the group first should obtain information about possible persons to be interviewed and should select interviewees with care. The interview should be planned well in advance. As an interviewer, you should know exactly what questions you are going to ask in the interview. You also should be aware of time limits and relevant information that is available in printed or other sources. Of course, you should also consider possible selectivity/screening devices which might affect both the interviewer and interviewee and examine information obtained in the interview accordingly.

Library sources. The library is probably the single most important and abundant source of information. However, you may waste considerable time in searching for material if you are not aware of various sources of information available in most libraries. Proper use of the card catalog can ensure efficient use of time, particularly when you are searching for material under a specific topic. Of course, the card catalog also contains a complete index of various sources of information by author and title as well as specific subject areas.

In addition to finding books and other printed material, you also will find various reference works to be very useful in gathering information for a group discussion. For example, encyclopedias such as *Britannica* and the *Americana* and their annual supplements are an excellent source of general information. Other reference works such as the *Encyclopedia of the Social Sciences* and encyclopedias on religions, education, and other subjects provide useful sources of information of a more specialized nature. Reference works such as *Who's Who in America* provide general biographical information, while specialized biographical information may be found in sources such as *American Men of Science, Leaders in Education,* and *Directory of American Scholars.*

Since most discussions deal with current problems, you will find various scholarly journals and magazines very useful in acquiring up-to-the minute information on current events. Large circulation magazines such as *Time, Newsweek,* and *U.S. News and World Report* are indexed by subject area in *Reader's Guide to Periodical Literature.* Articles appearing in specialized scholarly journals are indexed in such publications as *Psychological Abstracts, Education Index,* and *Agricultural Index.*

Pamphlets and other specialized printed materials also are very helpful in acquiring current information, although these materials often are more difficult to locate than books and magazine articles. Two reliable indexes for finding material of this nature are the *Public Affairs Information Service* and *H. W. Wilson Company's Vertical File.* Special interest groups also publish useful information on current topics. The names and addresses of such organizations may be found in the *World Almanac, Guide to Public Affairs Organizations,* and *Trade and Professional Associations of the United States.*

Considerable information may be obtained in various government publications such as the *Congressional Record.* An excellent source for locating various government publications is the *United States Government Publications* catalog.

Statistical information often is very useful in supporting ideas presented to a group. However, statistical information can be misleading, particularly if it is obtained from unreliable sources. Some dependable sources for statistical information of various sorts are the *World Almanac, Information Please Almanac,* and the *Statistical Abstract of the United States.*

You should become familiar with these and other useful sources of information that are contained in the library. Most university and public libraries provide brochures and pamphlets designed to aid researchers in finding various sources of information contained in the library. Of course, there are usually librarians available to assist you in finding information that is not readily accessible.

PRINCIPLES

1. Information is knowledge about objects and events and about the relationships between objects and events. Knowledge exists only in the mind of individuals and does not equate with reality.
2. There are four screening devices used to process information.
   a. Selective exposure is the tendency for people to avoid information which they feel is potentially nonrewarding or inconsistency producing.
   b. Selective attention is the tendency for people to focus their attention only on information consistent with their attitudes, beliefs, and values.
   c. Selective perception is the tendency to perceive what people want or expect to perceive and to interpret the information in a manner consistent with their expectations.
   d. Selective retention is the tendency to remember only information that is rewarding or consistent with initial attitudes and beliefs.
3. To avoid the four selectivity/screening processes when gathering information for discussion individuals should:
   a. Keep an open mind to the topic.
   b. Seek several credible sources from all sides of the issue.
   c. Be aware of possible initial biases.
   d. Check the interpretation of information with others.
   e. Obtain photocopies for exact information.
4. To avoid the four selectivity/screening processes when engaging in group communication individuals should:
   a. Organize the material to be presented.
   b. Duplicate and give copies of the material to all the group members.
   c. Avoid using emotional language.
   d. Provide opportunities for questions and feedback.
   e. Employ effective listening guidelines.
5. Valuable sources of information include personal knowledge, observation, interviews, and library sources.

DIFFUSION OF INFORMATION

Thus far our focus has been on the acquisition and processing of information. In this part of the chapter, we will consider *diffusion of information*, or the process of transmitting (i.e., communicating) information to other people.

When you desire to communicate information to another person, you need to overcome barriers which interfere with accurate transmission of the information. We already have discussed some of these barriers under the sections dealing with various selectivity and screening devices. In the remainder of the chapter, we will integrate concepts about selectivity/screening devices with some basic concepts about the nature of information diffusion. This should provide guidelines for diffusing information both within the small group and to individuals outside the group.

Information Diffusion Within a Group

More often than not a discussion group is faced with solving a complex problem in a relatively short period of time. One advantage of a collective problem-solving strategy is that considerable information can be located and synthesized by group members working independently or by subgroups assigned to research different aspects of the same problem. A method often used for capitalizing on this advantage of groups is to establish a *division of labor* for collecting information. Quite often a group will have members who are more knowledgeable in, or express an interest in, specific aspects of the group task. Special interests and abilities of group members should be examined in the systems analysis. It is usually a good idea to assign these individuals the job of collecting information about their respective areas of expertise and/or interest.

The division of labor perhaps should be given top priority during the group's initial meetings. This will ensure enough time for individual members or subgroups to gather relevant information concerning their respective topics. It is important to keep in mind that successful group discussion is dependent upon transmission of information among group members. A division of labor strategy generally will result in group members' having different, but compatible, pieces of information. A major task of the group is to ensure that each member obtains information relevant to the group's task.

Diffusion of information among group members is important for at least two reasons. First, it is essential that each member of a group be well informed about the nature of the problem to be discussed. Although it is efficient to divide the work load among individual group members, thus creating "experts" in subareas of a particular problem, it also is desirable (if not necessary) for each member to be well informed about all relevant areas of the problem. Successful group discussion is difficult to achieve otherwise. A second important reason for diffusing information among group members is related to the selectivity/screening devices discussed earlier in the chapter. Since people may consciously or unconsciously select and screen information, it is a good idea to have several persons examine the same information. This strategy may help to avoid inaccurate transmission of information due to the misperceptions or misinterpretations of one individual or a group of individuals.

There are a number of methods one can employ for diffusing information within a group. One reasonably successful method is to prepare and disseminate to all members of the group a collective bibliography of the most important sources of information concerning each topic researched by individuals or subgroups. However, the efficiency of this method of diffusion is affected by several factors. The accessibility of various sources of information to all group members certainly is an important consideration. For example, the method probably would be less efficient if there were only one copy of the source available, or if reference materials were not easily available in local libraries. Also, an extensive bibliography may impose time limitations on individual group members obtaining all the relevant information. In general, the collective bibliography method is used most effectively when a limited number of easily accessible sources are to be diffused to the group.

When the topic of group discussion is narrow in scope, such as in instances where case studies are used or all the relevant information for group discussion is contained in one source, an *information intermix* may be used to diffuse information among group members. In its most simple form, an information intermix involves two individuals. Each person is assigned a portion of materials, and each person then prepares a synthesis of his or her portion of the material and presents it to the other person. For example, a two-person intermix might be employed to diffuse the information contained in this chapter by assigning one half of the chapter to one person and the other half to another. Each person would then present a synthesis of the information contained in his or her assigned portion of the chapter to the other person, thus diffusing the relevant information.

The same procedure also can be used to diffuse information within large groups. Each member of the group is assigned a portion of the material and later paired with another person. The same basic procedure is followed as when only two persons are involved. All of the dyads are assembled in one room. The intermix begins by having members of the first dyad exchange information in the presence of the other dyads. When the information exchange within the first dyad is completed, the second phase of the intermix begins, whereby the first dyad again exchanges information, but this time they are followed by an information exchange by members of the second dyad. The same procedure is repeated again with the addition of each new dyad.

In the case of a six-member group information intermix, the first dyad presents their synthesized material three times, while the second dyad presents their material twice, and the third dyad only once. In this situation, therefore, it would make sense to assign the first dyad with the most important and/or complicated material so the redundancy of repeated presentations would increase the probability of accurate information diffusion to other group members. The information intermix used for diffusing information among group members can be used quite successfully with topics which are narrow in scope and do not require large amounts of diverse source material (e.g., case studies, simulation games).

Other suggestions for disseminating information within a group already have been provided under guidelines for engaging in group communication. In addition to these suggestions, principles discussed in other chapters of the book will provide further guidelines for maximizing information diffusion within a group. For example, Chapter 5 examines the concept of feedback and provides principles for maximizing feedback, and the information transmission, within a group. Chapter 9 considers various types of leadership and leadership functions which often affect the flow of information within a group.

Information Diffusion from a Group to an Audience

It was indicated in Chapter 1 that a major task of some small groups is to diffuse information to people who are outside the group. These special forms of group discussion are examined further in Chapter 11. For the present, however, it is important to note that when an audience is involved in a discussion, a number of additional elements are introduced into the communication process. All aspects of the group discussion process, from the initial planning stages to the final presentation, are influenced and modified in terms of the possible effects on the audience.

Perhaps the most important aspect of public discussions concerning the diffusion of information is that the initial information level, attitudes, and values of audience members must be taken into account in the planning and execution of the discussion. For example, a public discussion presented to persons knowledgeable about the topic may require less time discussing basic or fundamental concepts than may be required for a less sophisticated audience. Similarly, if the audience's attitudes about the discussion topic are negative, the group should expect more hostility from the audience than if their attitudes were neutral or favorable toward the topic. Recall from our examination of the various selectivity/screening devices that people may fail to process information which is nonrewarding or inconsistent with prior attitudes or information. Therefore, it is important in the discussion to present information that will not appear punishing and/or totally inconsistent to negative audience members.

Considerable research has examined ways in which information may be diffused efficiently and effectively to large numbers of people (see Rogers and Bhowmik, 1972; Rogers and Shoemaker, 1971). Although most of the research has investigated diffusion of information concerning political elections or acceptance of innovations relating to specialized fields (e.g., farming and medicine), many of the principles derived from the research apply to public discussions. Perhaps the most useful of these principles are concerned with the concepts of homophily and heterophily.

Homophily-heterophily. A fundamental principle of human communication is that accurate exchange of messages most frequently and effectively occurs between a source and receiver who are alike in various ways. This principle can be related to the coorientation-balance principle discussed in Chapter 2. For example, we might expect more effective communication to occur between two students who are about the same age and share similar interests than between two students from different cultural backgrounds and who share little in common. The term *homophily* refers to the degree to which people who interact are similar in attributes, beliefs, values, attitudes, social status, etc. Conversely, the term *heterophily* is the extent to which people are different with respect to these aspects.

Considerable research has suggested that greater homophily between source and receiver leads to increased accuracy of message transmission between source and receiver (Berscheid and Walster, 1978; Rogers and Bhowmik, 1972; Wheeless, 1974). The implication of this research finding for a group attempting to diffuse information to an audience is for the group to maximize the degree of homophily between it and the audience to whom information is to be presented.

While it is not always possible for group members to share characteristics with audience members to whom they present information, an attempt should be made to present the information in a manner consistent with the audience's background and expectations. For example, consider a situation in which a group presents information which is nonrewarding for or inconsistent with the prior convictions of audience members. The research on selectivity/screening devices would suggest that at least portions of the audience would fail to process the information accurately. Some audience members may misinterpret the information, others may forget the information very quickly, and others may not even "hear" the message. If any information at all was diffused further by various audience members (e.g., to friends and family), the chances for accurate information transmission would be slim. A diagram for the possible pattern of diffusion is presented in Figure 6.1.

In Figure 6.1 the broken lines represent inaccurate communication of information, circles represent members of the initial audience, and triangles

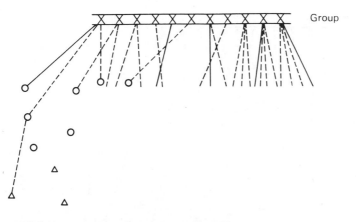

**FIGURE 6.1 A Hypothetical Heterophilic
Diffusion Pattern**

represent other people with whom audience members could later discuss the information. Note that most audience members processed the group's information inaccurately, some essentially received no message at all, and others received and processed the information accurately. Note also that relatively few audience members discussed the group's information with people who were not part of the initial audience.

Now consider a situation in which the group presents information in a manner which is rewarding for or consistent with the prior convictions of audience members.[1] In this situation, the group is acting more like an open system by adapting to the audience—an external variable. This change in environment, however, does not necessarily affect the ultimate outcome of the discussion. The ability to "start from different beginnings" and still reach the same end is a characteristic of an open system. The diffusion pattern might be diagramed as in Figure 6.2.

Figure 6.2 suggests that most of the audience members received and processed the group's information accurately. However, probably no communication event has perfect fidelity between source and receiver, even in a homophilous situation. Therefore, some audience members are shown as not receiving the message, while others are shown as having received or processed the information inaccurately.

Note that in the second situation the majority of initial audience members further diffused the group's information. Why? Recall the research finding regarding homophilous communication, which suggests that accu-

[1]We are not suggesting that the actual information being diffused in the second situation is different from the information in the first situation, but rather that it is presented differently (i.e., with consideration for the audience's prior convictions).

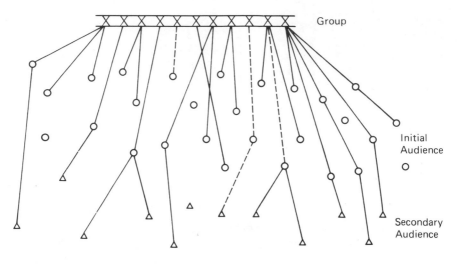

**FIGURE 6.2   A Hypothetical Homophilic
Diffusion Pattern**

rate communication occurs more readily between a source and receiver who are homophilous. Since in the second situation (Figure 6.2) the group's information was presented in a manner consistent with the initial audience's prior convictions, we would expect the information also to be consistent with the convictions of people with whom the initial audience is homophilous. Therefore, it is reasonable to assume that the initial audience probably would diffuse the information to other persons, particularly to those with whom they were homophilous.

Although these hypothetical situations serve to illustrate possible diffusion patterns, you should realize that numerous alternative diffusion patterns are possible in both situations. Therefore, you should consider the diffusion patterns illustrated in Figures 6.1 and 6.2 to be examples merely of what *might* happen. The key point to remember is that when a group attempts to diffuse information to an audience, the success of the group will be determined largely by the manner in which the information is presented to the audience. Below are some suggestions to consider when applying your knowledge of diffusion patterns in a group discussion:

1. Determine as completely as possible the initial information level and attitudes about the discussion topic that the intended audience already has. While this information sometimes may be difficult for the group to obtain, there are at least two strategies that may be employed. The group may conduct a survey of initial information and attitudes about the discussion topic from a sample of the intended audience. The list of suggested readings at the end of this chapter contains sources which will

provide you with additional guidelines for implementing this strategy. If a survey is impossible or impractical, the group should obtain as much information about the intended audience as possible. Some relevant information might consist of the audience's approximate education level, socioeconomic status, sex, and age. This type of general information typically is less difficult to obtain about a given audience. The group probably will know something about the intended audience simply by the nature of the discussion topic and the circumstances which dictated the need for public discussion. At the very least, the discussion topic and relevant conditions about the need for public discussion ought to allow the group to make inferences about the general nature of the probable audience members attending the discussion.

2. Utilize the information obtained about the audience to select: (a) sources of information for group discussion that the audience probably will recognize and respect, and (b) a strategy to maximize homophily between the group and audience when presenting information. The reason for selecting sources of information that the audience will recognize and respect centers on the nature of selectivity/screening process discussed earlier in the chapter. It is less likely that selectivity/screening processes will operate against the group if the information presented to the audience is supported by sources they perceive to be credible. Moreover, the group's perceived credibility will be increased if the group uses sources of information which the audience perceives as credible (McCroskey, 1969). It should be clear that this procedure also will tend to increase the degree of homophily between the group and the audience.

There are several other ways in which information about the audience can be used to increase homophily. One strategy is to relate the group's information about the discussion topic to similar information or attitudes which the audience already has. For example, if the group were presenting information to an audience of business people, a possible strategy might be to relate the group's information about the discussion topic to profits, management, economics, or some other issue appropriate to both the discussion topic and the audience's frame of reference.

3. Prepare written materials which summarize the most important information, and then disseminate the materials to the audience members.

4. Organize the discussion to maximize clarity in transmitting information to the audience (see Haynes, 1981).

5. Examine the physical characteristics of the room in which the discussion is to take place. Determine the seating arrangement, potential need for sound equipment, the overall comfort for audience members and group participants, potential outside interferences with the group discussion, etc.

PRINCIPLES

1. Diffusion is the process of transmitting information to other people.
2. Division of labor is an effective method of assigning individuals the job of collecting information about areas in which they are more knowledgeable or interested. A division of labor strategy will usually result in group members' having different but compatible pieces of information.
3. Diffusion of information among group members is important so that each group member will be well informed about the nature of the problem and to avoid selectivity/screening by having several persons examine the same information.
4. Information may be diffused in a group by compiling a collective bibliography of important sources; however, this method of diffusion is most effective when there is a limited number of easily accessible sources.
5. Information intermix may be used to diffuse information among group members. Each person is assigned a portion to synthesize and present to the group.
6. When diffusing information to an audience, the group should consider the initial information level, attitudes, and values of the audience members in the planning and execution of the discussion.
7. Homophily refers to the degree to which people who interact are similar in attributes, beliefs, values, attitudes, social status, etc. Heterophily is the extent to which people are different with respect to these aspects.
8. When a group attempts to diffuse information to an audience, the success of the group will be determined largely by the manner in which the information is presented to the audience.

The Role of Persuasion in Information Diffusion

Persuading people to accept and act upon information is important to all phases and aspects of small group communication. For example, a group member may have valuable information to share, but if he or she is unsuccessful in convincing others to accept and use the information, little is gained. Similarly, when information is disseminated to people who are outside the group, there is often a persuasive intent (i.e., the group expects the audience to *do* something with the information). In this section we will examine some essential factors to consider when the group desires to present information persuasively to an audience. Students interested in improving their individual persuasive efforts within the group should consult any one of several excellent textbooks on persuasion (e.g., Ross, 1974; Ross and Ross, 1981; Simons, 1976).

The line between persuasive communication and purely informative communication is often fuzzy (see Fotheringham, 1966; Simons, 1976). In the last section we assumed that a group only wanted to inform an audience. However, more often than not a group's intention goes beyond merely informing an audience. The group may also want the audience to use the information to act in a particular way. When a communicator (individual or group) has this added intention, the goal is one of persuasion.

Countless words have been written about persuasion for over two thousand years (see Golden, Berquist and Coleman, 1978). Clearly, we can only scratch the surface of this literature here; only the most basic considerations will be addressed. Perhaps most fundamental to all persuasion is that it is essentially a process of adaptation. By this we mean that a persuader must adapt his or her message to the audience's perspective in order to be successful. Even coercion, as a form of persuasion, must take the target's perspective into consideration or the coercer would not know what the target would perceive as threatening (see Burgess, 1972). The idea of adaptation was introduced in the last section by recognizing that any time a group disseminates information to an audience, it must consider the members' attitudes and initial information relevant to the topic. When the group's goal is persuasion, the need to adapt messages to the audience's perspective is even more critical, as the persuader not only wants understanding of the message but he or she also wants specific action on the part of audience members. We know from personal experience that most people will not change their behavior unless they can be convinced that a change is needed. The adaptation to an audience's perspective and the necessity of convincing them that action is needed are the two fundamental elements of all persuasion; they are called *audience analysis* and *rhetorical strategy*.

Audience Analysis

As the term suggests, audience analysis is concerned with acquiring information about an audience that is relevant to the persuader's desired goal(s). The objective of audience analysis is to learn about a target group so that the knowledge gained can be used to plan and execute a persuasive message(s).

Clearly, there is potentially an infinite amount of information about any given audience. How does the persuader go about selecting from this information reserve? The first step in conducting an audience analysis is to specify desired goals in clear, action terms. This will aid greatly in selecting the most relevant information to assess. In specifying goals, you should be as clear as possible about exactly what you want the audience members to *do* (hence, the use of action words). For example, does the group want audience members to donate money, write to their congressperson, volunteer time, or canvass a neighborhood? It is especially important for small group members to discuss intended goals and generally agree on what they are (see Chapter 3 for a discussion of goals). This will ensure a coordinated effort and increase chances of successful persuasion.

Once the goal(s) is determined, the group can discuss what information about audience members seems most important and relevant to the persuasion effort. Typically persuaders find two general kinds of information useful for audience analysis: demographic data and attitude data.

Demographic data consist of such factors as age, sex, income, and occupation. While persuaders usually cannot rely only on an audience's demographic statistics for audience analysis, often they will prove to be quite useful. For example, knowing that most of the audience will be women with children, between the ages of twenty-five and thirty-five, in a high economic class, can provide a persuader with considerable guidance for adapting a message. In addition, demographic statistics often are relatively easy to assess. If the group is presenting its message at a public forum it is usually not too difficult to obtain demographic data about the likely audience. This is especially true if known groups (e.g., Rotary Club, Knights of Columbus, Delta Gamma Sorority) are sponsoring the forum or have been contacted about attending the meeting. It may be a good idea to use the division of labor concept discussed earlier in this chapter to conduct audience analysis by assigning some group members the job of collecting demographic information while other group members collect other kinds of information.

Although demographic statistics can be quite useful for audience analysis, most persuaders are primarily interested in the audience's initial attitudes toward the topic of the message. The reason for this interest is that most approaches to persuasion focus on changing audience members' attitudes. The assumption is that by changing their attitudes, the persuader will produce a corresponding behavior change.

Unfortunately, the accurate assessment of a target group's attitudes is not always an easy thing to accomplish. First, the audience or even a sample of the audience is not always available for such an assessment prior to when the group must present its message. Second, there is error in all measurement techniques, but this seems to be especially so when people are asked to self-report feelings in interviews and on questionnaires. There is always the possibility of misunderstandings, lying, incomplete responses, and several other phenomena that can distort the validity of the information obtained. Nevertheless, if the group is able to use questionnaires and/or interviews to gather attitude information for audience analysis, they should by all means do so. At the same time, however, care should be taken to develop the most valid measurement techniques that time and resources will allow (see Kerlinger, 1979).

As indicated already, audience members may not be accessible to the group prior to the message presentation. In these instances, the group will likely have to rely on secondhand information about the audience's attitudes toward the topic. However, these secondhand sources often can provide valuable information that can make the difference between successful and unsuccessful persuasion. Perhaps the best sources for this information are representatives of the various groups that comprise the audience. For example, if the audience consists of fraternity and sorority members from the entire campus, it may be useful to contact the officers of these groups for information about their members' attitudes. In general, a good rule of thumb to follow is one based on the concepts of homophily and heterophily discussed earlier. The group should contact people who seem to be like the audience members in significant ways. Assessing these people's attitudes toward salient issues will likely provide useful information that can be generalized to the actual audience.

So far we have suggested that the group specify goals and collect relevant information about the audience's demographics and attitudes. The next step in conducting audience analysis is to examine the information obtained in light of the specified goals. This is extremely important in ascertaining the extent of initial compatibility between the group and the target audience. The group may find, for example, that its initial goals are not likely to be achieved and that it will have to settle for secondary goals or ones of less magnitude and scope (see Fotheringham, 1966). Once this assessment is done, the group is ready to plan its strategy for developing the persuasive message.

Rhetorical Strategy

The development of rhetorical strategies entails the use of information gained through audience analysis to plan and execute persuasive messages. A detailed account of various rhetorical strategies is far beyond the scope of this section. However, considerable research has been done on numerous attitude theories, and this research has resulted in general principles of attitude change (see Kiesler, Collins, and Miller, 1969; Karlins and Abelson, 1970). A few of the most salient of these principles are presented below.

1. In general, highly credible sources are more persuasive than moderate or low credible sources.
   a. The more extreme the behavior change requested by a highly credible source, the more actual change he or she is likely to get.
   b. Highly credible sources are likely to be less effective when audience members are highly ego involved in the topic (see Sherif, Sherif, and Nebergall, 1969).

2. In general, the greater the fear appeal used in a message, the more persuasive it will be.

   a. The level of fear used in a message should not exceed receivers' ability to cope with the threatening consequences.

   b. The more specific the recommendations for avoiding the threatening consequences, the more likely receivers will follow the recommendation.

3. Inclusion of evidence and supporting materials will increase the credibility and persuasiveness of a low to moderate credible source.

4. More attitude change is likely to occur if conclusions are explicitly stated rather than implied.

5. Two-sided messages (i.e., messages that recognize opposing arguments) are more likely to build resistance in the audience to subsequent, counterpersuasion messages.

It is important to stress that these and other principles (see Karlins and Abelson, 1970) should not be followed like a recipe. They are only intended to serve as general guidelines to persuasive message development. Final judgments about message development and execution must rest with the specific circumstances in which persuasion is to occur. Nevertheless, these principles often are quite useful in the initial drafting of message strategies and can prove to be effective if they are tempered with accurate audience analysis information.

The concept of division of labor should also guide the group's effort to develop persuasive messages. In most instances, all group members will be asked to present part of the message. Accordingly, it might be useful to divide the parts of the message among group members and have each work on a section of the presentation. Of course, it would be useful to assign members to tasks that relate to their respective areas of expertise and talent.

If a division of labor is used to develop the message, it will be necessary to meet once or twice before the actual presentation. During these meetings the parts of the message can be checked for consistency, accuracy, and compatibility with the group goal. Also, it would be a good idea to practice the presentation a few times. Although the research findings on the effects of delivery are somewhat ambiguous, it cannot hurt for the group to present the message in a pleasing style. Moreover, if the group can practice its presentation before an audience, it will provide a good opportunity to test the persuasiveness of the message.

In many instances time will be given for audience members to respond to the group's message. If this is the case, keep in mind that many persuasive battles have been won or lost during a question-answer period. Certainly little will be gained if the group's formal message is well received, but group members cannot answer questions to the audience's satisfaction. In some instances (e.g., when the audience is hostile), the question-answer period can be more challenging than any other part of the persuasive endeavor. The best way to prepare for such encounters is to be prepared. Know your material well and be able to cite credible sources to back up your assertions. However, it is important to "keep your cool" and not get into a shouting match with any audience member. The group stands to lose more from such encounters than it is likely to gain.

PRINCIPLES

1. The process of persuasion is essentially adaptive in nature; that is, the persuader must adapt his or her message to the audience's perspective.
2. Audience analysis is concerned with gathering goal-relevant information about an audience.
3. Fundamental steps in audience analysis are (1) goal specification, (2) collection of demographic statistics and information about the audience's attitudes toward the key issues, and (3) examination of collected information in light of intended goals.
4. Rhetorical strategy development entails the use of information gained through audience analysis to plan and execute persuasive messages.
5. There are several principles of attitude change that have relevance for rhetorical strategy development.

SUMMARY

In this chapter we examined information acquisition, processing, and diffusion. We defined information as knowledge about objects and events and about the relationships between objects and events, and we examined four selectivity/screening devices often used by people when they process information: selective exposure, attention, perception, and retention. It was stressed that the four selectivity/screening devices are best considered as tendencies rather than universal responses. However, the devices are considered potential barriers to effective information acquisition and processing prior to and during group discussion.

In the second part of the chapter, we focused our attention on the diffusion of information within a group as well as diffusion of information from a group to an audience. In examining diffusion within a group, we considered the concept of division of labor and how it may create a need to diffuse a degree of common information among group members. The principles of homophily and heterophily were examined with respect to diffusion of information from a group to an audience. It was stressed that the initial information level, attitudes, and values of audience members must be considered when information is diffused from a group to an audience.

Finally, the role of persuasion in information diffusion was examined. Suggestions were made for conducting audience analysis and for preparing messages that are intended to be persuasive.

IDEAS FOR DISCUSSION

1. What are some examples of selective exposure, attention, perception, and retention?

2. What are some sources of information that might be used for group discussion? How can the various selectivity/screening devices affect the way information is gathered and interpreted when these sources are used?

3. What are some methods for diffusing information within a group? In what ways are these methods similar to and different from methods for diffusing information from a group to an audience?

SUGGESTED PROJECTS AND ACTIVITIES

1. Observe a group discussion (tape record the discussion, if possible) and analyze the participants interaction for examples of the four selectivity/screening devices. In what way(s) could the group members have avoided the selectivity/screening devices?

2. Select two newspaper articles on the same controversial topic, but from different newspapers (one liberal and one conservative). Gather two groups of classmates, one group consisting of people with conservative views and the other consisting of people with more liberal views. Give the two newspaper articles to both groups and ask them to discuss the information reported in both articles. Observe the reactions and interpretations of both groups to the two articles. What concepts discussed in the chapter help to explain your observations?

3. Select and observe two or three television commercials and analyze each commercial by describing:

a. the type of person you think the advertiser was attempting to reach with the message.

b. how homophily was established (or attempted) between the advertiser and the audience.

How can the advertiser's strategy be employed in a public discussion?

4. Carefully select a topic about which you can start a rumor. You should avoid starting a rumor that will color another person's character or cause serious problems for anyone. Try to select a topic that will be of moderate interest to the persons to whom the rumor will be diffused. "Plant" the rumor with a few persons in your dormitory or apartment complex. Observe the ways in which the rumor is diffused throughout the dormitory or apartment complex. Consider these questions:

a. What type of people (e.g., friendly/unfriendly, popular/unpopular, etc.) seemed most involved in diffusing the rumor? Why do you think this was so?

b. How many people were reached by the rumor, and how long did it take?

c. What kinds of distortion occurred during the various stages of the rumor diffusion?

d. In what ways did the four selectivity/screening devices operate during the rumor diffusion?

REFERENCES

ASCH, S. E. The doctrine of suggestion, prestige, and imitation in social psychology. *Psychological review*, 1948, *55*, 250–278.

BERSCHEID, E., and E. H. WALSTER. *Interpersonal attraction*, 2nd ed. Reading, Mass.: Addison-Wesley, 1978.

BURGESS, P. Crisis rhetoric: coercion vs. force. *Quarterly journal of speech*, 1972, *59*, 61–73.

FESTINGER, L. *A theory of cognitive dissonance.* Stanford: Stanford University Press, 1957.

FOTHERINGHAM, W. C. *Perspectives on persuasion.* Boston: Allyn & Bacon, 1966.

GOLDEN, J. L., G. F. BERQUIST, and W. E. COLEMAN. *The rhetoric of western thought*, 2nd ed. Dubuque, Iowa: Kendall/Hunt, 1978.

HAYNES, J. L. Organizing a speech: a programmed guide, 2nd ed. Englewood Cliffs, N.J.: Prentice-Hall, 1981.

JANIS, I. L., and L. MANN. A conflict-theory approach to attitude change and decision making. In A. C. GREENWALD, T. C. BROCK, and T. M. OSTROM, eds. *Psychological foundations of attitudes.* New York: Academic Press, 1968.

KARLINS, M., and H. I. ABELSON. *How opinions and attitudes are changed*, 2nd ed. New York: Springer Pub., 1970.

KERLINGER, F. N. *Behavioral research: a conceptual approach.* New York: Holt, Rinehart & Winston, 1979.

KIESLER, C. A., B. E. COLLINS, and N. MILLER. *Attitude change: a critical analysis of theoretical approaches.* New York: John Wiley, 1969.

KING, S. W. *Communication and social influence.* Reading, Mass.: Addison-Wesley, 1975.

McCROSKEY, J. C. A summary of experimental research on the effects of evidence in persuasive communication. *Quarterly journal of speech*, 1969, *55*, 169–175.

ROGERS, E. M., and D. K. BHOWMIK. Homophily-heterophily: relational concepts for communication research. *Public opinion quarterly*, 1972, *34*, 523–538.

ROGERS, E. M., and F. F. SHOEMAKER. *Communication of innovations: a crosscultural approach*, 2nd ed. New York: Free Press, 1971.

ROSS, R. S. *Persuasion: communication and interpersonal relations.* Englewood Cliffs, N.J.: Prentice-Hall, 1974.

ROSS, R. S., and M. G. ROSS. *Understanding persuasion.* Englewood Cliffs, N.J.: Prentice-Hall, 1981.

SEARS, DAVID O., and JONATHAN L. FREEDMAN. Selective exposure to information: a critical review. *Public opinion quarterly*, 1967, *31*, 194–213.

SHERIF, C. W., M. SHERIF, and R. E. NEBERGALL. *Attitude and attitude change: the social judgment-involvement approach.* Philadelphia: Saunders, 1965.

SIMONS, H. W. *Persuasion: understanding, practice, and analysis.* Reading, Mass.: Addison-Wesley, 1976.

WHEELESS, L. R. The effects of attitude, credibility and homophily on selective exposure to information. *Speech monographs*, 1974, *41*, 329–338.

SUGGESTED READINGS

McCroskey, J. C. Human information processing and diffusion. In L. L. Barker and R. J. Kibler, eds. *Speech communication behavior*. Englewood Cliffs, N.J.: Prentice-Hall, 1970, pp. 167–181.

This article discusses the nature of information and diffusion. The article contains sections on learning theories, selectivity/screening, information processing, sources of information, and information diffusion.

Rogers, E. M., and D. K. Bhowmik. Homophily-heterophily: relational concepts for communication research. *Public Opinion Quarterly*, 1970, *34*, 523–538.

This article presents the effects on communication of similarity or difference between the communicator and the recipient of the message. The article also summarizes previous research and suggests needs for future study.

Rogers, E. M., and F. F. Shoemaker. *Communication of innovations*, 2nd ed. New York: Free Press, 1971.

This is an excellent source on diffusion research. Various diffusion models are presented along with several principles that are derived from research on diffusion.

Rosenfeld, L. B. *Human interaction in the small group setting*. Columbus, Ohio: Chas. E. Merrill, 1973.

Chapter 2, "Conceptual Orientations," includes a section on members' perceptions. Problems encountered in focusing on perceptions, effects of members' perceptions on behavior, and the various levels of members' perceptions are discussed with a technique for measuring perceptions.

Ross, R. S., and M. G. Ross. *Understanding persuasion*. Englewood, Cliffs, N.J.: Prentice-Hall, 1981.

Chapter 2, "Springboards of Motivation," includes sections on receiver characteristics and susceptibility to persuasion. Chapter 6, "The Persuasive Campaign," includes mass communication aspects.

Simons, H. W. *Persuasion: understanding, practice, and analysis*. Reading, Mass.: Addison-Wesley, 1976.

This is an excellent source on persuasion research and the pragmatics of planning and conducting a persuasive campaign.

Bill Fitz-Patrick/The White House

Problem
Solving

Study Questions

After you have read this chapter, you should be able to answer the following questions completely and accurately:

1. What are three general sources of problems?
2. What are the definitions of the following terms?
   a. *Problem*
   b. *Topic*
   c. *Proposition*
   d. *Decision making*
   e. *Solution getting*
3. What are three general types of problems?
4. What is evidence?
5. What are four rules that can help when opinions are used as evidence?
6. What are three tests to apply when "support testimony" is used as evidence?
7. What are three tests for all types of evidence?
8. What is the difference between inductive and deductive reasoning?
9. What are three types of reasoning in addition to inductive and deductive reasoning?
10. What are the eight major steps in systematic approach for problem solving in small group discussions?
11. What are four rules for engaging in the brainstorming process?
12. What is PERT?

"Rain, rain go away! Come again some other day." Unfortunately problems, like the rain in the children's rhyme, generally cannot be solved simply by telling them to "go away." Most problems have complex origins and require systematic thought, planning, and action to be solved or minimized. Problems which are purely personal in nature may be solvable by the individual who experiences them. However, many problems affect several people, large groups, or even society as a whole. These problems often can be resolved efficiently and effectively through group communication and problem solving. In a problem-solving group, the problem itself acts as an important variable which should be considered in a systems analysis. This chapter discusses many aspects of problem solving which should be examined in relation to other variables in your particular system or group.

SOURCES OF PROBLEMS

Problem solving is a primary objective of many small groups. The problems which groups attempt to solve evolve from an infinite variety of sources. However, three general sources of problems have been identified (Keltner, 1957, p. 44): *inherited problems, assigned problems,* and *self-discovered problems.*

In many organizations and small groups, discussions of "old business" bring many *inherited problems* to light. Some typical examples of such problems might be: "How can we get rid of the extra ten thousand fruit cakes that were left over from the Christmas moneymaking project?"[1] "Should we continue renting our present facilities?" "Does the group insurance plan our organization has had for the past thirty-five years still meet our members' needs?" Many such problems are passed on from previous groups composed of different people with different needs. In evaluating whether or not such inherited problems are worthy of group discussion, groups should assess the problems' current interest, appropriateness, and relevance to the present group or organization.

In small group communication and discussion classes, teachers often *assign* problems for students to discuss. This is perhaps the most common context in which a group is assigned a problem. However, in many other groups and organizations, problems are assigned or designated by chairpeople to subcommittees or subgroups for solution. In addition, outside forces may create or delegate problems for organizations to solve. Examples of such assigned problems are: "Develop a system to alleviate the traffic problem on the main street of campus." "Raise five hundred dollars for the children's home library." "Discover a method to decrease the student-police friction on

---

[1]The examples of problems in this section, in many instances, would need to be reworded in order to be appropriate for discussion. See pp. 138–139.

campus." Although groups who are assigned problems may have no choice in deciding whether or not to attempt to solve them, they still may want to ensure that the problem is clearly presented, that possible solutions previously attempted are identified, and that they know to whom the group is directly responsible.

Many problems arise as a result of everyday encounters, interactions, or pressures. Since these problems present what Dewey (1910) terms a "felt need" (i.e., an obvious or "pressing" need), they are generally more interesting to group members and, thus, are often afforded top priority for discussion. Teachers discover that students are not attending class and try to discover how to get them back. A fraternity finds that it cannot recruit enough new pledges to fill the house and tries to remedy the situation. A board of directors of a major bank learns that a financial loss was shown during the preceding quarter and wants to reverse the trend. These are only a few examples of typical *self-discovered problems.* When evaluating a self-discovered problem for potential discussion, group members should decide if the problem is related to the needs of the entire group or to only a few individuals, if it is of genuine interest and concern to the majority of the group, and if it is really within the ability or scope of the group to effect a solution.

Problems may arise from many sources in addition to these three suggested by Keltner (1957). These examples merely provide a foundation for further explanation of the problem-solving process via group communication and discussion.

PRINCIPLES

1. Three general sources of problems are: inherited problems, assigned problems, and self-discovered problems.

SOME DEFINITIONS

Before proceeding further, we will define several terms which will be used later in the chapter and/or which may be potentially confusing.

1. *Problem: a question proposed for solution or consideration implying certain obstacles which must be overcome.* A problem does not imply a difference of opinion, just an "imbalanced" state which creates tension, anxiety, danger, or discomfort for the group or others of concern to the group members.

2. *Topic: a description of an idea or concept to be discussed.* It is important to note that a topic is considerably broader than a problem. The topic of one discussion group was "Drug Usage on Campus." The broad topic of drug usage included a variety of potential problems for discussion such as, "How can the rate of drug abuse be reduced?" "How can drug pushers be stopped?" and so on. Thus, topics may suggest problems for discussion, but they are not the problems themselves. This distinction is important to remember, for later in the chapter the importance of stating the problem in a manner suitable for effective group discussion is noted.

3. *Proposition: a statement advocating a particular plan or point of view.* Again, it is important to note differences between propositions and problems. Propositions such as "We should require sterilization of all females after they have given birth to two children" require participants to take sides concerning the issue. On the other hand, if the same proposition were stated in a problem form such as, "What should be the role of the federal government in coping with the population explosion?" participants could explore all dimensions of the topic without being forced to take an initial stand on the issues. Thus, propositions indicate advocacy, whereas problem statements attempt to stimulate groups to determine the better of several possible alternatives.

4. *Decision making: the process of selecting among several alternatives.* There is considerable overlap in the terms *decision making* and *problem solving.* All problem-solving discussions require that the group make a decision. However, all decisions made by groups do not necessarily reflect the presence of problems. Decision making refers to the process a group follows in order to select among alternatives or chart a course of action. Problem solving involves the processes of problem identification, analysis, solution getting, and selection of the best solution from among those proposed. Thus, although decision making is a vital step in the problem-solving process, it may take place in group communication independent of problems or propositions.

5. *Solution getting: the process of discovering possible solutions relevant to a particular problem.* Solution getting is often confused with problem solving. However, it, like decision making, is only one step in the problem-solving process. It is relatively easy to discover possible solutions. In fact, if you ask a friend how to solve a specific problem, he or she probably will gladly suggest a ready solution. The only problem is that if you ask five different people for advice and all five have different solutions for the same problem, it is possible that some suggestions might work well, some might work "ok," and some might not work at all. Thus, in order to solve a problem, you must not only obtain a possible solution but you must also implement it and later evaluate it to determine whether it actually can solve the problem.

PRINCIPLES

1. A problem is a question proposed for solution or consideration implying certain obstacles which must be overcome.
2. A topic is a description of an idea or concept to be discussed.
3. A proposition is a statement advocating a particular plan or point of view.
4. Decision making is the process of selecting among several alternatives.
5. Solution getting is the process of discovering possible solutions relevant to a particular problem.

TYPES OF PROBLEMS

It is useful to examine several different types of problems in order to determine their appropriateness for discussion in small groups. Some types of problems *cannot* be solved through discussion, so it only wastes the group's time to talk about them. Other problems can be solved through discussion, but they require special sensitivity (or training) on the part of group members in order to make the discussion meaningful. Still other types of problems are extremely relevant for discussion by small groups. This section will discuss three general types of problems.

Problems of Fact or Perception

Facts refer to events, happenings, or objects. They generally may be verified through empirical or scientific methods. In addition, facts are generally thought to be synonymous with "the truth." If, in reality, the truth can be known or discovered, it makes little sense to waste time in discussion "guessing" the answer to a factual question (problem). What is called for in this instance is not talk but action. For example, instead of discussing "What is the present position of the Republican party on school desegregation?" it would make more sense to go to the library for a copy of the Republican party's platform for the next (or last) election and read what Republican leaders have said about the issue. Such factual information may be obtained through research, not through discussion.[2]

On the other hand, much information that we consider factual only may be *perceived* to be the truth. In instances where the absolute truth never can be discovered, factual problems may be discussed to learn different people's perceptions of the problem in question. For example, if a group contained two members who purported to observe a speech by a Republican leader concerning the issue of school desegregation and reported different

---

[2]This assumes that a knowledgeable Republican party officer is not present in the group to present "expert" testimony.

perceptions, it might be fruitful to probe deeper to determine which observer's perceptions were based on more objective and/or verifiable data. Problems of fact also may be discussed to help share information or to reinforce important points for group members to remember. However, when the purpose of a discussion is to inform, the facts discussed do not take the form of a problem, but merely become a topic for discussion.

Problems of Attitude, Feeling, or Value

In problems involving attitudes and value judgments, objective facts may not be available. For example, the problem "How can the grading system used in this class be made fair for all students?" cannot be solved simply by accumulating some facts. In the final analysis, it rests on the class members' perceptions of the term *fair*. In a sense, it is somewhat dangerous to spend time discussing problems involving feelings or emotions. Unless all group members share the same emotions, or unless persuasion takes place within the group, no consensus can be reached through extended discussion. The primary value in considering this type of question for discussion is to help understand others' feelings and attitudes. However, groups must be sensitive to the dangers of discussing problems which have no real solution and must attempt to avoid letting interpersonal disagreements lead to interpersonal dislike.

Problems of Policy or Behavior

It is this type of problem which is best suited for discussion in small groups. In policy problems, facts may be brought to bear on possible solutions, reasoning may be applied, and group consensus can be gained through interpersonal communication. Some problems—"What role should the president of the university play in regulating student publications?" "What strategy should the coach take to win Saturday's football game against a team averaging over 250 pounds per man?" "What regulations should the library establish to avoid the theft and destruction of books and magazines?"—all involve issues which may be objectively analyzed, studied, and finally solved. A major value of problem solving in groups is that by bringing more insights to bear on a problem, groups reap a greater variety of possible solutions. More drawbacks to the suggested solutions also may be discovered by groups than by single individuals. The "two heads are better than one" argument is relevant here.

Problems of policy take several different forms. One form asks the group to make a decision from several proposed alternatives. For example, "Should we bank our money or buy preferred stocks?" Another type of problem of policy demands that the group bring together knowledge or facts from a variety of sources in order to solve the problem (e.g., "Why are we having a difficult time recruiting members for our organization?"). Still another type of problem of policy involves an objective or implied action. For example, "How can we raise enough money to send our foster child to camp?" Regardless of the form this type of question takes, the problem-solving approach is relatively similar. Suggestions for specific procedures to follow in group problem solving are provided later in the chapter.

PRINCIPLES

> **1.** Three general types of problems are: problems of fact or perception, problems of attitude, feeling of value, and problems of policy or behavior.

EVIDENCE AND REASONING: ESSENTIALS FOR PROBLEM SOLVING

In discussing problems via small groups, it is essential that group members possess (a) relevant facts or evidence and (b) the ability to reason logically. Evidence consists of facts and opinions used to prove some contention. It provides a solid foundation for logical reasoning.

Evidence

As was stated previously in this chapter, facts and perceptions are often confused. Evidence consists of both facts and perceptions (opinions). However, the two forms of evidence differ in their nature, persuasiveness, and potential value.

Remember that facts only "approach the truth." Some examples of facts which may be used as evidence include statistics, recordings (books, records, tapes), objects, graphs and diagrams, and pictures. Although these examples of "factual" evidence are generally thought to be objective and unbiased, they still must be relevant to the issue being discussed before they are valuable. A common problem with factual evidence is people's tendency to "twist" a piece of evidence to prove a related point.

Because opinions are obviously more subjective than facts, they must be used with more caution. These rules can help when using opinions as evidence:

1. Use opinions of experts whenever possible.
2. Do not base an argument (or case) exclusively on opinion.

3. Make sure the experts are asked to offer opinions in their particular field of competence.

4. Be sure that you quote experts accurately and in the proper context.

Opinions of nonexperts also may be used as evidence, but their impact or credibility may be insufficient to be persuasive.

Testing evidence. Below are some tests you can apply to determine the validity of evidence (McCroskey, 1972, pp. 161–163; Bradley, 1981, pp. 249–264).

The first three tests are suggested when "support testimony" is used as evidence:

1. Is the authority biased? In other words, does the authority have a vested interest or a potential reason for taking a certain stand. If the authority is genuinely impartial, his or her opinion and testimony will have more credibility.

2. Is the authority intellectually sound? An entertainer who does a low-calorie soft drink commercial may have some positive appeal to the TV viewers, but his or her ability to make scientific judgments regarding the chemical additive used to replace sugar and the general healthfulness of the soft drink may be questionable.

3. Is the authority qualified by training and/or experience? In essence, this test asks the question "What special opportunities has the authority had to enable him or her to speak with authority?"

The last three tests are appropriate for all types of evidence:

4. Is the evidence probable? Regardless of how objective a piece of evidence may appear, it still must be viewed in light of prior experience and knowledge. A piece of evidence which does not coincide with logical expectations should be carefully examined.

5. Is the evidence consistent? Consistency may be gauged both internally and externally. Internal consistency primarily refers to consistency within a given written or spoken message. If a witness is self-contradictory, the testimony will be questionable. Similarly, external evidence may be inconsistent if two experts in the same area have different perceptions of a particular concept or event. In the case of differing opinions among experts, either a third expert must be brought in, or the credibility of the two differing experts must be examined to determine which is the more qualified.

6. Is there a sufficient quantity of evidence? This test is self-explanatory. If a case is based on a single bit of testimony, it may be insufficient to

persuade the others in the group. Generally, the more evidence of fact and opinion you can provide, the more persuasive you will be.

Reasoning

Although facts and opinions may provide a basis for a given argument, the reasoning process is generally used to demonstrate how the evidence proves a particular point. Reasoning involves cognitive appeals for the purpose of influencing belief. Most forms of reasoning may be classified as either inductive or deductive. *Inductive reasoning* proceeds from a number of specific statements to a general conclusion, whereas *deductive reasoning* begins with a general observation and leads to a specific conclusion.

Below are examples of inductive and deductive reasoning:

Induction

1. Public schools in Florida are integrated.
2. Schools in Alabama are integrated.
3. Public schools in Georgia are integrated.
   (*specific statements or premises*)

   Conclusion: Public schools in the South are integrated.
   (*generalization*)

Deduction

1. Public schools in the South are integrated.
2. Alabama is a state in the South.
   (*general statements*)

   Conclusion: Public schools in Alabama are integrated.
   (*specific statement*)

It should be noted in the above examples that conclusions from inductive reasoning often provide premises for deductive reasoning. Similarly, conclusions from deduction may provide premises for induction. Ideally, a combination of both types of reasoning will be used to help develop a case or argument.

In addition to being able to reason inductively and deductively, you can reason (1) from analogy, (2) from cause to effect, and (3) from effect to cause. Reasoning from *analogy* simply involves the assumption that if two concepts are shown to be similar in several respects, they will probably be alike in other unknown respects. Analogies may be either literal or figurative. Literal analogies are based on similarity of two objects or events in the same "class." Figurative analogies compare objects or events in different "classes." A literal analogy might be made between two professors, one of whom is known to be successful in stimulating students. The analogy begins by demonstrating that the second professor possesses the qualities which made the first professor successful. It ends by concluding that the second professor also must be successful. A figurative analogy is often presented in parable form. The parables in the teaching of Christ are among the most widely known figurative analogies. "Building a house on solid rock" is analogous to building one's life on a solid faith in God. Both analogies may be used in reasoning, but their effectiveness depends on (1) the relevance of the analogy, (2) the accuracy of the analogy, (3) and the degree of the relationship implicit in the analogy.

Reasoning from *cause to effect* involves the isolation of variables which are thought to cause a certain phenomenon and demonstration of the logical relationship between the causes and their effects. Two questions must be answered in testing reasoning from cause to effect: (1) Is the cause of adequate strength to produce the effect? (2) Are there any restrictions which would prevent the cause from producing the effect? An example of cause to effect reasoning is: The electricity was off for twenty-four hours. Consequently, the food in the freezer thawed out and spoiled. The causal relationship between the lack of electricity and the food spoilage is a logical one which also satisfies the two test questions posed above.

Reasoning from *effect to cause* involves observing a known effect and inferring its probable cause. For example, if a college president observed repeated protests and sit-ins on campus, he or she might attempt to isolate the causes such as prominent national or international events (wars, assassinations, etc.) or local campus events (restrictions on student rights of visitation, voting). In testing the validity of reasoning from effect to cause it is necessary to ask: (1) Is the alleged cause of sufficient strength or importance to produce the observed effect? (2) Could other causes possibly have produced the known effect? In the case of the example of the college president, it would be very difficult to determine that a single cause produced this observed effect. Thus, reasoning from effect to cause can be misleading at times and should be used with caution.[3]

PRINCIPLES

1. Evidence consists of facts and perceptions (opinions).
2. Four rules that can help you in using opinions as evidence are:
   a. Use opinions of experts whenever possible.
   b. Do not base an argument (or case) exclusively on opinions.

[3] This section is derived with some adaptation from Wiseman and Barker, 1974, pp. 213–216.

    c. Make sure the experts are asked to offer opinions in their particular field of competence.

    d. Be sure that you quote experts accurately and in the proper context.

3. Three tests to apply when "support testimony" is used as evidence are:
    a. Is the authority biased?
    b. Is the authority intellectually sound?
    c. Is the authority qualified by training and/or experience?

4. Three tests for all types of evidence are:
    a. Is the evidence probable?
    b. Is the evidence consistent?
    c. Is there a sufficient quantity of evidence?

5. Inductive reasoning proceeds from a number of specific statements to a general conclusion.

6. Deductive reasoning begins with a general observation and leads to a specific conclusion.

7. In addition to inductive and deductive reasoning, it is possible to reason from analogy, from cause to effect, and from effect to cause.

A SYSTEMATIC APPROACH TO PROBLEM SOLVING

In Chapter 2 the concept of systems was discussed. In this section the term *systematic* overlaps somewhat with the concept of system previously presented, but it has a more limited meaning. Here we will suggest a step-by-step plan for approaching problems in small group discussions. Such a systematic plan has been termed an *agenda* by some experts. A specific plan or agenda is useful when the group members understand the steps, have time to use them completely, and see their usefulness in a particular instance. However, you should be aware that many problems do not lend themselves to the use of a complete agenda, so its use might be adapted to the particular problem, environment, and group.

The following steps are based in part on those proposed by Dewey (1910). The major additions are based on current thought concerning creative thinking and problem solving. This creative aspect of problem solving will be amplified below.

Define the Problem

This step involves delineating the exact nature of the problem and defining terms in the problem statement. Only the definition of terms will be discussed at this point, because delineation of the problem relates not only to specific terms in the problem statement but also to problem limitation and analysis. In defining the key terms of the problem, you should observe the following rules (Keltner, 1957, pp. 53–54):

1. State the distinguishing attribute of the thing to be defined.
2. Do not use in the definition the name of the thing to be defined or any word which in any way is synonymous with it.
3. Do not include more than the category to which the object belongs or less than what the category includes.
4. State the definition in unambiguous language.
5. State the definition in the form of a positive statement.

Dictionaries may be used to derive definitions, but generally an operational definition proposed by the group will be more appropriate.

Attempt to phrase the problem statement in such a way that it cannot be answered by yes or no. In other words, instead of stating it as "Should the U.S. Government Initiate Trade with Communist Nations?" you should state the problem as "What Should Be the Role of the U. S. Government in Trading with Communist Nations?" Whereas the first phrasing asks participants to take a position immediately (i.e., yes or no), the second phrasing helps keep the problem on an objective plane and allows all facts to be brought forth before solutions are suggested or positions are taken.

After the problem is stated properly and key terms are defined, the next step is to limit the problem.

Limit the Problem

Most complex problems cannot be solved in a brief period of time. Therefore, it is important to make initial decisions concerning the most critical aspects of the problem which must be considered. Limitation of the problem area should be made in light of the following considerations:

1. relevance to group interests and needs
2. importance of the specific issue to group or others
3. amount of time allowed for discussion and/or action

In classroom discussion, it is important to limit the scope of a problem so that it can be covered adequately during the class period. In real-life groups, time is also an important variable, so topic or problem limitations also must be made on a pragmatic basis.

A topic of national or international scope such as "What Should Be the Role of the United Nations in Managing World Crises?" obviously could generate discussion for days, months, or even years. Such a topic, if used in a discussion or small group class, should be limited substantially, perhaps by taking a specific subarea and limiting discussion to only that area. An example might be, "What Should Be the Role of the United Nations in Negotiating Prisoner of War Exchanges Between Country X and Country Y?"

Once the problem is limited to a manageable size, it is necessary to begin problem analysis.

Analyze the Problem

Problem analysis is at the core of the problem-solving process. Unfortunately, many group members tend to slight or completely ignore this area and jump immediately into suggesting solutions. Unless the problem is completely understood, it is unlikely that the solutions proposed will serve to solve the problem adequately. The basic purposes of the analysis step are to collect evidence and facts which will help describe and clarify the problem and to explore the scope and dimensions of the problem.

When possible, it is desirable for group members to divide the labor of collecting information and evidence relevant to the problem. Once information is collected and ordered in a manageable form, it should be used to help isolate causes of the problems as well as to identify the major effects produced by the causes. The more thorough a job of analysis a group performs, the more time it will save later in obtaining relevant solutions. In fact, in some rare instances, a complete analysis of the problem can almost serve to solve the problem.

After evidence and information have been collected, examined, and evaluated, and the cause-effect relationships relevant to the problem have been examined, it is necessary to suggest specific criteria which will guide the selection of the final solution(s).

Establish Criteria

Some writers refer to this step as the "problem reformulation phase." It is the step which requires the group to set specific objectives which any or all solutions must meet. The specific objectives or criteria may be derived directly from the problem analysis step or may be generated independently. Establishing criteria or specific objectives in advance of establishing solutions is not only logical but timesaving as well. If solutions are simply suggested without any basis for evaluation or completeness, it may take the group a long time to ferret out those solutions that will do the job.

Refer back to Chapter 3 on group goals for more information concerning this important aspect of group problem solving. Obviously, the first procedure involved in this step is to determine what is required of the proposed solution(s). Often it is more efficient to employ the brainstorming technique (discussed later in this chapter) in order to get a large number of criteria "on the floor" for later evaluation. Remember that if the brainstorming technique is to be successful, all group members must reserve judgment about the quality of the criteria until all have been proposed.

After the criteria have been suggested, the next step is for the group to decide on those criteria which are most important and relevant. Although criteria must be established specifically for each problem, two general ones which are often employed are: (1) the proposed solution should be workable and feasible (in terms of resources, time, and money), and (2) the solution should not protect the majority at the expense of the minority (or vice versa).

Generally, specific criteria should be employed in addition to more general ones. Below are examples of specific criteria for solutions related to the problem of "What Should Be the Role of the State in Creating New Water Recreational Facilities During the Next Five Years?"

The solution should:

1. ensure that taxes are not raised
2. ensure that the natural ecology is not disturbed significantly (i.e., any disturbing of natural balance during construction phase will be restored upon completion)
3. not involve only lands owned or farmed by low income groups and minority groups
4. not provide a basis for personal gain for large real estate corporations, particularly those with direct personal friends in state government
5. provide equivalent facilities for people in all different geographic regions in the state

Note that some criteria are stated in negative terms, implying what the solution should avoid. Others are stated in positive terms, suggesting what the solution should include. A good set of solution criteria will provide a balance of both negative and positive points.

Suggest Possible Solutions

The "solution getting" phase of the problem-solving process should begin with an exploration of general classes of solutions which may be useful. Then specific solutions appropriate to each general class should be examined. Once again, it often is desirable to employ the brainstorming technique in order to obtain a large quantity of potential solutions. Remember to defer judgment until all solutions have been proposed. At this stage, seek quantity rather than quality. Don't be afraid to improve or "piggyback" on ideas suggested by others. When all possible solutions have been brought to light, then—and only then—should the evaluation process be initiated. The first step is to check each solution against the criteria previously established.

Check the Solutions Against the Criteria

It is at this point that critical evaluations are again called for. However, try to keep criticisms aimed at ideas rather than personalities in order to keep the evaluation phase more efficient and effective. If possible, each specific solution should be compared to all of the established criteria. Those solutions which do not satisfy the critical criteria should be discarded, and the remaining solutions should be ranked according to their satisfaction of the criteria.

Finally, those solutions which seem to meet the criteria must be evaluated on different bases to determine the one(s) most feasible and desirable. Considerations such as cost of implementation, ease of implementation, short-range versus long-range effects of the solution, and predicted adequacy of the solution should be considered. The final solution may be a combination of several different solutions.

Once a plan of action or solutions has been agreed upon by the group, the next step is to implement it (them).

Implement the Solution(s)

In some classroom discussions, the implementation and evaluation phases of problem solving may not be executed. However, in real-life groups these phases are probably the most important. If an idealized solution cannot be implemented successfully, it cannot help to solve the problem.

The group must strive to discover the most efficient and effective plan for implementing the solution. If money is a factor, costs must be considered; if time is important, it also must be taken into account. When all contingencies are accounted for, the group must finally agree on one or more plans of implementation. One model for implementation is discussed later in this chapter (PERT). Other plans may be adapted for individual group use. Once the plan has been implemented, it must be evaluated to determine whether the problem really has been successfully solved.

Evaluate the Success of the Solution

It is important to wait a sufficient length of time after a solution has been implemented to give it a chance to work before attempting to evaluate its success. Obviously, some proposals are long term, whereas others yield immediate results. Tests for the solutions must be devised (see Chapter 3). The criteria agreed upon should be examined to see if the solution has met them adequately. Other questions which may be asked include: "Can improvements or alterations be made on the implemented solution to increase its effectiveness?" "Is the cost of the plan (in money, time, or energy) commensurate with the results obtained?" and "Has the plan created new problems which are equal to or more disturbing than the original problem?" In other words, the evaluation step requires the group to make a final decision concerning whether to keep the present plan of implementation in force or to alter, replace, or repair it in order to help it meet the needs.

It is only after evaluation has taken place and effects of the plan are known that the worth of a solution can be determined. If the plan works, the problem has been solved. If it does not work, the group must go back to their list of possible solutions and try another, and keep repeating the process until something is finally found to be effective.

PRINCIPLES

1. The eight major steps in the systematic approach (i.e., agenda) for problem solving in small group discussions are:
   a. Define the problem.
   b. Limit the problem.
   c. Analyze the problem.
   d. Establish criteria.
   e. Suggest possible solutions.
   f. Check the solutions against the criteria.
   g. Implement the solution(s).
   h. Evaluate the success of the solution.

BRAINSTORMING: CREATIVE SOLUTION GETTING

Most of the emphasis on creative thinking and the brainstorming process has been derived from Alex Osborn's text *Applied Imagination* (1962). Osborn and his colleagues conducted considerable research using brainstorming techniques and, in most situations, they were found to be up to 44 percent more effective than traditional problem-solving methods. The major premise behind the brainstorming method is that everyone should experience total freedom to express ideas without fear of personal embarrassment or criticism from others. Osborn suggests the following rules for engaging in the brainstorming process:

1. Defer judgment on all ideas presented until everyone has had a chance to contribute.

2. Seek to obtain the greatest possible quantity of ideas.
3. Use the "chain reaction" technique associated with "freewheeling" (i.e., let your mind flow freely without precensoring ideas).
4. Try to combine and improve on the ideas of others.

In general, groups employing the brainstorming process will want to set a specific time limit for this phase of the solution (or criteria) getting process. Generally, a brainstorming session should last for no longer than five to seven minutes. During this intensive ideation period, one or two persons may be asked to serve as recorders of ideas. If two people are recording ideas, they can take turns recording in order to more efficiently commit to paper the suggestions which have been made.

Remember that the brainstorming session is a true verbal free-for-all. Criticism is ruled out, and all ideas are permitted without condemnation or ridicule. It generally takes a few trials or practice sessions for the group to get used to the idea of free expression without criticism. If possible, groups should pick topics with simple solutions to practice in preparation for engaging in brainstorming concerning more complex problems.

Some key questions members can ask themselves in an attempt to stimulate further ideation include: "Can I adapt something? reverse it? substitute something? modify it? rearrange it? combine it with something? minimize it? magnify it?" By rearranging your habitual thoughts about a problem, you may be able to come up with a new technique or slightly different solution.

A note should be made regarding the size of an ideal brainstorming group. In general, brainstorming groups with more than five people are difficult to manage. In larger groups, several people often do not get a chance to express their ideas. The ideal size is probably four or five, with one or more participants serving as recorders as well as contributors.

Leadership in a brainstorming group generally is not necessary, although at times a "regulator" may be necessary in groups just learning the brainstorming technique. A regulator should try to help remind the members of the group of the rules that must be followed in order for the session to be productive.

If your group tries brainstorming and it doesn't work for you, there is a variation that might help: have all group members work independently, with each person generating as many ideas as possible. Some research has found that this method produces more solutions than when group members work cooperatively (Jablin and Seibold, 1978). If your group uses this variation, you can regroup and try to build on each other's ideas, and then move on to the next stage of problem solving.

After the brainstorming session, the solution(s) or criteria advanced then may be evaluated. The evaluation stage may follow immediately after the ideation or brainstorming stage. However, in some instances it is useful to allow for an incubation period before beginning evaluation.

PRINCIPLES

1. Four rules for engaging in the brainstorming process are:
   a. Defer judgment on all ideas presented until everyone has had a chance to contribute.
   b. Seek to obtain the greatest possible quantity of ideas.
   c. Use the chain reaction technique associated with freewheeling.
   d. Try to combine and improve on the ideas of others.

PERT — AN IMPLEMENTATION STRATEGY

You will recall, in the problem-solving sequence suggested earlier, that *implementation* is a critical step. This section describes a specific systematic plan for the orderly implementation of a solution.

PERT (Program Evaluation and Review Technique) was introduced by the U. S. Navy in 1958 in order to solve some of the problems which were noted in the Polaris missile program (Ivars, 1962). The technique has been used since then by other government agencies, including the air force, as well as by private, social, and business groups. The method basically is designed to systematically analyze (if possible through the use of a computer) impending problems or bottlenecks which may be encountered in implementation of a solution and to test the feasibility or logic of the proposed plan or procedure. PERT is based on a probability concept employing project feasibility estimates. Through PERT planning, illogical or unfeasible steps may be determined in advance and eliminated.

One advantage of the PERT technique is that it forces groups to commit to paper the specific details of plans. This step alone probably helps to increase precision. Even if all of the PERT steps are not followed, it can be valuable in helping groups visualize their total plan.

The PERT system is somewhat complex, but it is worth learning in situations where the product of the group effort is very important. For a concise overview of the PERT system and a detailed list of steps to follow, consult Phillips (1965).

PRINCIPLES

1. PERT (Program Evaluation and Review Technique) is a specific systematic plan for the orderly implementation of a solution.

A NOTE OF CAUTION

Problem solving, at best, is a difficult issue to approach on any level. In this chapter we have suggested that a system may be devised to approach problems logically through group interaction and discussion. However, there is little data to suggest that the *only* valid method of approaching problems through group discussion is through a step-by-step plan similar to the one presented in this chapter. We believe that you should examine the composition of your group, the nature of the problem, the time and energy available to solve the problem, the resources available to implement the solution, and the battery of other issues which may be relevant to your group in a given context, before deciding upon a specific approach or approaches to solving the problem. All of these factors can affect the productivity of your group and should be examined with a systems analysis approach. Although some of these factors have been discussed in other chapters of this book, it is important to note here that well-acquainted groups make better decisions than ad hoc groups (Hall, 1971). Consequently, your group should not try to rush the problem-solving process if it is not absolutely necessary.

In general, we feel it is desirable to follow a systematic step-by-step program in solving problems, but we want to encourage creativity in approaching problems through communication. It is probable that a combination of creative and systematic approaches to problem solving will stimulate the best possible solutions. The key is not to be tied to any specific system so that it serves as a straitjacket for the group. Any approach employed should serve as an aid, not a constraint, in the problem-solving process.

SUMMARY

This chapter focused on problem solving in small groups. It began by examining three general sources of problems for small group discussion. Next, definitions of and distinctions among such terms as *problem, topic, proposition, decision making,* and *solution getting* were provided.

It was emphasized that certain types of problems are more appropriate for discussion than others. Consequently, types of problems appropriate for discussion were examined.

Evidence and reasoning were discussed next, particularly as they relate to small group problem solving. Distinctions were made between facts and opinions. Several tests of evidence also were provided.

The reasoning process was described and several examples of various types were provided. Inductive and deductive reasoning were defined, as were reasoning from analogy, cause to effect, and effect to cause.

A major portion of the chapter was devoted to the delineation and explanation of a systematic approach to problem solving. This eight-step approach, if followed, helps guide groups systematically in problem solving from definition of the problem through checking on the effectiveness of solutions.

Brainstorming techniques were discussed, including rules for their use and some guidelines for effective brainstorming. Finally, PERT, an implementation strategy, was described in detail. Advantages and disadvantages of the PERT system also were discussed.

IDEAS FOR DISCUSSION

1. What is the relationship between facts and evidence?

2. What are some examples of the use of testimony in radio and television advertising?

3. What types of topics are most suitable for brainstorming sessions? Give some specific examples.

4. What is the difference between problem solving and solution getting?

5. What are the major advantages of the PERT approach? What are the major disadvantages?

6. Which steps in the agenda for discussion presented in this chapter are absolutely necessary to follow? Which may be skipped on occasion?

7. What are some examples of inductive reasoning? What are some specific examples of deductive reasoning?

SUGGESTED PROJECTS AND ACTIVITIES

1. Using other textbooks for resource materials, compile a list of as many techniques and/or rules for problem solving in groups as you can find. Then, prepare a chart which illustrates the similarities and differences among the different systems. Finally, compose your own technique for group problem solving based on your research.

2. Observe three different problem-solving discussion groups in action. Record the steps they followed (if any) in attempting to solve their problem. Prepare a brief paper comparing and contrasting the effectiveness of each method observed.

3. In a four- to six-person group, conduct a five-minute brainstorming session to find as many ways as possible to get evidence.

REFERENCES

BRADLEY, B. E. *Fundamentals of speech communication: the credibility of ideas*, 3rd ed. Dubuque, Iowa: Wm. C. Brown, 1981.

DEWEY, J. *How we think*. Lexington, Mass.: Heath, 1910.

HALL, J. Decisions, decisions, decisions. *Psychology today*, 1971, *5*, 51–54, 86–88.

IVARS, A. The management side of PERT. *California management review*, 1962, *4*, 16.

JABLIN, F. M., and D. R. SEIBOLD. Implications for problem-solving groups of empirical research on "brainstorming": a critical review of the literature. *Southern speech communication journal*, 1978, *43*, 327–356.

KELTNER, J. W. *Group discussion processes*. New York: Longmans, Green, 1957.

McCROSKEY, J. C. *An introduction to rhetorical communication*, 2nd ed. Englewood Cliffs, N.J.: Prentice-Hall, 1972.

OSBORN, A. F. *Applied imagination*. New York: Scribner's, 1962.

PHILLIPS, G. M. PERT as a logical adjunct to the discussion process. *Journal of communication*, 1965, *15*, 89–99.

WISEMAN, G., and L. BARKER. *Speech—interpersonal communication*, 2nd ed. New York: Harper & Row, Pub., 1974.

SUGGESTED READINGS

APPLEBAUM, R. L., E. M. BODAKEN, K. K. SERENO, and K. W. E. ANATOS. *The process of group communication*. Chicago: Science Research Associates, 1974.

Chapter 5, "Problem Solving," investigates elements of the problem solving of a small group. The definitions, interaction roles, three approaches, and several patterns of problem solving are discussed.

BRILHART, J. K. *Effective group discussion*, 2nd ed. Dubuque, Iowa: Wm. C. Brown, 1974.

Chapter 5, "Organizing Group Discussion," presents several problem-solving methods as well as offering general problem-solving principles including PERT.

GOLDBERG, A. A., and C. E. LARSON. *Group communication: discussion processes and applications*. Englewood Cliffs, N.J.: Prentice-Hall, 1975.

Chapter 4 presents a short discussion on reasoning, its types and fallacies. Chapter 7 explains factors that inhibit or enhance problem solving. This chapter also includes alternate processes and systematic methods of problem solving.

HARNACK, R. V., T. B. FEST, and B. S. JONES. *Group discussion: theory and technique*, 2nd ed. Englewood Cliffs, N.J.: Prentice-Hall, 1977.

Chapter 8 defines, discusses, and compares evidence, and also includes the presentation, believability, and discovery of evidence. Chapter 9 discusses inductive and deductive reasoning and reviews common reasoning fallacies. Chapter 10 discusses the definition and phrasing of a discussion problem and offers two methods for discussing and solving the problem.

Ken Karp

Laimute E. Druskis

Marc P. Anderson

Marc P. Anderson

Nonverbal
Communication
in the
Small Group

Study Questions

After you have read this chapter, you should be able to answer the following questions completely and accurately:

1. What is nonverbal communication?
2. How does "masking" relate to small group communication?
3. What are Knapp's four functions of eye contact as related to group communication?
4. What is the "look and look away" technique of eye behavior in interpersonal communication?
5. What are two factors that appear to influence the meaning of a movement?
6. In what way do group members use touch?
7. What feelings may group members express through touch?
8. What are artifacts?
9. What are stereotypes?
10. When are stereotypes harmful?
11. What is one factor that tends to affect the impression you form of an individual based on his or her clothing?
12. How does your physical appearance relate to your participation in small groups?
13. What information may group members infer from another member's vocal qualities?
14. What emotions may group members infer from the voice?
15. What is the difference between territory and personal space?
16. What are four variables which appear to affect how comfortable you are with the distance at which another individual stands or sits?
17. What are two potential effects of seating arrangement on communicative interactions?
18. What are two variables that may affect the seating position you choose in relation to other persons?

Picture yourself participating in a group discussion concerning the role of nonverbal communication in interpersonal relationships. In the discussion of the topic, you are asked to estimate the amount of time the average person spends speaking words each day. What would your answer be? Two hours? One hour? One-half hour? Ray Birdwhistell (1970), a noted authority on nonverbal behavior, estimates that the average person actually speaks words for a total of only ten to eleven minutes daily. If we speak words for a relatively short period of time, how do we communicate the rest of the time? In general we spend most of our time communicating nonverbally.[1]

In most small groups, only one person at a time communicates orally. You probably have realized that a group member can simultaneously communicate a nonverbal message and a verbal message (the person may gesture, for example). However, while one person is communicating orally, you may tend to overlook the nonverbal communication of other group members. A group member's smile, frown, or deadpan expression communicates a loud nonverbal message.

The study of nonverbal communication is relatively new and has only recently been examined in connection with small group interaction. However, it is of significant importance in the small group setting. Stein (1975) found that when observers were given records of a group's nonverbal behavior, they could accurately identify emerging leadership. Furthermore, the observers could accomplish this without knowing how frequently group members participated.

As you can see, nonverbal communication does play an important role in small group communication. In this chapter we will relate some other topics to the small group setting under the general headings of physical behavior, physical appearance, vocal behavior, territory and personal space, and environmental variables. When conducting a systems analysis, you should take these factors into account.

PHYSICAL BEHAVIOR

A member of a group can affect the group's deliberations without saying a word. For example, he or she may have a bored expression, stare out the window, and sit apart from the group. If that person is an influential member, the other members may attribute his or her boredom to any number of factors, among them that the group is only repeating what has already been said. Group members usually make inferences about other members' internal states through such physical behaviors as: *facial expression, eye contact, body movement,* and *touching.*

---

[1]Although there have been various definitions for nonverbal communication, the definition we feel is suitable for the purpose of small group communication is: all communicative forms other than the written or spoken word which impart meaning to an individual or group.

Facial Expression

You probably depend on facial expressions to gain additional information about a verbal message or the source of the message. Albert Mehrabian (1981) provides us with the following formula to describe how we interpret others' feelings:

$$\text{TOTAL FEELING} = 7\% \text{ verbal feeling} + 38\% \text{ vocal feeling} + 55\% \text{ facial feeling}$$

We will address the importance of vocal behavior later in this chapter. Right now we are concerned with the 55 percent of feeling which is communicated through our facial expressions.

Knapp (1977) notes that at least six categories of emotion can be accurately detected from facial expressions: happiness, anger, surprise, sadness, disgust, and fear. Most likely you unconsciously rely on certain areas of the face to predict certain emotions. For example, you may infer surprise from a raised eyebrow. Or, you may infer that a group member is happy by his or her "smiling" mouth and eyes. Sometimes, however, you may look at these facial "cues" and misinterpret the group member's emotional state.

Misinterpretation of a group member's emotional state may occur because the face may display several emotions either at one time or in rapid succession. For example, a group member's eyes and eyebrows may be displaying an emotion such as surprise while the mouth may be suggesting happiness by smiling. Or a group member's face may display several emotions in rapid succession such as when a sneer is quickly covered up by a smile. Displaying several emotions, either at once or in rapid succession, may result from the attempt (and perhaps momentary failure) to control facial expressions.

Most people learn how to control or "mask" facial expressions early in life. For example, you might recall a time as a child when you pretended to be asleep and tried hard not to smile when your parents came in the room, so they wouldn't detect your charade. On the other hand, you were taught to smile throughout your waking hours: we try to smile when people hurt our feelings, we try to smile at jokes that really disgust us, and we try to smile when we're angry enough to hit someone.

Group members may display facial expressions that differ from their true feelings for a variety of reasons—in order to avoid hurting someone's feelings, for example. A group member may poke fun at a solution to the problem that you offered and, rather than show how angry you really feel, you smile. Another reason that group members "mask" is to conceal information. For example, you may know that one group member's statistics are out of date but nod your head in agreement in order not to embarrass that person.

Lack of perceptiveness and sensitivity to masked facial expressions has several consequences for group members. For example, suppose that one person embarrasses another group member; that person is insensitive to the masking smile and continues to hurt the individual's feelings. The hurt individual may withdraw from group participation. Or, on the other hand, the hurt individual may become aggressive, begin blocking proposals, and be insensitive to the feelings of other group members in addition to the feelings of the group member who caused the hurt.

Another consequence of lack of perceptiveness and sensitivity to masked facial expression in this example may be merely spending needless time resolving interpersonal problems. Other consequences might be not resolving the problem in a satisfactory manner and having one or more members leave the group. Therefore, try to be attentive to masked facial expressions in order to avoid potential interpersonal problems.

PRINCIPLES

1. Group members depend on facial expressions to gain additional information about a verbal message or about the source of the message.
2. Six categories of emotions that can be accurately detected from facial expressions are: happiness, anger, surprise, sadness, disgust, and fear.
3. A group member's face frequently will display several emotions either at the same time or in rapid succession.
4. Group members frequently will "mask" their true feelings by displaying a facial expression that is different from what they inwardly believe or feel.
5. Group members may mask for reasons such as to avoid hurting another group member's feelings or to conceal information.
6. You should try to be attentive to masked facial expressions in order to avoid potential interpersonal problems.

Eye Contact

The significance of eye contact traditionally has been recognized by communication teachers and scholars. For example, students in public speaking courses are taught to maintain eye contact with their audience. They learn to shift their glance from one part of the audience to another without appearing mechanical. Lack of eye contact or artificial eye behavior would distract from the speaker's verbal message and potentially cause ineffective communication.

Eye contact also affects interpersonal communication. Early in life we are taught that it is not polite to look or stare at other people in certain situations. Mehrabian (1981, p. 54) explains that "elevators tend to be uncomfortable for most people; forced into a small space with strangers, they avoid each other's gaze by staring at the floor or watching the lighted, floor indicator panel above the doors."

Social scientists also have been concerned with the importance of eye contact or gaze during interactions. Knapp (1977) explains that eye gaze behavior can serve to: (1) regulate the flow of communication; (2) monitor feedback; (3) express emotions; and (4) communicate the nature of the inter-personal relationship. We can readily apply these general functions of eye behavior to a small group setting.

Regulating the flow of communication between group members. When the speaker of a group discussion stops speaking and looks directly at another group member, it usually indicates that it is the other group member's turn to speak. For example, at the beginning of a group discussion, the secretary may review what occurred at the last meeting. At the end of the review, he or she might turn to the leader and look into his or her eyes. Almost immediately after eye contact is made, the leader might say, "Thank you, Jerry, for reading the minutes. And now for the business of today." Although Jerry never said, "I'm finished," the leader knew it was his or her turn to take the floor. Simply by looking at the leader, Jerry managed to regulate the flow of communication in the group discussion. This behavior might occur when you are talking about something and "get stuck" for a word. You might look at a friend in the group to help you out.

Monitoring feedback. The importance of feedback to a group was discussed in Chapter 5. However, it is important to highlight the role which eye contact plays in transmitting feedback. In group situations, it is difficult for more than one member to speak at a time. It is difficult to have the entire group verbally express agreement with an idea. Consequently, the speaker often relies on "reading" the faces of the members. Perhaps the easiest way to tell if someone understands is to look him or her in the eye. The speaker might say, "Am I making my point clear?" and look into the eyes of the group members to determine if the message is indeed getting through.

Expressing group members' emotions. Although it is often difficult to read an individual's emotional state by looking at the eyes in isolation from the rest of the face, the eyes are still a strong indicator of certain feelings. Previously we indicated that there are six basic categories of emotions which can be accurately perceived on one's face: surprise, disgust, anger, happiness, sadness, and fear (Knapp, 1977). These emotions are interpreted in conjunction with eye movement and placement. For example, even though you might not be able to explicitly detect a look of disgust in a group member's eyes, you still could tell that the individual was dissatisfied with the solution. How often have you said to someone, "Don't look at me that way." The other person responded, "What way?" Although you could not verbally describe the emotion in the eye behavior of the other person, you knew it when you saw it. Often group members send emotional feeling through their eye behavior without even realizing it.

Communicating the nature of interpersonal relationships between group members. Have you ever been in a group where two of the members "went together"? You probably were able to tell that they were a couple just by observing their eye behavior. Have you ever been in a group where two of the members disliked each other? Again, by observing their lack of eye contact, you probably were able to determine the nature of their interpersonal relationship. Generally we look more at people we like, and less at people we don't like. Exline and Winters (1965), for example, reported that subjects avoided eye contact with an interviewer who had commented unfavorably on their performance. Consequently, in group settings we can be expected to turn to our friends for potential reinforcement and avoid our enemies for potential punishment.

At this point you may be wondering what the optimum length of a gaze is in small group communication. Usually a "normal" gaze lasts no more than ten seconds. Most often a group member will look at the listener or listeners when beginning to speak and then will look away. Nielson (1962) suggests that a speaker looks away so that he or she won't be distracted or lose the train of thought. Then the group member will briefly gaze at the listener at the ends of phrases to see if the listener understands and/or agrees. After once again looking away, the speaker will signal the end of the speech with a rather long look. In other words, a speaker looks at the listener, looks away to lessen distraction, looks back at the listener seeking feedback, looks away, and then looks back at the listener to signal the end of the speech. This technique may be termed the "look and look away" technique of eye behavior in interpersonal communication.

Violation of the "look and look away" technique may occur in your small groups as a result of both individual and cultural differences. For example, you may have been in small groups with an individual who did not follow the "look and look away" technique. Until group members who were new to the group recognized that this was the style of the particular individual, they may have displayed signs of nervous tension. When the new members became accustomed to this individual's steady gaze, they probably would suggest that he or she simply seemed to be more interested in them than most other people. You also might encounter violations of the "look and look away" technique if you participate in group discussions with people of different cultures. For example, some French people tend to maintain longer eye contact, while Americans tend to have less eye contact. The important thing to remember is that these differences are individual and cultural and may have little direct relationship to invitation for interaction, liking or disliking, believability, or the task.

PRINCIPLES

1. As related to one's participation in small group interaction, Knapp explains that eye contact can:
   a. Regulate the flow of communication between group members.
   b. Aid in monitoring the feedback of group members to the speaker.
   c. Serve as a method of displaying and expressing one's emotions.
   d. Indicate the nature of the interpersonal relationships which exist within the group.
2. When a group member employs the "look and look away" technique of eye behavior in interpersonal communication, he or she looks at the listener, looks away to lessen distraction, looks back at the listener seeking feedback, looks away, and then looks back at the listener to signal the end of the speech.
3. Violation of the "look and look away" technique occurs in groups as a result of both individual and cultural differences.

Body Movements

Our society is one which seems to depend a great deal on body movement as a form of communication. The hitchhiker's thumb, the student's raised hand, and the discussion leader's nod communicate as clearly as words. In addition, the performance of ordinary activities such as walking into a room, shaking hands with someone, and sitting in a chair communicates messages. Whenever one person visually observes another, there is a continuous flow of information about that person.

Body movements are important for feedback purposes in small groups. The term *requesting* refers to any behavior which serves to tell other members of the group that you want to speak. Suppose, for example, you are involved in a heated discussion concerning the building of a new football stadium. You have some statistics indicating that a strong football program would increase all the programs at the university. No one, however, will recognize you and give you the opportunity to speak. You're sitting on the edge of your chair, visually following the verbal interactions of the other members and waving your hand in order to attract attention. This behavior eventually attracts the attention of the other members and you are given the opportunity to speak. Without ever saying a word, you nonverbally requested the floor.

Body movements also communicate affective states (e.g., moods or emotions). Suppose you are discussing a topic which makes you feel nervous or uptight because of relevance to your personal life. Body movements such as swinging your leg, tapping your fingers, or playing with your hair might indicate to the other group members that you are uncomfortable with the discussion. Burgoon and Saine (1978) explain that the lower body parts, or the trunk of your body, indicate the *intensity* of an emotion. Swinging your leg frequently, for example, would indicate a more intense emotion than would a simple, occasional tap of your foot. If a group member's movements suggest nervousness or tension, you may decide to soft-pedal it until that person is more comfortable. Body movements serve as cues that help you respond in interpersonal communication settings.

Both researchers (e.g., Birdwhistell, 1970) and popular writers (e.g., Fast, 1970) have emphasized the variability in meaning of body movement. Two of several factors which appear to influence the meaning of a movement are (1) the context in which the movement occurs and (2) individual learning.

The meaning of a movement primarily seems to depend on the context in which the movement occurs. Ray Birdwhistell (1970), who is best known for his research in the area of body movement, notes that a body movement may mean nothing at all in one context and yet may be extremely significant in another context. For example, parents who observe their son sticking out his tongue at himself in the mirror probably will smile and attach little significance to the event. However, if the child sticks out his tongue at the parent after a reprimand, the movement probably communicates a significant message!

The meaning of a particular movement also may vary according to the differing contexts of discussions. For example, a group member who leans backward and away from the group in an informal group discussion held outdoors may be perceived to be relaxed. However, a similar movement in the formal context of a conference room may indicate lack of involvement or boredom. Therefore, you should exercise caution in applying generalizations of meaning to all group members in all situations.

The meaning of a movement also seems to depend on learning or the meaning that we have come to associate with a particular movement. Former president Nixon learned this principle when he visited a Latin American country. As he departed from the plane, he signaled "A-OK" with his hand to symbolize good faith. Unfortunately, he failed to realize that in that particular country, the "A-OK" gesture stands for an obscene act. Although learning differences are most prevalent in intercultural communication, they also exist in small group discussion. Group members should be aware of different meaning for movements in order to avoid potential misunderstandings.

PRINCIPLES

1. Through their body movements group members can: send feedback, communicate affective states (e.g., moods or emotions), and request permission to speak.
2. The context in which a movement occurs and individual learning appear to influence the meaning of a movement. Therefore, you should exercise caution in applying generalizations of meaning to all people in all situations.

Touching

Touch is one of the child's primary means of communicating with the environment. When children cry, they receive consolation by stroking and patting. When they explore the world, they touch and perhaps taste whatever is within their grasp. Children learn through touching and through being touched.

As children grow, touching is reduced. The mother may substitute a verbal "You're all right" for a comforting pat. The response "Don't touch that," instead of a hand slap as a child reaches for an object, increases in frequency. In general, verbal language replaces much of tactile communication.

Group members also rely more on verbal language than on touch to communicate in small groups. You can imagine the confusion that would result if group members expressed agreement or disagreement tactilely instead of through verbal language. While touch is not a primary means of communication in small groups, group members do use touch to reinforce verbal comments. For example, a group member may place his arm around the shoulders of another group member as he or she verbally expresses consolation for a rejected proposal. Group members also use touch as a means for communicating feelings such as encouragement, emotional support, or happiness.

Because touch plays an extremely important role in interpersonal relationships, the potential effects of touch on group members should be examined. Have you ever sat next to a "chronic toucher"? Although this individual may have intended nothing more than casual friendship, you may have misinterpreted the friendly pat as an aggressive come-on. Noise may be created in the communication system when a group member misinterprets the intention of the touch. Although touch may be more effective than words in many ways, touching a group member at the wrong time may be as detrimental as any negative verbal comment.

PRINCIPLES

1. Group members rely more on verbal language than touch to communicate in small groups.
2. Group members may use touch to reinforce verbal comments.
3. Group members may communicate feelings such as consolation, encouragement, emotional support, or happiness through touch.
4. Touching a group member at the wrong time may be as detrimental as any negative verbal comment.

PHYSICAL APPEARANCE

It is Saturday night, and a young woman is preparing for a dance. She spends nearly two hours combing her hair and "putting on her face" (from skin freshener to false eyelashes). Finally, she steps into the new formal that she is able to wear after three weeks of crash dieting. She is determined to beat the female competition. Several weeks later during exam week, the young woman is again busy in front of the mirror. This time, however, she carefully places blue-green shadow beneath her eyes and uses baby powder on her face to achieve a "pale and hungry" look. Finally, she dresses in her oldest, most wrinkled clothing. After all, there is no time for beauty while studying for exams.

Our fictitious young woman illustrates the idea that most individuals manipulate their physical appearance in an attempt to communicate messages to other individuals. For example, the young woman may be trying to send a message such as "I am a very desirable woman" to her boyfriend or "Look how much time I spent studying, I deserve a good grade" to her professor. However, has communication occurred? In other words, do people look at an individual's physical appearance and make inferences or judgments about that individual?

Clothing and Stereotypes

Suppose you have been invited to participate in a group discussion about the university's policy toward having rock and roll bands perform on campus. You are the first to arrive and observe the other group members walk into the room. The first person to enter is a young black man with an Afro-style haircut, dressed in a dashiki shirt and African trading beads. The second person to arrive is a female wearing jeans and a T-shirt with "ERA—NOW" printed on it. The third person to enter the room is a female wearing a "preppie" skirt and shirt. The fourth person has very short hair and is dressed in his ROTC uniform. As each person enters the room, you size them up and make inferences about them as individuals and as members of the group. You probably inferred that the first two individuals were more "liberal" and the second two individuals were more "straight."

Several investigators have studied similar situations. Kelley (1969) questioned whether people make inferences about a person's liberalism or conservatism based on that person's physical appearance. He discovered that people associated an orientation toward traditional "fun and football" college culture with conventional dress; moreover, they associated "against the war in Viet Nam," "label self a radical," and "used marijuana" with less conventional dress. Therefore, it would appear that people do make inferences about other people based on physical appearance.

Even small details of clothing may affect interpersonal perceptions. In the early 1980s, for example, you might have inferred that a group member was a "punk rocker" if he wore a safety pin through his nose. Objects with which people adorn themselves are called *artifacts*. An artifact can be a wedding ring, perfume, or even a guitar embroidered on the back of a shirt. All of these objects provide information about the other group members. Impressions quickly formed from physical appearance or from artifacts frequently are termed *stereotypes*.

You probably have been taught that stereotypes are harmful, and this is true when the stereotypes are inaccurate. For example, suppose you are a member of the hiking club at your school. One of the new members comes to the first meeting dressed in a tailored business suit. Would you assume that you have little in common with this individual? Would you wonder why someone dressed like that had joined the club? As group members become acquainted, however, you learn that this individual just interviewed for a job and feels foolish in the suit. Under these circumstances, you might be inclined to reexamine your initial appraisal of the person. One potential negative consequence of inaccurate assessments of group members is that the group may waste much time in polite conversation before discovering that there was only a difference in style of dress and not a difference in opinion.

There seems to be less reliance on clothing factors in forming impressions of group members as more information is gained about the individual. Suppose the individual in the previous example was a friend of yours. Although your friend usually dressed in jeans and a T-shirt, he came to the group meeting dressed in a business suit. More than likely you would inquire as to why he was "all duded up." You would not assume that he had become a different person overnight. However, since we initially know nothing about strangers, we often use dress as a method of assigning accurate or inaccurate personality traits to them.

Personal Appearance and Projected Self-Concepts

This discussion primarily has focused on physical appearance and the effects it has on the impressions you form of group members. However, the effect that your own physical appearance has on your self-image should not be overlooked. How you feel about the way you look can directly affect your behavior in communication situations. If you feel as though you look attractive, you probably are more confident of yourself and may participate more often in your group's discussion. If you spilled chili on your shirt at lunch, you may feel self-conscious and are less motivated to interact with the group. This self-image (confidence versus insecurity) may affect communicative interactions with other group members. Thus, physical appearance may affect small group behavior through reaction to impressions formed of group members and through actions resulting from a group member's self-image.

PRINCIPLES

1. Individuals manipulate their appearance to achieve an effect.
2. Group members make inferences about other members based on physical appearance.
3. Impressions quickly formed from physical appearance or details of clothing are termed *stereotypes*.
4. Stereotypes are harmful when they are inaccurate.
5. The amount of information you have from observation of a group member's behavior tends to affect the impression you form based on physical appearance.
6. Your physical appearance may affect your self-image and your self-image may affect your interaction with group members.

VOCAL BEHAVIOR

Imagine a small group discussion about an emotional topic. One female is particularly ego-involved with the topic. She responds to a challenge in a high, squeaky voice, "I am *not* upset." However, you realize that she *is* upset and suggest that the group take a short coffee break. Perhaps without realizing the contradiction between the verbal and vocal message, you relied on the vocal message as an indication of true feeling. In addition, you probably have noticed that your vocal message sometimes contradicts your verbal message.

Vocal Contradictions

The contradiction between verbal and vocal messages may be intentional or unintentional. The previous example illustrates unintentional contradictions. Unintentional contradictions also may occur in the group situation when you are angry but the group context dictates that you speak cordially. You may be able to fake a polite verbal message but you may slip and let your anger show through in your vocal qualities. One type of intentional contradiction between the verbal and vocal messages is sarcasm. For example, you may say, "This group is really motivated," and mean that the group lacks motivation. If the other group members perceive the meaning is in the way you say the words rather than in the words themselves, you have transmitted information about yourself (e.g., you are angry, or you may be a sarcastic individual) as well as about your observation.

Even when you do not consciously try to manipulate your voice, you transmit information about yourself. Group members estimate the occupations, sociability, intelligence, and level of education as well as many other qualities from the vocal characteristics of the other group members. For example, you may recall someone making inferences about a man who had a high, effeminate voice or about a woman who had a deep, masculine voice. Perhaps unconsciously we form impressions of people based on their vocal qualities and, right or wrong, we relate to these people as if the impressions were accurate.

Vocal Qualities

Your voice also transmits information about your emotional state. Research has indicated that through differences in rate and the use of pauses and pitch, the voice conveys emotions such as contempt, anger, fear, grief, and indifference. For example, you may have recognized that a group member was angry or afraid by his or her faster rate, shorter comments, and more frequent pauses or use of "uh" and "um." An increase in the number or length of pauses in a group member's speech may indicate indecision, tension, or resistance. If a person is indecisive, for example, you most likely would not want to push him or her into making a decision on a critical issue. By perceiving and being sensitive to vocal qualities, you may be able to guide your responses constructively to avoid potential communication problems.

A word of caution is in order, however. When you make inferences about group members based on their vocal qualities, you should be aware that the vocal expressions vary from individual to individual in the group. For example, within the broad concept of "anxiety" there are wide individual differences. In your group discussions you probably have observed that some anxious members talk slower and have a lot of silent pauses and/or nonfluencies while other anxious members do not. Thus, prior knowledge of the individual in situations other than the group context should affect your perception of the individual.

Silent Messages

At this point you may think that avoiding verbal interactions is the answer to the possibility of misunderstanding of your vocal messages. No such luck! Silence can be as loud as words. For example, silence may communicate that you are listening attentively or that you are too angry to speak. Silence also communicates that you are thinking or that you are not paying attention. Silence as well as vocal behavior can be misunderstood, and the meaning of your silence should be made clear to the other group members.

The vocal behavior you use in small groups probably will not be the only factor influencing your effectiveness in the discussion. However, it probably will influence the perceptions that the other members hold of you. For example, unless the members know that you talk loudly in all situations, they may think that you are upset or aggressive. Whether or not in fact you are aggressive is less important than the fact that the other members hold that perception. Individuals respond to others in terms of perceptions rather than reality. Vocal behavior is only a part of the total behavior of an individual, and therefore interacts with other behaviors to influence the responses of other individuals. Remember that individuals as well as groups are open systems with many interacting elements.

PRINCIPLES

1. When your vocal message contradicts your verbal message, the contradiction may be intentional or unintentional.
2. Group members may infer occupation, sociability, intelligence, and other qualities from a group member's vocal qualities.
3. Group members may infer emotions such as contempt, anger, fear, grief, and indifference from differences in rate, pauses, and pitch.
4. Silence also communicates messages.
5. There usually are wide individual differences in vocal expression.

TERRITORY AND PERSONAL SPACE

Have you ever had someone take "your" parking place, sit in "your" seat in class, or put their books on "your" desk? What was your reaction? Obviously, you cannot physically move someone else's car (unless the keys are in it).

However, you may ask an individual to change his or her seat or you may move someone else's books.

This type of aggressive behavior frequently is used to respond to an invasion of one's "territory." The term *territory* may be thought of as a given area over which ownership is felt. Generally an individual feels compelled to defend the area against those who may invade it. Ownership may be felt over a large area such as a home, or a small area such as a favorite chair.

You should be aware that group members also may "claim" territory. For example, a group member may think that a certain chair or position at the conference table is his or hers. If you occupy that chair, the person might ask you to move. Or, initially repressing aggressive feelings, the group member may display aggression in the discussion although he or she ordinarily is not an aggressive individual. Group members who notice and try to cope with the aggressive behavior may be totally unaware of the precipitating cause.

The concept of personal space differs slightly from the concept of territory. Personal space may be thought of as a "bubble of air" surrounding the individual which expands and contracts according to certain variables (these variables will be discussed later in this section). Whereas invasion of territory may result in aggression, invasion of personal space usually leads to withdrawal. For example, you may recall a group member who moved his or her chair too close to yours. You probably remember that your reaction was subtle rather than aggressive—perhaps tapping a pencil, swinging a crossed leg, or in some cases moving your chair away from the "invader." You may have responded to the invasion of personal space by withdrawing from the discussion. You may have become preoccupied with an anxious feeling and lost interest in the discussion even if you could not perceive the cause of your anxiety. On the other hand, probably you can recall a similar instance in which a group member moved his or her chair too close to yours but you didn't feel threatened.

There are several variables which appear to affect how comfortable you are with the distance (i.e., whether or not you are "threatened") at which another individual stands or sits. Four of these variables (Argyle and Dean, 1965) are: *sex of the interactants; nature of the interpersonal relationship; topic or task;* and *setting for the interaction.*

Sex of the interactants.   You probably have noticed that in our society female group members sit closer to other females than to male group members (where group members know each other slightly). In a group discussion in which all group members are females, the members would tend to sit closer together than if there were both males and females in the group. In the same fashion, an all-male discussion group would probably have greater physical distance between individual members because males tend to interact at greater physical distances than females.[2]

Nature of the interpersonal relationship. You probably have noticed that there usually is greater physical distance between group members who do not know each other or who dislike each other. If unfriendly group members are forced to sit together, the individuals may lean farther backward or face in the direction away from each other in an attempt to put as much space between them as possible. As group members become acquainted and friendlier, however, they tend to sit closer together.

Topic or task. There usually is greater physical distance between group members discussing impersonal topics; individuals discussing intimate topics usually stand or sit closer together. Suppose that two groups who knew each other equally well were formed. One group was given an intimate topic for discussion and the other was given an impersonal topic. It would seem logical that you would be able to determine which group was discussing the intimate topic by observing how close together the chairs were in each group. We would like to remind you, however, that the sex of the interactants and whether or not they know or like each other interact with this variable. A group composed of males who did not know each other probably would not sit as close together as a group of females who knew each other—regardless of the intimacy of the topic.

Setting for the interaction. The comfortable distance between individuals also seems to vary from situation to situation. If you were to observe one individual in all the groups to which he or she belongs, you probably would notice that the individual allowed group members to stand or sit closer in some situations than in others. For example, a group member might allow group members to sit closer if an informal meeting were held outside under a large shade tree. On the other hand, a group member might keep group members at a greater distance if the group meeting were held around a conference table in an average size room. Thus, the distance between individuals also varies from situation to situation.

The next time you are in a group situation, try to observe the distance between group members. You might observe other variables than the ones discussed in this section as affecting the distance for interaction. Burgoon and Saine (1978) explain that age, race, culture, status, personality, and mood of the interactants also affect the distance at which people interact. In addition, the setting for the interaction has a direct effect on the amount of personal

[2]See Hayduk (1978) for an excellent discussion of personal space.

Introversion-extroversion. Cook (1970) found that extroverts chose opposite seats or chose positions which would put them in close physical proximity. Introverts generally chose positions which would keep them more at a distance. Because individuals who withdraw from small group communication do not make a full contribution to the group, the group may not realize its potential.[3]

Knowledge of the effects of seating arrangement on interaction can be beneficial to the group member participating in a small group discussion. For example, if the leader knows of two talkative group members (extroverts), he or she may choose to minimize interruptions to the discussion by having them occupy seats at some distance from each other. Similarly, the leader may want to encourage group members who are shy by placing them toward the center instead of at the corners of a rectangular table. Or, for example, if the leader knows of potentially hostile group members, then this hostility can be prevented or minimized by physical separation of the unfriendly group members. A careful systems analysis of the group will help the leader limit the communication between hostile group members, perhaps by focusing the discussion only on the task and giving the most knowledgeable group members the most access to communication.

PRINCIPLES

1. Communicative interaction can be affected by the environment in which the interaction occurs.
2. The leader or someone chosen by the leader should give considerable thought to the interior decoration of the room prior to the discussion.
3. Seating arrangement and interaction are related; individuals tend to interact more frequently with people seated opposite them; individuals who sit at the corners of a rectangular table tend to contribute the least to the discussion.
4. Leadership and introversion-extroversion are two variables which tend to affect the seating position you choose.

SUMMARY

This chapter has focused on nonverbal communication as it relates to your participation in small groups. The first section discussed various physical behaviors as they relate to small groups. Group members rely on facial

---

[3]Systematic desensitization has been found to help reduce withdrawal behaviors. McCroskey (1972) proposed a program for implementation of systematic desensitization for communication anxiety.

expression, eye contact, body movement, and touch to communicate messages about their own internal states and to make inferences about the internal states of other group members. Sensitivity to these physical behaviors may help you to avoid potential communication problems in small groups.

The second section discussed the idea that individuals manipulate their physical appearance in an attempt to communicate messages to other individuals. Group members observe an individual's physical appearance and form an impression. Inaccurate impressions present problems for group members.

The third section discussed vocal behavior. Group members make inferences about other members based on vocal qualities. Sometimes there is a contradiction between verbal and vocal messages. Group members also rely on these contradictions to form impressions.

The fourth section examined the role of space as it relates to the small group context. When a group member invades your territory, you may react aggressively. However, if a group member were to invade your personal space, you would probably retreat. Variables were identified which appear to affect comfortable interaction distance.

The final section of the chapter provided you with information about the importance of the environment and physical arrangement of the group. Generally the leader, or someone assigned by the leader, assumes responsibility for environmental conditions surrounding the discussion. Seating arrangement is an important variable in small group communication.

The purpose of this chapter has been to increase your awareness of nonverbal communication, especially in small groups, rather than to present an overview of the field.[4] It seems obvious that the total nonverbal behavior of the group member (in part culturally learned) affects other members' responses to any one behavior. Thus, the preceding chapter is only an appetizer for the total field of nonverbal communication.

IDEAS FOR DISCUSSION

1. What is the role and significance of nonverbal communication in small group communication?
2. What are possible explanations for the behavior of:
   a. an overtalkative group member?
   b. a silent group member?

[4]Several books which take different approaches to the study of nonverbal communication are available for further study. Birdwhistell (1970) takes a more systematic approach while Fast (1970) is a popular best-seller. Perhaps the most recent book which contains a summarization and explanation of research findings is Malandro and Barker, 1983.

    c. an aggressive group member?

    d. a group member who laughs even when something funny has not been said?

3. What are several ways that you express your boredom with a group discussion through physical and vocal behaviors?

4. How do you know when someone is interested in talking with you if he or she does not verbalize an interest?

5. What nonverbal factors have you noticed in people of different cultures that might cause problems in group discussions with people of your culture?

6. What personality factors would you assign to:

    a. an obese group member?

    b. an athletic and muscular group member?

    c. a thin group member?

    How might each of these persons react during a tense moment in a group discussion?

7. What nonverbal cues do you rely on to tell if a group member is lying?

8. What are other environmental variables that might affect the group discussion?

9. Do you think total darkness would be beneficial or detrimental to group discussions? Under what, if any, conditions might it be beneficial?

SUGGESTED PROJECTS AND ACTIVITIES

1. Conduct a five-minute small group meeting about the group's social climate without talking. After the time is up, conduct a follow-up discussion to determine the accuracy of messages received during the no-talking period. Did the group understand more or less than they would have predicted in such a restricted communication setting? What kinds of messages were most easily transmitted and received during the no-talk period? What kinds of messages were hardest to communicate?

2. In a group of from five to seven members, prepare a discussion to be presented in front of the rest of the class in which the members of the group deliberately attempt nonverbally to mask their true feelings and role play different ones. After the discussion, ask the class members who were observing if they could detect any masking behavior in the group. Discuss the relative success of the group's attempt at masking and role playing.

3. In groups of three to four, conduct a study in a local restaurant. Order something to eat and watch for the effect of clothing on the service that customers receive (e.g., liberals—jeans, sandals, T-shirts—versus conservatives—coats, ties, dresses, etc.). Observe carefully the facial expression of the waiter or waitress, the verbal behavior, and the apparent attitude toward the customers. On the basis of this study, what conclusions can you draw about the effect of clothing on attitudes of waiters and waitresses and the consequent service you obtain?

4. Have one member sit on the floor in the middle of the group while the rest of the group sits on regular chairs and has a group discussion. Then have the group sit

on the floor around a group member who is sitting on a chair and continue the discussion. What effects, if any, did the different heights of members in relation to the rest of the group have on the interaction and content of the discussion?

REFERENCES

ALLIGERIES, A. R., and D. BYRNE. Attraction toward the opposite sex as a determinant of physical proximity. *Journal of social psychology*, 1973, *90*, 211–219.

ARGYLE, M. *The psychology of interpersonal behavior*. Baltimore: Penguin, 1967.

ARGYLE, M., and J. DEAN. Eye contact, distance and affiliation. *Sociometry*, 1965, *25*, 289–304.

BIRDWHISTELL, R. L. *Kinesics and context*. Philadelphia: University of Philadelphia Press, 1970.

BURGOON, J. K., and T. SAINE. *The unspoken dialogue: an introduction to nonverbal communication*. Boston: Houghton Mifflin Co., 1978.

COOK, M. Experiments on orientations and proxemics. *Human relations*, 1970, *23*, 61–76.

DAVIS, E. *The elementary school child and his posture patterns*. New York: Appleton-Century-Crofts, 1958.

ECKMAN, P., P. ELLSWORTH, and W. V. FRIESEN. *Emotion in the human face: guidelines for research and an integration of findings*. Elmsford, N.Y.: Pergamon Press, 1971.

Educational Facilities Laboratories, Inc. *School environments research*. Ann Arbor, Mich.: University of Michigan, 1965.

EXLINE, R., and L. WINTERS. Affective relations and mutual glances in dyads. In S. Tomkins and C. Izard, eds. *Affect, cognition and personality*. New York: Springer Pub., 1965.

FAST, F. *Body language*. New York: M. Evans, 1970.

HAYDUK, L. A. Personal space: an evaluative and orienting overview. *Psychological bulletin*, 1978, *85*, 117–134.

GOFFMAN, E. *Behavior in public places*. New York: Macmillan, 1963.

KELLEY, J. Dress as nonverbal communication. Paper presented to the Annual Conference of American Association for Public Opinion Research, May 1969.

KNAPP, M. L. *Nonverbal communication in human interaction*, 2nd ed. New York: Holt, Rinehart & Winston, 1977.

MALANDRO, L., and L. L. BARKER. *Nonverbal communication*. Reading, Mass.: Addison-Wesley, 1983.

MASLOW, A. H., and N. L. MINTZ. Effect of aesthetic surroundings: I. Initial effects of three asethetic conditions upon perceiving "energy" and "well-being" in faces. *Journal of psychology*, 1956, *41*, 247–254.

MEHRABIAN, A. *Silent messages*, 2nd ed. Belmont, Calif.: Wadsworth, 1981.

MICHELINI, R., R. PASSALACQUA, and J. Cuismano. Effects of seating arrangement on group participation. *Journal of social psychology*, 1976, *99*, 179–186.

MINTA, N. L. Effects of aesthetic surrounding: II, Prolonged and repeated experience in a "beautiful" and "ugly" room. *Journal of psychology*, 1956, *41*, 459–466.

NIELSEN, G. *Studies in self-confrontation*. University of Copenhagen, Psychological Laboratories, 1962.

PATTERSON, A. H., and W. E. BOLES. The effects of personal space variables upon approach and attitude toward the other in a prisoner's dilemma game. *Personality and social psychological bulletin*, 1974, *1*, 364–366.

SILVERSTEIN, C. H., and D. J. STANG. Seating position and interaction in triads: a field study. *Sociometry*, 1976, *39*, 166–170.

SOMMER, R. *Worm runners digest*, 1960, *2*, 45–49. Reprint from *The Canadian Archives*, 1960, 76–80.

STEIN, R. T. Identifying emergent leaders from verbal and nonverbal communication. *Journal of personality and social psychology*, 1975, *32*, 125–135.

SUGGESTED READINGS

BELLAK, L., and S. S. Baker. *Reading faces.* New York: Holt, Rinehart & Winston, 1981.

This popular book contains a step-by-step method for reading faces. Examples are given for well-known individuals, and pictures are provided.

BIRDWHISTELL, R. L. *Kinesics and context.* Philadelphia: Philadelphia Press, 1970.

In this book, the father of kinesics presents essays on body motion communication. The book includes methods of isolating behavior, approaching behavior, collecting data, and research.

KNAPP, M. L. *Nonverbal communication in human interaction,* 2nd ed. New York: Holt, Rinehart & Winston, 1977.

Along with coverage of the major areas of nonverbal communication, this book also provides a good review of the literature within each chapter. The chapters include discussions of such areas as the environment, physical behaviors, face and eye behaviors, vocal cues, etc.

LEATHERS, D. G. *Nonverbal communication systems.* Boston: Allyn & Bacon, 1976.

This text includes an overview of the areas of nonverbal communication. Besides traditional areas such as facial expression, hand and body movements, proxemics, etc., this book also discusses telepathic communication and basic measuring instruments.

MALANDRO, L., and L. L. BARKER. *Nonverbal Communication.* Reading, Mass.: Addison-Wesley, 1983.

This book is an excellent introduction to the study of nonverbal communication. Each chapter is concerned with exploring research and the pragmatics of the codes of nonverbal communication.

MEHRABIAN, A. *Silent messages,* 2nd ed. Belmont, Calif.: Wadsworth, 1981.

This book explores three metaphors of nonverbal communication and how they relate to our nonverbal behavior. The book discusses research which substantiates the metaphors of immediacy-liking, power-status, and dominance-submission.

Ken Karp

9 Leadership in Small Groups

Study
Questions

After you have read this chapter, you should be able to answer the following questions completely and accurately:

1. What is the trait approach to defining leadership? What problems result from viewing leadership as traits?
2. What are three leadership styles?
3. What problems result from viewing leadership as an official position?
4. What is a definition for leadership?
5. What are task needs? What are four actions which a group member can perform to satisfy task needs?
6. What are maintenance needs? What are four behaviors which a group member can perform to satisfy maintenance needs?
7. What is the dilemma for leaders regarding task versus maintenance needs?
8. What are guidance needs?

Your favorite television program is interrupted one evening with an announcement. You hear the voice of the press secretary: "Ladies and gentlemen, the President of the United States." Most individuals would agree that the president is the recognized leader of our country. Consider the cabinet meetings, however. Does the president exert leadership or does he merely preside over the cabinet meetings? Is he the only individual in the cabinet to influence the group, or are there other individuals who also perform leadership functions? This chapter is intended to help you answer these questions. We will consider approaches to defining leadership, identify three types of leadership needs which small groups have, and suggest some actions which have been demonstrated to satisfy the leadership requirements of small groups. After performing a systems analysis of the leadership needs of groups in which you participate, you may decide to perform leadership functions yourself.

APPROACHES
TO DEFINING LEADERSHIP

Most people, when reading the term *leadership*, tend to think of a single individual. The thought of a sorority or fraternity president, a teacher or an employer may come to mind. An image may form of a person who has been elected or appointed to the task of assuming major responsibilities for the group's activities. Before we propose our preferred definition of leadership, we would like to look at some previous approaches to the study of leadership.

Leadership Traits

The trait approach to the study of leadership was the first serious attempt to understand leadership. The approach seems to be based on the notion that leaders are born and not made (the phrase "a natural, born leader" illustrates the point). Studies were conducted to identify traits or characteristics which leaders possess. The investigations have attempted to learn whether leaders are more popular, intelligent, aggressive, self-confident, enthusiastic, or physically attractive than those they lead. Such leadership qualities seem reasonable. The research studies, however, have failed to achieve consistent results. Although many different physical and personality traits have been examined, few were found which could be used for *consistent* identification of leaders.

An earlier draft of this chapter was prepared by Ronald E. Bassett, University of Texas at Austin, and we gratefully acknowledge his contribution.

Leadership Styles

The styles approach to the study of leadership, like the previous traits approach, assumes that there is one person in the leadership position. This approach, however, seeks to determine which of three styles of leadership is most effective.

The three styles of leadership that have been investigated include the democratic, the autocratic, and the laissez-faire styles. Many generalizations emerged from these studies. A democratic leader was conceived to be a "guide" not a "controller." Democratic leaders seek group participation and tend to guide through the use of questions (e.g., "Are we ready to suggest criteria for solutions to the problem?"). Autocratic leaders, however, tend to give orders (e.g., "We will now begin listing our criteria."). Laissez-faire leaders were the most difficult to analyze because this style implies that the leader leads through not leading at all. Essentially, a laissez-faire leader performs leadership functions only when requested. In many cases, the group does not request the assistance and it therefore becomes a "leaderless group."

Each of these three styles of leadership varies in effectiveness according to the type of group and the task. It is obvious that a military leader should not be democratic in the height of battle (e.g., "Excuse me private, do you think you could shoot your gun and kill some of the enemy?"). It's probably just as obvious that people in community groups don't like to be given orders (e.g., "We're having a yard sale on Saturday. I want your things priced and at my house by 8:30 A.M. You have the noon till 2:00 P.M. shift."). An analysis of leadership is potentially useful in identifying relationships (and problems) between group leaders and group members.

Leadership As an Official Position

The traits approach and the styles approach to the study of leadership assume that the person occupying the official position of power (i.e., the leader's office) is considered the leader and therefore the person exerting leadership. Sometimes the occupant of the leader's office does in fact provide leadership for the group. However, at other times, problems arise in viewing leadership in this way. For one thing, in many small, informal, or newly formed groups, a formally designated leadership position may not exist. Consider, for instance, a group of four undergraduate women who decide to spend Saturday afternoons cleaning up litter along local roadsides. In such a group it is doubtful that there will be a designated leader's position (e.g., a chairperson). Are we to conclude then that this group *cannot* have a leader? Obviously not.

The second problem in viewing leadership in terms of official positions is that some research suggests that sometimes persons occupying the designated leadership position are not the most influential members of the group (Collins and Guetzkow, 1964). For example, the young lieutenant fresh from ROTC may be designated leader of a company of soldiers, but the seasoned sergeant may have the most influence on actual combat decisions and troop morale. Therefore, we believe that it is inadequate to look only at the occupant of the leader's office to study leadership. We propose another perspective to the concept of leadership.

Definition of Leadership

Leadership is influential behavior, voluntarily accepted by group members, which moves a group toward its recognized goal and/or maintains the group. Let us make certain that the terms used in our proposed definition are clear. *Influential behavior* refers to actions performed by one person which cause others to respond in a desired fashion. For example, suppose you have just lighted a cigarette and another group member informs you that he or she is allergic to tobacco smoke. If you extinguish the cigarette because of that statement, then the group member may infer that he or she has caused you to respond in the way which he or she intended (i.e., another person's behavior has influenced yours).

Voluntarily accepted by group members means that the participants in a group accept the influence without force or threat of force. The guard on a prison work crew may influence prisoners to break more rocks by refusing to give them water, but his influence is certainly not voluntarily accepted by the prisoners.

Moves a group toward its recognized goal assumes that the group has some purpose and that this objective is known to the group members.

Maintains the group refers to actions which aid the group members in working together as a unit (e.g., establishing warm interpersonal relations). Some examples of specific types of behaviors which move groups toward goals and help to maintain groups as harmonious social systems will be examined later in this chapter.

Our definition of leadership does not assume that only the person occupying the leader's office influences the group. Neither is the definition based on the premise that there are *natural leaders*—persons with traits that enable them to influence all persons in all situations. In fact, viewing leadership as influential behavior does not assume that only *one* person influences the members of a group. To the contrary, it recognizes the possibility of all members contributing to the process by which groups seek and achieve goals. In summary, leadership consists of actions which help the group move toward its goal and/or help group members to work together. It is a dynamic variable in group process and should be studied by a systems approach to small group communication.

Problems in Learning
to Become a Better Leader

In the next section of this chapter, you will find descriptions of leadership behavior as well as some suggestions for what you should do if you want to perform leadership functions. Most of the descriptions of what leaders actually do have been based on observations made in laboratory or field research settings. However, many of the suggestions regarding what leaders *should do* are based on less systematic and less controlled observations of actual working groups. As a reader you are cautioned to refrain from interpreting discussions of leadership behaviors in this chapter as "surefire ways" to leadership success. The existing knowledge of small group process is still too incomplete to make error-free prescriptions for the leadership behavior appropriate for any one group.

Several situational factors will influence the leadership behaviors which are appropriate to a given set of circumstances. Fiedler (1964, 1967) has developed a model identifying factors upon which leadership behaviors are contingent. The first factor is *leader-member relations*, which includes the affective or emotional relations between the leader and the members. How they feel about each other will affect the leadership. Another factor is the *task structure*, or what external demands are placed upon the group. The final factor is *position power*. This is the amount of actual power inherent in the leadership position. For example, the president of the United States has a great deal of position power, while the leader of a sensitivity group has very little. Other factors which could influence leadership behaviors are

1. the members of the group and their relation to one another
2. the situation or context in which the group functions
3. the distance between the group's present position and goal attainment

Attempting to employ behavior which may be very effective in one set of circumstances can have disastrous results in an entirely different situation. *Leadership must be viewed as actions which satisfy the needs of a particular group, at a particular point in time.*

PRINCIPLES

1. The trait approach to the study of leadership attempted to identify traits or characteristics which leaders possess. Few traits were found which could be used for *consistent* identification of leaders.
2. The styles approach to the study of leadership attempted to determine whether the democratic, the autocratic, or the laissez-faire leader was most

effective. The styles of leadership vary in effectiveness according to the type of group and the task.

3. Investigating leadership by studying the occupant of a recognized position of power has two shortcomings: first, some groups do not have official leaders; second, in some groups the person occupying the leader's office may not be providing leadership for the group.

4. Leadership is influential behavior, voluntarily accepted by group members, which moves a group toward its recognized goal and/or maintains the group.

5. Leadership should be viewed as actions which satisfy the needs of a particular group, at a particular point in time.

GROUP NEEDS
AND LEADERSHIP BEHAVIORS

Small groups have three basic leadership needs: task needs, maintenance needs, and guidance needs. Task needs are satisfied by leadership behavior which moves the group toward its recognized goal or objective. Maintenance needs, in contrast, require leadership behavior which enables the group to develop and preserve harmonious relations among members. Guidance needs are satisfied by leadership behavior which enables the group to move in an *orderly fashion* toward its objective.

The labeling of any one particular function as serving either the task or maintenance needs of a group is difficult and probably requires an oversimplification of the complex leadership process. However, recognizing that groups have needs related not only to goal achievement but also to interpersonal relations may aid you in conceptualizing the various leadership functions which must be performed in groups.

Task Needs

In this section we will examine in some detail four important leadership behaviors which have been demonstrated to satisfy task needs (i.e., behaviors which aid the group in achieving its goals). These behaviors are diagnosing the situation and proposing action, seeking information, stimulating action, and handling crisis.

Obviously there are many more leadership functions which could have been included. However, due to the limited space, we have chosen a few behaviors and then tried to draw implications from the research findings which might aid you in obtaining a more in-depth knowledge of the actions task leaders perform.

Diagnosing the situation and proposing actions. Carter et al. (1968) observed groups in which leaders were appointed and others in which leaders were not appointed, but emerged as the group worked on its task. The groups they studied also differed in the nature of the task assigned to them. One task involved mechanical assembly, another required a high amount of reasoning, and still another required a high amount of discussion. Regardless of whether the leader was appointed or emergent and regardless of the nature of the task assigned to the group, two types of actions were consistently associated with leadership: diagnosing and making interpretations of the situation and giving information for carrying out actions.

It is easy to see how these behaviors relate to our definition of task leadership as behavior which moves the group toward its goal. Diagnosing the situation and making an interpretation requires that the leader know where the group is in discussion at any point in time. For example, group members may be confused about ideas or plans that are being discussed at the present moment. When group members are confused, the group leader must be able to detect this condition, determine its cause, and then attempt to correct it. Often, the leader can eliminate confusion by restating comments which have been made or by stopping the discussion for a moment to clarify the line of thought.

In addition to being able to analyze the group's condition at the present moment, the task leader may need to assess the group's *progress* toward the objective. This may require summaries provided either by the leader or by a group secretary who keeps track of the discussion. The leader may summarize the group's actions several times before the end of the meeting to point out the group's progress (or lack of progress) in a given area and to determine what needs to be done to complete a particular task.

The task leader must also diagnose the past and present condition of the group's achievement in relation to the stated goal to determine when *new actions* are required. For example, when a particular plan has ceased to be productive, the task leader must know when to abandon it. Likewise, the task leader must determine when sufficient time has been spent on one aspect of the task and when solutions may be threatened by insufficient time. In summary, one aspect of task leadership which seems to be performed by leaders under widely differing circumstances is the analysis of the group's performance in relation to its stated goal.

Another behavior most frequently performed by persons providing task leadership is giving information on how to carry out action. This simply means that persons performing task functions are able to move the group toward its goal by providing plans for putting their ideas, as well as the ideas of others, into effect. However, a cautionary note is in order. Suppose you are extremely motivated to accomplish the task. At the first meeting you spring all your ideas on the group while the other members are just getting acquainted with one another. You find your ideas being ignored or rejected without fair evaluation. A group member who is more interested in the task when the other group members are interested in interpersonal relationships may be perceived as a know-it-all. An awareness of group needs is important.

Seeking and obtaining information. Individuals work in groups because often the group product is superior to what any individual member of the group could produce working alone. The production of superior thinking and decisions is dependent in part on the pooling of the total resources of the group. To achieve this end, the task leader must seek out all relevant information which group members possess. However, merely asking questions is not sufficient to ensure that the total resources of the group will become available. The leader must learn to ask questions which specify the information wanted. Keltner (1970) has summarized some of the basic principles of effective questioning: First, use language that both you and the respondent understand. If you truly want information, don't try to impress others with the size of your vocabulary. This is a quick way to turn them off. Second, keep questions simple and easy to understand. This requires that you know what information you want before you can expect others to provide it. Third, ask questions which you expect your respondent to be able to answer. If you put a person on the spot by asking a question that he or she can't answer, that person may interpret your action as a put-down and refuse to give you information that he or she does have.

Stimulating action. One of the greatest threats to goal achievement is apathy. It cannot be assumed that simply because a person attends a group meeting, he or she is concerned about the group or its goals. However, research indicates that when group members feel the group's task is important to them, overall satisfaction with group interaction is higher (Collins and Guetzkow, 1964). We can expect higher morale and higher quality decisions from a group whose members are genuinely concerned about the outcome of the group's performance. If the group's goal is truly important, then it is the leader's obligation to show each member how the goal is related to the members' needs. We are all basically selfish and motivated by the desire to satisfy our own needs and interests. Whether or not participants ask, each wonders, *What's in it for me?* Even if the value of the goal seems to be self-evident, making certain that each member realizes the importance of the goal in meeting his or her own needs is vital.

In addition to demonstrating the relationship between the group's goal and the members' needs, research has indicated three other techniques relevant to motivating the group.

1. There is some evidence that groups with feedback become more motivated and involved in the task than groups without feedback. Furukawa (1972) suggests that the nature of the feedback (rewarding or punishing) may be an important consideration in determining its effect on group motivation. It seems logical to assume that a group which achieves success may raise its level of aspiration and become more motivated. Many tasks and subgoals exist and success in these limited but related areas may increase the group's motivation level and stimulate action toward the group goal.

2. Several experimental studies have indicated that groups which are well organized will be motivated and productive (Goodacre, 1953; Horwitz et al., 1953). Organization of the group includes clarification of group goals and individual roles. In other words, you should inform the group of its purpose (e.g., to select quality control standards for the business) and the individual members of their tasks (e.g., to present the management point of view). In general, groups which are well organized are more motivated and productive not only because they have clear direction to the goal but also because clearly defined roles lessen the possibility of wasted time due to power struggles. Interpersonal competition to be the chosen leader is one of the most obvious power struggles.

3. Experimental studies also have indicated that moderate competition between groups may increase cohesiveness and serve as a motivating force (Kahn and Ryen, 1972). College sports rivals serve to illustrate the point. Too much emphasis on competition, however, can cause stress and be detrimental to motivation. In your systems analysis, you should look at group goals and personalities of group members to determine the potential effectiveness of intergroup competition.

Handling crisis. As we have stated several times before, the power of a task leader rests in his or her ability to move the group toward its goal. When a serious threat to goal achievement is perceived by the group, the leader must respond *at once* to continue to move the group forward, or the group may turn to other sources for leadership (Gulley, 1969).

Experimental support for this assertion is provided by Hamblin (1968) who placed subjects into three-person teams to play a game. Midway through the game, the rules were changed, thus creating threat and a crisis of sorts for the teams. Hamblin recorded attempts by team members to influence team playing strategies. The observations indicated that team members with high influence in the first half of the playing period had even greater influence in the crisis condition (i.e., rules change). However, persons with high influence established before the rules change lost their influence if they were unable to solve the problems created by the rules change.

Blythe (1975) also found that a leader who did not come to the aid of a faltering discussion group created indignation and disappointment on the part of group members. When you are a group leader, you should try to respond to the constantly fluctuating conditions of your group/system.

PRINCIPLES

1. When group members appear unclear about the topic under discussion, restate previous comments or stop the discussion to clarify the line of thought.
2. Provide summaries of the group's progress toward its goal.
3. Analyze the relation of the group's present position to its desired ending state to determine when a plan has ceased to be productive and when goal achievement is threatened by insufficient time.
4. Suggest plans for putting your ideas as well as the ideas of others into action.
5. Ask specific questions to seek out all the relevant information members possess.
6. Make certain that each member realizes the importance of the group's goal to satisfying his or her own needs.
7. Three techniques which are relevant to motivating the group include: providing positive feedback, organizing the group, and moderating competition with another group.
8. Respond at once to any threat to group goal attainment by employing all available efforts and resources to keep the group moving toward its objective.

Maintenance Needs

Leadership behaviors which promote morale and harmonious social conditions in the group are as important as task-related leadership functions. An individual who exerts leadership in the area of group maintenance is sensitive to other individuals. In this section, we will discuss four leadership behaviors which affect the maintenance of the group. These behaviors include: climate making, regulating the discussion, stimulating involvement, and resolving conflict.

Climate making. Several kinds of leadership services go into creating an emotional atmosphere that is conducive to productive discussion. One of these services is to be honest, yet tactful, in the way you present your ideas. A cold, impersonal approach can discourage interest and participation by others while a warm and friendly approach can promote interpersonal trust

5. Place the hesitant member in a favorable position in the communication net. Individuals who occupy the more central positions in a communication net' send a greater number of messages (see Chapter 4). In other words, increasing the involvement of a hesitant group member may be as simple as having him or her sit at the head of the table. Obviously the group member who occupies the position at the head of the table is not necessarily the most verbal. However, other things being equal, individuals who occupy central positions interact more frequently than do other individuals.

Resolving conflict. Although resolving conflict is the subject of Chapter 10, it is important to mention it as a maintenance need. Most discussion groups that have a long history of working together experience conflict to some degree. Keeping the proper perspective on conflict is important. There is a fine line between a healthy exchange of ideas and an ugly scene that can damage egos and hinder the group's ability to work together. When conflict occurs, an effective mediator should try to keep the attention on the issues and not on the persons advocating the opposing ideas. A good strategy to use is for the leader to state the problem as he or she sees it and then to invite those persons who hold opposing positions to clarify their views. The leader may then lead the entire group in a step-by-step examination of the problem, attempting to ascertain the specific points on which members agree and disagree. The role of the "peacemaker" is very important to the survival of the group.

PRINCIPLES

1. Present your ideas in an honest yet tactful manner.
2. Provide emotional support to other group members.
3. Most overly talkative group members will be quiet if their interaction with others is restricted either through seating arrangement or by visually ignoring them. Reprimands should be carefully worded since rude remarks could cause serious repercussions.
4. Suggestions for stimulating individual involvement in the discussion include the following:
   a. Make sure that each member has an equal chance to participate.
   b. Make sure that each member is aware of the obligation to participate.
   c. Be sensitive to attempts to participate.
   d. Reinforce early attempts to participate.
   e. Place the hesitant member in a favorable position in the communication network.
5. When conflict occurs, an effective mediator keeps the group's attention on the issues and not on the persons advocating the opposing ideas.

Conflict Between Task
and Maintenance Needs

In Chapter 1, we discussed some of the reasons people may decide to work as a small group rather than as individuals. For whatever reasons individuals join groups, members tend to remain part of the group only as long as group membership is a rewarding experience. Group membership is rewarding for most people when they like other group members.

Developing interpersonal relations requires time which could have been spent on the task. As the group continues to meet, additional time must be spent on sustaining pleasant relations. When an individual works alone, he or she may devote attention solely to the task. When that person works in a group, he or she must divide attention between the task and the other group members. The presence of others can motivate the individual, distract the individual, or make him or her defensive, but whatever the outcome, the mere presence of other persons requires adjustments or adaptations in a person's behavior.

There is a basic conflict between task and maintenance needs. The conflict lies in the fact that a disproportionate amount of time spent on either set of needs is disruptive to group process. If the leader concentrates on the task and ignores group maintenance needs, the establishment and continuance of interpersonal relations will suffer, with the possible consequence of lower group morale. On the other hand, if the group neglects the task to concentrate on interpersonal relations, then goal achievement is delayed or perhaps becomes impossible. The problem for the leader is to maintain a satisfactory balance in meeting the task as well as the maintenance needs of the group.

As we pointed out before, the nature of the leadership functions and the distribution of the functions among group members differ with each group. Task functions and group maintenance functions may be performed by one or several members. The two types of leadership functions may also be performed at the same time. For example, a group member may help to arbitrate a dispute (a maintenance function) by clarifying the issues (a task function) which are the cause of the dispute. Consider the following example:

A group of student government representatives, five whites and two blacks, were bitterly divided over the amount of money which should be given to the Black Student Union (BSU) on campus. The black representatives felt that the budget for the BSU should be increased, while the white representatives felt that the BSU's present budget was adequate. After an hour of argument, the blacks accused the whites of being racists, and the whites accused the blacks of wanting special treatment for their organization. The group's appointed leader (the student body president) finally stepped in to arbitrate the dispute. He pointed out that the real problem confronting the group was not racial bias but the absence of a set of guidelines for determining the way funds should be distributed among all student groups. He noted that the BSU was the first group whose budget requests had been considered in the meeting. He predicted that unless a set of guidelines for matching student government funds to student group needs was established, the representatives could expect arguments over the budgets of other campus groups, e.g., the judo club, the sailing club, etc.

The two factions agreed to cease their argument long enough to consider some guidelines. A short time later, the group outlined a set of guidelines and, using these, decided unanimously that the BSU should be granted an increase in money, but a lesser increase than had originally been argued for. Thus, in this illustration, the leader successfully balanced task and maintenance leadership functions by clarifying the goal and the path for attaining it (see Anderson, 1975). The group moved more efficiently toward its objective of distributing funds to student groups, and both blacks and whites were able to end their interpersonal conflict.

There were alternative courses of action open to the designated leader in the example just given. On one hand, the leader could have decided that the group had wasted too much time on arguing and called for a vote on the BSU budget. Given the heated tempers on both sides, we could probably expect the five whites to vote to deny the BSU's budget increase request. Since the whites were in the majority, the issue could be officially closed, and the budgets of other campus groups could then be considered. Such actions would have advanced the group toward their goal of allocating funds. However, interpersonal relations between black and white members would have probably been damaged beyond repair. Without satisfactory interpersonal relations, the ability of the group to perform its subsequent tasks would be substantially impaired.

Now consider what the consequences might have been if the leader had emphasized *only* maintenance functions. He might have suspended the planned agenda and asked both sides to engage in a dialogue in an attempt to understand the other's position. If such a tactic was successful, pleasant interpersonal relations might have been restablished, but the task would have been neglected.

In summary, there is a dilemma for leaders. If task functions are not performed, the group fails to move toward its goal. On the other hand, if maintenance functions are not performed, interpersonal conflict may occur and result in lower morale and inferior quality decisions (Gulley, 1969). Thus, effective group leadership requires that task *and* maintenance needs be balanced. Your systems analysis should focus on both types of needs and how to fulfill them.

Task versus maintenance leaders. Although we noted that both task and maintenance functions may be performed by the same person, Bales (1965) found that two types of "influence specialists" often emerge in problem-solving groups which do not have a designated leader. One leader in Bales's study was typically an "idea person," and he was held in high regard by the group for his performance of task functions (e.g., suggesting the best ideas and emphasizing goal achievement). The other leader was considered the "best liked" member of the group. Cartwright and Zander (1968) have suggested that the top contributor of ideas may be so aggressive that he or she alienates other group members (see also Russ and Gold, 1975). Thus, although the top "idea person" moves the group toward goal achievement, his or her emphasis on the task may result in inadequate attention to maintenance needs. Therefore, to establish equilibrium between the task and interpersonal needs, a less aggresive person may assume maintenance functions for the group, relieving tensions produced by the task functions leader.

Guidance Needs

In addition to task and maintenance needs, groups also have guidance needs. Guidance needs are satisfied when the group's activity is sufficiently controlled to permit *orderly movement* of the group toward its objective.

A first step in assisting the group toward its goal is to start the meeting. Whoever does this exerts considerable influence because opening statements tend to set the tone or climate of the entire meeting. Opening statements should provide some indication for the purpose of the meeting. If the group is meeting together for the first time and there are group members present who do not know each other, they should be introduced. At this point, generally the group also reaches an agreement regarding the time length of the meetings. Although the opening statement may only take a matter of minutes, it is a very important first step.

The next guidance function involves a plan for conducting the group meeting. A written plan consisting of topics that the group hopes to discuss during the meeting is often referred to as an *agenda*. If an agenda has not been set before the meeting, then one of the first tasks for the group members is to agree upon what they will attempt to cover in the meeting.

How closely groups follow their agendas varies from group to group, however. Some groups have a high need for procedural order and stick closely to their agendas. Other groups seem to dislike rigid structure (see e.g., Bormann, 1975) and spend time on maintenance needs. This should not imply, however, that members of groups with a high need for procedural order are inflexible and antisocial. It may mean " . . . that other climate factors, i.e., use of agendas, task lists, deadlines are more prevalent than are concerns with flexibility and socio-emotional issues" (Putnam, 1979, p. 217). Once again balance and goals should be considered. If crisis appears imminent and the group is pushing toward its goal, the group probably will adhere closely to the agenda. On the other hand, if disruptive conflict has occurred recently, the group may prefer to "cool off" for a while by straying from the agenda.

An important variable affecting the guidance functions a leader must perform is *group size*. As the number of group members increases, the leadership of the group must correspondingly change. For example, when the number of members multiplies from four to twelve, the leader must devote more attention to seeing that all members have access to the discussion. As group size increases, each member will have fewer opportunities to speak. A lag may exist between the time a member wishes to speak and the point at which he or she is actually permitted to do so. In this condition, comments which would have been pertinent to the discussion at an earlier time may actually be irrelevant at a later time and may sidetrack the group from the topic currently under discussion. It should be noted that there is some evidence which suggests that as group size increases, the members may become more tolerant of authoritarian behavior from the leader in regulating the topics under discussion and the participants' access to the discussion.

You have probably correctly concluded by now that guidance functions overlap with both task and maintenance functions discussed earlier. All three types of functions have been shown to affect member satisfaction with group participation. In an extensive study of seventy-two business and government conferences, three specific guidance functions were found to be strongly related to participant satisfaction (Collins and Guetzkow, 1964):

1. *The quicker the agenda topics are dealt with and completed, the higher the member satisfaction.* This should not suggest that leaders should emphasize speed over high quality decisions which are often obtained only after extensive periods of hard thinking and group interaction. Rather, it suggests leaders should encourage members to direct attention to topics under consideration and avoid aimless digressions, which may be momentarily pleasant, but which may eventually reduce member satisfaction.

2. *Orderly, rapid, and efficient problem solving increases member satisfaction.* This condition cannot be achieved unless both leader and participant come to meetings adequately prepared to work on the group's task. Leader preparation may include making arrangements for a suitable environment in which the group may work, and making certain that each member knows what topics will be discussed. Member preparation requires that members have at least done their "homework" on tasks assigned to them and that they come prepared to discuss problems and make suggestions.

3. *Shorter meetings are more satisfying than longer ones.* After a meeting has continued for a long period of time, members obviously will become fatigued. As a result, morale may be lowered and members may be willing

to settle for less than the best efforts of the group in problem-solving and goal-seeking behaviors. Topics placed last on the agenda of a long meeting may simply not receive attention proportionate to their importance. Therefore, except in unusal circumstances, leaders would be wise to avoid lengthy sessions, and either take a brief recess or adjourn the meeting when members become tired.

The Role of Leader

Our perspective on leadership in this chapter suggests that any person in the group may exert leadership. One group member may influence other group members through task, maintenance, or guidance functions. In some groups, a leader may emerge because of abilities he or she may have in satisfying the needs of the group. Research does indicate that emerging leaders perform behaviors associated with group procedure (Knutson and Holdridge, 1975). A group leader may know very little about the specific problem, yet know a great deal about organizing the information presented by other group members.

At the beginning of this chapter, we asked you to reflect on the leadership of the president of the United States. He could not possibly know all there is to know about all governmental agencies and foreign policy commitments. His role as leader of the president's cabinet is to organize the contributions of the other group members who do have the specific information. Although the president is an example of an assigned leader (he is the leader of the cabinet because he has been elected president), the example also applies to emerging leaders. Emerging leaders follow agendas and notify the group of their progress toward the goal. Emerging leaders stimulate involvement of group members and help to resolve disruptive conflict. You probably can perform these leadership functions yourself. Remember, however, that leadership is only part of the complex system of group process. Your decision to lead a group should be made only after consideration of the many other variables in the system.

PRINCIPLES

1. When beginning the first group meeting, state the purpose of the meeting, introduce members who do not know each other, and agree on a time limit for the meeting.
2. Agree on a plan or agenda to organize the group's activity. How closely the group chooses to follow the agenda depends on the group's need for procedural order.
3. As group size increases, regulate the topics under discussion and participant access to the discussion more closely.

those of your fellow students. Do they differ? If you had been a member of the group, what actions would you have taken to satisfy group needs?

REFERENCES

ANDERSON, A. B. Combined effects of interpersonal attraction and goal-path clarity on the cohesiveness of task oriented groups. *Journal of personality and social psychology*, 1975, *31*, 68–75.

BALES, R. F. The equilibrium problem in small groups. In A. P. HARE, E. F. BORGATTA, and R. F. BALES, eds. *Small groups: studies in social interaction.* New York: Knopf, 1965.

BLYTHE, P. W. Silence is golden. *Canadian counselor*, 1975, *9*, 69–70.

BORMANN, E. G. *Discussion and group methods: theory and practice.* New York: Harper & Row, Pub., 1975.

CARTER, L., W. HAYTHORN, B. SHRIVER, and J. LANZETTA. The behavior of leaders and other group members. In D. CARTWRIGHT and A. ZANDER, eds. *Group dynamics: research and theory*, 3rd ed. New York: Harper & Row, Pub., 1968.

CARTWRIGHT, D., and A. ZANDER. Leadership and performance of group functions: introduction. In D. CARTWRIGHT and A. ZANDER, eds. *Group dynamics: research and theory*, 3rd ed. New York: Harper & Row, Pub., 1968.

COLLINS, B. E., and H. GUETZKOW. *A social psychology of group processes for decision making.* New York: John Wiley, 1964.

FIEDLER, F. E. A contingency model of leadership effectiveness. In L. BERKOWITZ, ed. *Advances in experimental social psychology.* New York: Academic Press, 1964.

————. *A theory of leadership effectiveness.* New York: McGraw-Hill, 1967.

FURUKAWA, H. The effect of success or failure evaluation upon followers' morale and perception of leadership function. (Japanese) *Japanese journal of experimental social psychology*, 1972, *11*, 133–147.

GOODACRE, D. M. Group characteristics of good and poor performing in combat units. *Sociometry*, 1953, *16*, 168–178.

GULLEY, H. E. Discussion leadership: achieving a moving equilibrium. Unpublished manuscript, University of Kentucky, 1969.

————, and D. G. LEATHERS. *Communication and group process: techniques for improving the quality of small group communication*, 3rd ed. New York: Holt, Rinehart & Winston, 1977.

HAMBLIN, R. L. Leadership and crises. In D. CARTWRIGHT and A. ZANDER, eds. *Group dynamics: research and theory*, 3rd ed. New York: Harper & Row, Pub., 1968.

HORWITZ, M., R. V. EXLINE, and F. J. LEE. *Motivational effects of alternative decision-making processes in groups.* Urbana, Ill.: Bureau of Educational Research, University of Illinois, 1953.

JONES, S. E., D. C. BARNLUND, and F. S. HAIMAN. *The dynamics of discussion*, 2nd ed. New York: Harper & Row, Pub., 1980.

KAHN, A., and A. H. HYEN. Factors influencing the bias toward one's own group. *International journal of group tensions*, 1972, *2*, 33–50.

KELTNER, J. W. *Interpersonal speech communication: elements and structures.* Belmont, Calif.: Wadsworth, 1970.

KNUTSON, T. J., and W. E. HOLDRIDGE. Orientation behavior, leadership, and consensus: a possible functional relationship. *Communication Monographs*, 1975, *42*, 107–114.

PUTNAM, L. L. Preference for procedural order in task-oriented small groups. *Communication Monographs*, 1979, *46*, 193–218.

RUSS, R., and J. A. GOLD. Task expertise and group communication. *Journal of psychology*, 1975, *91*, 187–196.

VERPLANK, W. The control of the context of conversation: reinforcement of statements of opinion. *Journal of abnormal and social psychology*, 1955, *51*, 668–676.

ZIBMARADO, P. G. *Shyness*. Reading, Mass.: Addison-Wesley, 1977.

SUGGESTED READINGS

CARTHCART, R. S., and L. A. SAMOVAR. *Small group communication: a reader*, 3rd ed. Dubuque, Iowa: Wm. C. Brown, 1979.

Part IV, "Group Leadership," includes articles discussing historical perspectives of leadership, various theories, and styles of leadership.

FIEDLER, F. E., M. M. CHEMERS, and L. MAHAR. *Improving leadership effectiveness: the leader match concept*. New York: John Wiley, 1976.

The book is a manageable self-teaching guide with discussions and exercises to help improve leadership effectiveness.

GOLDBERG, A. A., and C. E. LARSON. *Group communication*. Englewood Cliffs, N. J.: Prentice-Hall, 1975.

Chapter 6, "Leadership," provides information on leadership styles, network models, rating scales, behaviors, and theories.

FISHER, B. A. *Small group decision making: communication and the group process*, 2nd ed. New York: McGraw-Hill, 1980.

Chapter 7, "Leadership and Status," provides an excellent discussion of perspectives on leadership. The chapter also presents in a tongue-in-cheek manner "principles for avoiding the leadership role."

TRAMMEL, M. E., and H. REYNOLDS. *Executive leadership: how to get it and make it work*. Englewood Cliffs, N. J.: Prentice-Hall, 1981.

The authors of this book have applied research in the area of leadership to business environments. The book contains many practical suggestions for executive leadership.

United Press International Photo

Robert E. Murowchick/Photo Researchers, Inc.

10

Conflict
Management
and Resolution
in Small Groups

Study
Questions

After you have read this chapter, you should be able to answer the following questions completely and accurately:

1. What is task conflict?
2. What is interpersonal conflict?
3. What is procedural conflict?
4. What are three positive effects of conflict?
5. What is groupthink?
6. To what extent can conflict in groups be potentially negative?
7. What are five decision-making strategies in groups?
8. What is the difference between conflict resolution and conflict management?
9. What are nine suggestions for conflict management in small groups?

Radio and television news thrives on conflict between persons and between nations. However, only the most serious conflicts make the headlines. It's no wonder that the term *conflict* has negative connotations for most of us.

Obviously, all conflicts are not the same. We face minor conflicts each day in our personal relationships. We may have disagreements with our families, friends, or employers. An employee who requests a 20 percent raise, for example, probably will experience conflict with his or her employer. If the employer agrees to the raise, the conflict has been resolved. However, as you already know, conflicts rarely are resolved this easily. Most conflicts are "managed" as individuals work out differences and reach agreements that are acceptable to both parties.

Conflict resolution, in groups, often is difficult. Through the decision-making process, group members work together to find a solution that is acceptable to the group. This process often involves managing conflicts. In this chapter, we will discuss various types of conflict and examine some of the advantages of conflict. We also will look at some of the procedures groups use for making decisions. Finally, we will present some suggestions for conflict management.

TYPES AND VALUES OF CONFLICT

Think for a moment about the small groups to which you belong. Are most of those groups ongoing groups or are they "one-time meeting" groups? You probably belong to groups which meet together over time—perhaps even on a regular basis (e.g., weekly). Most individuals who spend considerable amounts of time in interpersonal relationships will experience periods of tension, anger, or anxiety (Doolittle, 1976). In other words, periods of conflict are inevitable as individuals interact with each other on a continuing basis. In this section, we will identify the types of conflict groups may experience, and examine the positive values of conflict.

Types of Conflict

In the previous chapter, we identified three basic group needs: task needs, maintenance needs, and guidance needs. *Task needs* refer to the movement of the group toward its goal or objective. This is the first area for potential conflict among group members. Group members may disagree about facts or opinions from authorities. The interpretation of evidence may be questioned. In other words, disagreement about the substance of the discussion is called "task conflict." Task conflict can be productive and improve the quality of decisions through "idea testing." This value of task conflict will be discussed in the next section.

Groups also experience *maintenance needs.* Maintenance needs refer to the interpersonal strengthening of the group as members develop and preserve harmonious relations. This is another potential area for conflict, and the term *interpersonal conflict* is used to indicate the disagreement that most people call a "personality clash." The clash may take the form of antagonistic remarks that relate to the personal characteristics of a group member. Frequently, however, the conflict is expressed through more subtle nonverbal behaviors. There may be icy stares or, at the other extreme, an avoidance of eye contact. Interpersonal conflict may be inevitable, but it is not as useful to the group as task conflict.

The third need groups experience is in the area of guidance. *Guidance needs* refer to the orderly movement of the group toward its goal or objective. "Procedural conflict" exists when group members disagree about the procedures to be followed in accomplishing the group goal. New procedures may be formulated and a new agenda suggested. Even the group goal may be modified. Procedural conflict, like task conflict, may be productive.

Sometimes what appears to be task conflict or procedural conflict in the group is a result of hidden agendas or personal goals. For example, a group member may desire to be the most influential member of the group. If the desire is blocked or challenged by another member, conflict is likely to occur. Initially it may appear that the individuals are challenging the merit of ideas. A close look at personal motives, however, may reveal the true nature of the conflict.

Because small group communication acts as a system, no single variable operates in isolation. A change in one variable may produce changes in others. Because the system is continuously changing, a small group could possibly experience more than one type of conflict simultaneously (Knutson and Kowitz, 1977). In the next section, we will examine some of the positive aspects of conflict.

Some Advantages of Conflict

In the previous section, we noted that conflict could be productive and have positive effects on groups. Three of these positive effects are: improving the quality of decisions, stimulating involvement in the discussion, and building group cohesion.

Improving the quality of decisions. Suppose your group is discussing the issue of "student enrollment at your school." You and another member disagree about the number of students attending your college. What would you do? Would you continue affirming your position or would you walk to the telephone and call the Registrar's Office to request the enrollment information contained in their records? Most group members will look for more information to resolve task conflict. Often this means that the group must a moderately sized cooperative with a small run-down storefront in the downtown area, approximately two miles from campus. Although the majority of the members are students, some nonstudent families are joining the cooperative to take advantage of the savings on cheese, juice, and other food items. All members are required to work at the store a given number of hours each month. With increasing numbers of customers, workers have experienced difficulty keeping the small food bins adequately stocked, and the customers are finding the aisles a "tight squeeze." The storeroom is no longer large enough to store food from one delivery until the following delivery. All board members have agreed that the cooperative needs more space.

Various solutions to the problem have been suggested and all but two of them have been rejected. One potential solution involves renting a warehouse some distance from the store for food storage and expanding the back wall several feet into the alley behind the store. The other solution involves moving the store to a location in a small shopping center. The second proposal would cost considerably more than the first proposal but would provide space for a juice and sandwich bar (i.e., health food/fast food). There are several ways of resolving the disagreement concerning the two proposals. In the following section, we will discuss some of the ways groups make decisions, and then we will present some suggestions for conflict management.

Decision Making

Groups make decisions in a variety of ways. Five decision-making strategies include: force, majority vote, compromise, arbitration, and consensus. Let's look at each of these ways in more detail.

Force. Suppose the president of the board of directors in the previous example said: "The board has been discussing expansion versus moving to a new location for the past three meetings and obviously cannot reach a decision. Since this group elected me president, I am going to make the decision." As a member of this group, how would you feel? Angry—because someone was making a decision that you should participate in? Depressed—because this is one more group that's been "spinning its wheels"? Anxious to hear the president's decision—what if he or she disagrees with your point of view? Anger, depression, and anxiety are not positive feelings and tend to adversely affect group morale. When group members don't feel good about a decision, they generally don't want to work to implement the decision. The decision may have been made, but it's generally not worth much.

The above illustration concerns, in part, the effect of *status* on conflict and decision making. If you perceived yourself equal in status with the president of the cooperative, your dissatisfaction with the decision would be increased. Conversely, were the president of obviously higher status (with "deserved" power), you might be more willing to accept authoritarian decisions he or she might make without discontent.

Majority vote. As you read of the disagreement among the board members concerning the proposed move to a larger location, you might have thought: *Take a vote.* The democratic ethic seems to center around voting. Certainly when time is at a premium, majority vote allows a group to make a decision quickly. It also seems reasonable to assume that as members of ongoing groups, sometimes an individual will be on the side of the "winning" majority and sometimes he or she will be on the side of the "losing" minority. Sometimes, however, a member loses more than wins. When the losses are taken as personal defeats (i.e., a rejection of my ideas is a rejection of me as a person), then majority rule can be destructive.

Compromise. The members of the board of directors could compromise and agree to rent a warehouse and look for a suitable location for a juice and sandwich shop. No one completely wins but no one completely loses, either. Half of a falafel sandwich is better than none, right? While the compromise solution *is* better than doing nothing at all, compromise is not solving the additional storefront problems of inadequate space for food bins and crowded aisles. Realizing that the solution is not going to completely solve the problem, and feeling as though they gave more than they gained, *both* sides of the controversy may have low motivation to implement the solution. Although group members often can work together to find much better solutions, compromise may be the best possible solution in some conflicts. Compromise, for example, can be useful as a temporary solution. The board may use the time to investigate other rental possibilities.

Arbitration. If the board members see no way to resolve their differences and are becoming bitter about the continuing conflict, the group may have to resort to arbitration. During arbitration the group brings in a disinterested third party to make the decision. Labor-management disputes are often handled in this manner. Arbitrators generally resolve disagreements at some middle-ground position, and often the decision seems like compromise in that no one completely wins and no one completely loses. Potential low group motivation toward implementing the decision may result here as well.

Consensus. In contrast to the previous decision-making strategies, consensus initially centers on goals rather than on alternatives. Conflicts involving "my way" versus "your way" often result in discussion of the superiority of personal solutions. When members shift their attention from solutions per se to the goals, solutions can be developed which permit both sides to obtain their goals (See Chapter 3 for a discussion of goals).

Suppose the board of directors for the food cooperative is meeting. The members seem to have become divided into the expansion versus new location viewpoints. At this point a group member asks each other member to state his or her goals. The members favoring expansion generally indicate their concern over finances; their goal is to keep the monthly rent within reasonable limits (feelings are that rent is too high in a shopping mall). The members favoring a new location generally want a nicer looking storefront and an increase in membership; their goal is an attractive store in a location with good customer traffic. After some discussion, the meeting adjourns with group members feeling positive about group progress and agreeing to investigate other rental possibilities before the next meeting.

At the next meeting, other alternatives are discussed. One alternative is a storefront two blocks from campus. Customer traffic is good and the store is large. The rent is reasonable because the inside of the building is in need of repair. Because of the member work requirement, labor to repair and paint the inside of the building is available. Several cooperative members are experienced construction workers and could provide the necessary labor. After perceiving that many members favor the proposal, the president asks if the group consensus is to move to the near-campus location or if anyone wants to "block" the move. Although one group member doesn't like one of the businesses adjoining the prospective store, he doesn't block and agrees to give his assistance to the group effort. Both the group goal (i.e., more space) and individual goals (i.e., reasonable rent and an attractive location with good customer traffic) are achieved. Group morale is high and group members leave the meeting with eager anticipation to accomplish the many necessary tasks before the cooperative opens its doors for business in its new location.

Consensus is a desirable decision-making method but far more difficult than the other methods of making decisions. Each member must be responsible both for expressing his own needs openly and honestly and for listening openly to the needs of other members. Each group member also should understand him- herself well enough to know when he can agree to work for group effort (although he may not totally agree with the proposal) and when his or her personal viewpoint differs to the point that blocking is necessary. Consensus seems to work best in mature, ongoing groups where honest expression (at the risk of interpersonal conflict) is valued, and commitment to the group is strong.

There is no single strategy for decision making which should be used by all groups. Nor is there a strategy for decision making which should be used by any one group to make all of its decisions. We have suggested that consensus has certain benefits which may make it most desirable. It enhances creativity, promotes understanding, and provides an atmosphere which promotes trust and cooperation. However, it also seems to work best in mature groups and is time consuming. In situations where the group is under a time pressure, majority vote may be the preferred decision-making strategy. Decision-making strategies are tools. It is important to select the right tool to get the job done and then use it as skillfully as possible.

PRINCIPLES

1. Five decision-making strategies include: force, majority vote, compromise, arbitration, and consensus.
2. Force generally is an ineffective decision-making strategy because group members often do not support decisions they do not make.
3. Majority vote can save time when a quick decision is necessary, but the strategy can be destructive when group members take losses as personal defeats.
4. With compromise solutions, no one completely wins and no one completely loses. If group members feel as though they gave more than they gained and/or that the problem is not completely solved, motivation to implement the decision may be low for both sides of the controversy.
5. During arbitration, the group brings in a disinterested third party to make the decision. Sometimes arbitration has the same effects as compromise in that no one completely wins, and no one completely loses.
6. Consensus initially centers on goals rather than alternatives, and the group attempts to formulate a new solution that will meet the goals of both sides to the controversy.

Conflict Management

The perspective on conflict in small groups has changed in recent years. Sociologists initially viewed conflict as a disruptive force in society (Coser, 1956). Conflict in groups was once seen as an undesirable (although sometimes necessary) temporary occurrence. The objective was to resolve, or bring the conflict to an end. More recently, conflict has been viewed as an inevitable and integral part of group process. Many conflicts (e.g., the struggle for civil rights in this country) cannot be brought to a speedy conclusion. Sometimes, finding ways in which the parties to the controversy can communicate is more important than immediate resolution of the conflict with a single solution. Whether the issue is civil rights, labor-management relations, or campus concerns, people do sit down and talk. In this way, the conflict becomes "managed." Conflict management does not exclude attempts to resolve conflict, but the emphasis is on communication rather than on termination of the disagreement.

Conflict cannot be managed unless communication channels are kept open. To walk out of a group meeting or to refuse to confront the issues, creates more problems than it solves. Communication by itself has an effect on cooperative resolution of the conflict (Steinfatt, et al., 1974). Because of the importance of communication to conflict management, we offer the following suggestions to increase your effectiveness with this important variable in group process.

Identify your problem and desires.   Stop and think before you speak. Is the problem that is creating the conflict in you? Are *you* the person who doesn't agree with the group? Why? Perhaps, for example, you don't agree with the group because you feel that you will have to do most of the work; you feel that the group is taking advantage of you. After you are clear about your desires, you may be more ready to state those desires or needs in a descriptive way.

Describe your problem and state your desires.   If you disagree with the group, the group cannot work through the conflict unless you communicate what you want. It is up to you to describe the situation as specifically as possible. You might say, for example, "I have a problem. It really upsets me that the rest of the group wants to do another mailing to the cooperative membership. Last time we did a mailing no one helped, and I'm concerned that I will have to do the mailing by myself again. I would like to help, but I'm carrying eighteen hours at school this term and can't do the mailing by myself." This expression explains what is going on inside of the group member. It's amazing how many group members argue without ever sharing what is *really* bothering them.

Express disagreement tactfully.   Filley (1975, p. 14) states: "The most important consideration in determining the outcome of the conflict is whether the situation is personalized or depersonalized." Personalized situations are situations in which the whole being of the group member is threatened (i.e., the individual rather than the idea is what is being judged). In depersonalized situations, the group member's behavior is described as creating a problem. "You are careless" is a personalized situation. "It's difficult for me to keep up with you. When you stuff these envelopes so fast, some of the zip codes get out of order," is a depersonalized situation. Some authorities refer to depersonalized situations as "sticking to the facts, not criticizing the personalities." Personalized situations (criticizing personalities) often result in interpersonal conflict. Depersonalized situations (discussing behaviors) lend themselves to conflict management.

Listen actively.   Active listening was discussed in Chapter 5. Active listening requires that you attend to the feelings and emotional tone of the message as well as to the content of what the other group member is saying. Sometimes contradictions are apparent between what group members say verbally and what they say nonverbally (see pp. 161–162). Perhaps a group member is unwilling to disagree because of the fear of personal rejection. Some group members would rather not express disagreement than have a friend no longer like them. Be supportive, encourage the individual, and listen. Understanding the desires and needs of another member is necessary if you are to offer solutions which can potentially meet those desires and needs.

Persuade others of the value of conflict. How group members view conflict determines to a large extent how they deal with it and how successful they are in managing it. If a member views conflict as something to be avoided, he or she may respond defensively. The group member may even pretend that everything is fine and that the group is sailing along a "smooth ocean." "Choppy waters" and cohesiveness are not necessarily opposites. Avoiding conflict may appear effective in the short run. It generally is not satisfactory in the long run with ongoing groups.

Develop intragroup trust. Conflict is not a fight that should be avoided or a fight to be won at another's expense. Group meetings are not the place for personal vendettas. Conflict should be viewed as cooperative problem solving. The degree of trust within your group will be directly related to the group's ability to handle conflict constructively.

Don't take disagreement as personal rejection. If group members disagree with what you say, you may think that they don't like you or are "out to get you." The perceptions we hold of ourselves are a result of years of conditioning, and cannot be changed immediately. Be careful not to let your ego interfere with the goals of the group.

Demonstrate cooperativeness if your plan is rejected. Cooperativeness is your responsibility to group effort, even though your personal opinions may not be in agreement with the group opinion. In essence, the group goal becomes more important than personal opinions.

Structure the group carefully. If possible, you should choose group members who get along. Sometimes, however, you are unable to select participants. If you are aware that potentially hostile individuals are group members, you may wish to separate them from each other.

One solution to conflict, which usually is not desirable but ends conflict, is to dissolve the group. Individuals may choose to leave the group rather than to conform to group opinion. Research (Hare, 1976) indicates that there are at least three cases in which an individual is more likely to conform to group opinion: if the member must make his or her opinion public, if the majority holding a contrary opinion is large, and if the group is especially

DOOLITTLE, R. J. *Orientations to communication and conflict.* Modcom Modules in Speech Communication. Chicago: S.R.A., 1976.

DOOLITTLE, R. J. Conflicting views of conflict: an analysis of basic speech communication textbooks. *Communication education*, 1977, *26*, 121–127.

FILLEY, A. C. *Interpersonal conflict resolution.* Glenview, Ill.: Scott, Foresman, 1975.

FISHER, B. A. *Small group decision making: communication and the group process*, 2nd ed. New York: McGraw-Hill, 1980.

FROST, J. H., and W. W. WILMOT. *Interpersonal conflict.* Dubuque, Iowa: Wm. C. Brown, 1978.

HARE, A. P. *Handbook of small group research*, 2nd ed. New York: Free Press, 1976.

JANIS, I. L. Groupthink among policy makers. In N. SANFORD, C. COMSTOCK, and ASSOCIATES, eds. *Sanctions for evil.* San Francisco: Jossey-Bass, 1971.

JANIS, I. L. *Victims of groupthink: a psychological study of foreign policy decisions and fiascoes.* Boston: Houghton Mifflin Co., 1972.

KNUTSON, T. J., and A. C. KOWITZ. Effects of informational type and level of orientation on consensus-achievement in substantive and affective small group conflict. *Central states speech journal*, 1977, *28*, 54–63.

MILLER, G. R., and H. W. SIMONS, eds. *Perspectives on communication in social conflict.* Englewood Cliffs, N.J.: Prentice-Hall, 1974.

STEINFATT, T. M., D. R. SEIBOLD, and J. K. FRYE. Communication in game simulated conflicts: two experiments. *Speech monographs*, 1974, *41*, 24–35.

SUGGESTED READINGS

FILLEY, A. C. *Interpersonal conflict resolution.* Glenview, Ill.: Scott, Foresman, 1975.

Although this book was written for use in the field of organizational management, the material is applicable to small groups as well. Chapter 2, "Methods of Conflict Resolution and Problem Solving," discusses "win lose," "lose lose," and "win win" strategies for dealing with conflict. Chapter 4, "Personal Styles of Conflict Resolution," discusses individual styles of conflict resolution.

FROST, J. H., and W. W. WILMOT. *Interpersonal conflict.* Dubuque, Iowa: Wm. C. Brown, 1978.

Chapter 5, "Analyzing Issues and Setting Goals," explains the difference between goals and issues and develops strategies for goal setting in conflict management. Chapter 6, "Strategies and Tactics," discusses the overall game plan (strategy) in conflict and the communication moves (tactics) which relate to the conflict strategies.

PHILLIPS, G. M., D. J. PEDERSON, and J. T. WOOD. *Group discussion: a practical guide to participation and leadership.* Boston: Houghton Mifflin Co., 1979.

Chapter 3, "Managing Conflict in Discussions," discusses groupthink. Symptoms of groupthink are presented and correctives to groupthink are discussed.

SMITH, M. J. *When I say no, I feel guilty.* New York: Dial Press, 1975.

This book is a popular best-seller on assertiveness training. Chapter 1, "Our Inherited Survival Responses; Coping With Other People by Fight, Flight or Verbal Assertiveness," discusses three responses to conflict. Additional chapters discuss assertive rights and how to cope with criticism.

Photo courtesy of The National Broadcasting Company, Inc.

11

Special Forms of Small Group Communication

Study
Questions

After you have read this chapter, you should be able to answer the following questions completely and accurately:

1. What is a definition of a forum? What is its purpose or function, and when would you be likely to use a forum alone?
2. What are the characteristics of a forum?
3. What is a definition of a panel? What are some purposes the panel might serve effectively?
4. What are the characteristics of the panel and its operations that make it unique?
5. What is a definition of a symposium? What purpose does it serve most effectively?
6. What are the distinguishing characteristics of the symposium and its operation?
7. What is a definition of a colloquium, and what special purposes does it serve usefully?
8. What are the unique characteristics of the colloquium?
9. What are the characteristics of a forum, panel, symposium, and colloquium that differentiate each from the others? What are the similarities across two or more of these four forms of public discussions?
10. What is the distinction between a public discussion and a private discussion?
11. What is a sensitivity training group? What are some common goals or purposes of most sensitivity groups?
12. How does a sensitivity training group differ from a therapy group?
13. What are some unique aspects of the sensitivity training group that distinguish it from other forms of small group discussion?
14. What is role playing, and why is it considered under the category of "private discussions"?
15. What are some common personal and group goals associated with role-playing techniques?
16. What are the steps in developing successful group role playing?
17. What is a buzz session? What are the purposes of buzz sessions?
18. What are two important factors to control when buzz sessions are used?

In earlier chapters we have examined the nature of small group communication and attempted to suggest principles designed to improve the effectiveness of its operation. Most of our attention has been centered on those factors which influence the effectiveness of small group deliberations. Because you are likely to engage frequently in both informative and problem-solving discussions, we have devoted a chapter to each of these formats and processes. However, there are still other forms of small group communication to which you can successfully apply the concepts and principles discussed earlier.

In this final chapter, we will describe some of the selected special forms of small group communication. Special forms of public discussions are examined first; these include consideration of the forum, panel, colloquium, and symposium. The second section deals with special forms of private discussions, including a description of sensitivity training groups, role-playing groups, and buzz sessions. For each of the special forms of small group communication we will define the form, specify its purpose or function, identify its characteristics, and then provide an example of its use.

SELECTED PUBLIC DISCUSSIONS

Our primary focus throughout this book has been on the interpersonal level of communication as it is applicable to small groups. In addition, we have tended to emphasize a setting or context that may be characterized as "private." By this latter statement, we mean that our comments thus far have stressed the operation of small groups in seclusion from the presence, sight, or intrusion of others. Obviously, small groups can and do function in public as well as in private settings. In this section we will examine four common forms of public discussions in which you will probably be asked to participate within the next few years. These forms are labeled "public" because the discussions take place in the presence of an audience. Some types of public discussions invite and depend upon audience participation. We will consider the forum, the panel, the colloquium, and the symposium.

Forum

A forum is a general form of public discussion in which the full audience participates from the outset of the meeting under a chairperson's leadership. In its pure form you will find that there are no formal presentations by either individuals or a group. Rather, under the leadership of a chairperson or moderator, the members of the audience examine a subject, topic, or problem by giving impromptu speeches from the floor, taking issue with what has been said, asking and answering questions, and responding briefly to questions and comments. So, the general purpose of a forum in its pure state is to provide the audience with an opportunity to share information on a topic or problem. Wagner and Arnold have provided an excellent summary of purposes of the forum:

> a) To enable an audience to gain supplementary information from experts or knowledgeable persons, since in no form of public discussion can those who participate in the stimulation stage express all their knowledge, views, and preferences.
>
> b) To give final form and organization to the views and information which the listeners derive from pre-forum discussion.
>
> c) To provide an opportunity for correcting intentional or inadvertent bias, distortion, or misunderstanding.
>
> d) To give an opportunity for verbal expression by the audience, an important adjunct to silent thinking (Wagner and Arnold, 1965, pp. 182–183).[1]

The forum is seldom implemented as a separate form of public discussion, although it may be so used in rare instances. Typically you will observe the forum used in combination with other types of public discussion, as in a panel-forum or symposium-forum. When used in combination with other types of public discussion, a period of time usually is set aside for the forum. This period of time ranges widely, running from twenty minutes to forty-five minutes, depending on various conditions. Essentially the forum, whether employed as a separate form or in combination with other types of public discussion, may be conceived of as the audience's participation time (Sattler and Miller, 1968).

Heavy responsibility falls on the shoulders of the chairperson or leader of the forum. The chairperson begins by gaining control of the audience. Next he or she provides a brief orientation to the topic or problem and the occasion. Then he or she instructs the audience on the "rules of the game" for the forum concerning procedures for questioning, responding to questions, making remarks, and any other appropriate limitations placed on the forum's methods of operation. The chairperson also stimulates the members of the audience to get the forum underway and keep it moving along, by asking leading or provocative questions, and by identifying key issues. The chairperson is similarly responsible for controlling and guiding the discussion. In meeting these responsibilities, he or she will attempt to keep questions, responses, and remarks on target and framed in a clear and concise manner. Obviously, with many unknown audience members participating in a forum, a comprehensive systems analysis is virtually impossible. However, during the meeting, the leader should try to identify people with different viewpoints and give all factions access to communication. Other duties of the chairperson and the audience participants are summarized below.

---

[1]From Russell H. Wagner and Carroll C. Arnold, *Handbook of Group Discussion*, 2nd ed. Boston: Houghton Mifflin Co., 1965, pp. 182–183. Reprinted by permission.

1. The forum is a general form of public discussion in which the full audience examines a topic or problem by giving impromptu speeches, taking issue with what has been said, asking and answering questions, and responding to comments under a chairperson's leadership.

2. The forum is seldom employed separately, and it typically is used in combination with other types of public discussion, such as the symposium-forum or panel-forum, for the general purpose of sharing information on a topic or problem.

3. The physical environment of the room or auditorium should be arranged so that the audience can see and hear one another and the leader easily.

In addition to the above principles, Wagner and Arnold have provided an excellent summary of practices relevant to the forum. They note that these guidelines are appropriate for any forum, whether it is employed separately or in combination with other forms of public discussion.

The duties of the chairman or forum leader include:

a) Responsibility for instructing the audience as to the mode of participation desired—whether informal discussion, questions and answers only, comments from the floor, or some combination thereof. The chairman should also advise the audience of any limitations on questioning or speaking which will apply during the forum period.

b) Responsibility for asking leading questions, offering striking statements, posing the issues brought out in the previous discussion, etc., to stimulate participation.

c) Encouraging brevity, clarity, and integration of ideas through apt questions, suggestions, restatements, interpretations, and transitions.

d) Guiding the progress of questioning or discussion as in any group discussion. It is especially important that the chairman keep questions and comments, and the length of the forum as a whole, within reasonable bounds. He must deal tactfully but firmly with irrelevant, obscure, emotional, and other difficult questions and comments. His objective should be to encourage free and frank participation without allowing a few tiresome persons to monopolize the time or defeat the majority's effort to explore the main questions.

e) If informal discussion is the objective of the forum, the chairman should emphasize the importance of selecting a preferred solution. By doing this he can increase the audience's reflective thinking and bring about a certain degree of organization and progress.

f) Rephrasing and restating questions and comments whenever there is any doubt that all have heard and understood what was asked or said.

g) Taking responsibility for referring questions and statements to the proper person if an answer or comment seems to be needed. (Naturally, those who ask questions or offer comments should be free to direct their remarks to persons of their own choice.)

h) Bringing the forum to a satisfying close by summarizing aptly and briefly while there is still a lively interest in the problem. Only in this way can the audience be sent away still thinking about the subject. Forums which drag on too long can diminish interest in the subject and thus defeat their main purpose.

Those who participate as members of the audience should:

a) Ask questions useful to themselves *and others*. The interests of the *group* are paramount; personal, trivial, irrelevant questions and comments are out of place.

b) Phrase their questions and comments clearly, simply, briefly, and interestingly.

c) Phrase questions and comments in such a way as to maintain a reflective attitude on the part of everyone. Good taste and good temper should be maintained no matter how controversial the problem may be.

Those who respond to audience questions and statements are duty bound, as in informal discussion, to be:

a) Free from contention and dogmatism in their comments.

b) Helpful in maintaining the climate of opinion conducive to group thinking. (See precautions enumerated in (d) under duties of chairman above.)

c) Frank and cooperative in providing the data and advice needed for effective problem solving (Wagner and Arnold, 1965, pp. 183–184).[2]

With some basic understanding of the forum, let's now consider an example of this form of public discussion. The forum can serve as a useful form of public discussion for providing both access and input to some individual or group charged with making recommendations or decisions concerning a problem or topic. Suppose you were appointed by the president of your university to a task force on student publications composed of faculty and students. During an early phase of the task force's work, the group decides to hold an open meeting on the campus to permit students, faculty, and staff to express their views relevant to the current operation of student publications.

The chairperson of the task force might very logically select the forum as the type of public discussion to be used in this instance. The forum would provide an opportunity for interested individuals of the campus community to express their views on matters relevant to student publications, thus providing access and input to the task force for later deliberation. The chairperson of the task force might serve as the moderator for the forum, performing all those duties described previously for the forum leader. Note that in this example the forum was used as a form separate from other types of public discussion. Later in this section we will consider examples in which the forum is used in combination with other forms of public discussion.

[2]From Russell H. Wagner and Carroll C. Arnold, *Handbook of Group Discussion*, 2nd ed. Boston: Houghton Mifflin Co., 1965, pp. 183–184. Reprinted by permission.

FIGURE 11.1   The Forum

Panel

A panel is a form of public discussion in which a group of four to eight persons, including a leader, discusses a problem in front of an audience (Utterback, 1964). The presence of the audience can act as an important external variable on the panel, and significantly affect the discussion. Consequently, its potential effect on the group members should be considered in a systems analysis. On the basis of such an analysis, the leader may decide to exclude from the panel any members who tend to be nervous or excitable. The members of the group are usually either experts or reasonably knowledgeable concerning the problem under discussion, and their views on the problem may vary widely. They follow the problem-solving format described earlier, proceeding through the discussion in an orderly and logical manner. You will find no prepared speeches and no particular order designated for individuals in the group to speak. As in private discussions, the interaction

217

among members is informal, characterized by frequent interruptions and substantial give-and-take under the leadership of a moderator or chairperson.

Panels are *public* discussions and as such they are presented for the benefit of the audience (Gulley, 1968). Accordingly, the primary purpose of a panel usually is to give or share information concerning a problem and its possible solutions with the members of the audience. While the members of the panel attempt to solve a problem (one level of purpose), they do so for the purpose of informing the audience (another level of purpose). Thus, it is possible for you to conceive that the panel has two simultaneous levels of purpose or a kind of dual purpose, with the essential purpose being that of informing the audience.

Clearly, the panel does not present its discussion exclusively for the purpose of its own edification or entertainment, which is a potential difficulty you should not overlook as a member of a panel. Auer (1954) and Wagner and Arnold (1965) appropriately suggest that in addition to the purpose of informing the audience, the panel sometimes may seek to stimulate the audience to participate with them in the actual process of problem solving. The leader might pursue this purpose by having the audience and panel work together in the discussion of key issues or possible solutions. In special instances the panel may also have as its purpose to persuade the audience. But, more typically, the primary purpose of the panel is to inform the audience about the problem.

Because a panel is presented before an audience, it is important that all its members be seen and heard by those observing the event. For this reason, the panel is sometimes seated on a platform in the front of a room. Tables and chairs are arranged so that the panel members may see one another easily and so that all members of the panel may be seen by the audience.

These environmental conditions may somewhat affect the informal group process when the group is transplanted onto the public platform in front of an audience. As you might expect, some of the informality present in group discussions conducted in private is reduced in panel discussions conducted in public. For example, all members must speak loudly enough to be heard by the audience. The public nature of panel discussions also tends to place a constraint of time limits on the meeting. Usually an hour to an hour and a half is a good guideline for the time limit for a panel discussion when it is planned as a single event. However, panels are generally planned with a forum to follow. Something less than an hour devoted to the panel discussion and probably not more than forty-five minutes designated for the forum are reasonable guidelines for the time limits when a panel-forum discussion is planned. Of course, these time limits are only suggested guidelines, because the needs for more or less time will be dictated by the constraints of individual situations.

Earlier we noted that panel discussions proceed in an orderly and logical manner, but some planning is necessary to help ensure the desired outcome. The first phase of planning incorporates all the general suggestions made in Chapter 7 on problem solving. It may even be a good idea in some situations for you to end this phase with a brief outline prepared for a problem-solving discussion.

A second phase of preplanning is also necessary for panel discussions. As a member of the panel you are generally well advised to have a short planning meeting prior to the panel discussion, particularly if your group has not previously worked together. At this meeting, members of your group should reach agreement on any essential definitional matters and place some limits on the problem to be discussed.

Next, the topic questions or issues to serve as the central focus in the discussion should be agreed upon and ordered as they will be introduced into the discussion. Care should be taken to determine that you can cover the selected topics concisely and efficiently during the panel discussion. Then, to help ensure that the selected topics will get discussed, your group should specify some general guidelines regarding the time allocated for each topic or question. Again, these time limits are only guidelines, and they will be useful only to the extent that each member observes them within reasonable limits.

Once this procedural outline of the group's plan is completed, the members of your panel are ready to go do some independent thinking about their individual contribution. Clearly, the development of the procedural outline is not followed by a rehearsal session. There has to be some balance between the preplanning of the panel and the spontaneity desired during the actual panel discussion. Responses from you and other members during the panel discussion should appear to be improvised and extemporaneous, rather than rehearsed like a play. Your actual panel discussion should be characterized by flexibility with a freshness of both ideas and interactions, yet prepared, without appearing to be rigid.

The chairperson or moderator is the person to whom both your panel and the audience look to get the discussion under way. After saying a sentence or two to quiet the audience, he or she should announce the topic and introduce the members of the panel. Next the leader would be seated with the panel, open the discussion with a few introductory sentences, and then involve other members in the panel discussion. The chairperson should operate in the panel discussion as we suggested in the chapters on problem solving and leadership, remembering that there are special requirements imposed on the public discussion. Particularly, the chairperson must be sensitive to the audience's needs for summaries, for reiteration of ideas to improve clarity, for transitions between topics, and for emphasis in steps being followed in the discussion process. After the chairperson gives the final summary for the panel discussion, he or she then may turn to the audience, either to make concluding remarks (if only a panel discussion is scheduled) or to follow the procedures stated earlier for the forum (if a panel-forum is scheduled).

PRINCIPLES

1. The panel is a public discussion in which a group of four to eight experts discuss a problem, following the problem-solving format, in front of an audience under a chairperson's leadership.

2. Experts should participate on the panel and follow the problem-solving format (utilizing its informal style of interaction) for the purpose of sharing with the audience information concerning a problem and its solution.

3. The physical environmental conditions should be arranged so that the panel members may see and hear one another easily (ideally, on a platform) and so that the panel can be seen and heard by the audience.

4. When possible, a panel-forum combination should not run longer than an hour and forty-five minutes.

5. Planning for the panel's discussion is in two phases. In the first phase of planning, all the principles listed in Chapter 7 on problem solving are considered, ending the session with a brief outline for the problem-solving discussion. At the second planning session, the panel should agree on essential definitions, limitations of the problem, topic questions or issues and their order of introduction into the discussion, plans to cover pertinent topics, and time limits for topics.

6. The chairperson for a panel discussion should get the meeting under way, orient the audience to the topic or problem, introduce the panel's members, and follow the general principles for a moderator/chairperson specified in Chapter 9 on leadership. In addition, the chairperson should follow many of the principles listed for the forum, since the panel is a public discussion, and follow *all* of them when a panel-forum is employed.

We conclude this section by describing an example of a panel discussion in which you might be interested. Let us assume that some group of faculty and students in your university believes that the role of students in the decision-making processes of the university should be increased, but other groups disagree with this view. Students and faculty have requested that the administration invite several experts to the campus to discuss the matter. The president of the university has complied with this request and appointed a committee composed of students and faculty members to implement the suggestion. You are appointed to the committee.

After substantial discussion, the committee agrees to invite four experts

FIGURE 11.2   The Panel

from outside the university's community to participate in a panel-forum discussion. The topic selected for the panel-forum discussion is: What Should Be the University's Attitude Toward Increasing Student Involvement in Decisions Concerning the University's Affairs? The committee might then agree upon a list of specialists who could serve effectively as panel members, and invite them to participate in the panel-forum discussion. After the chosen individuals accept invitations to participate in the panel-forum, the committee might select from the campus community a person who was knowledgeable about the topic and possessed group leadership skills to serve as the chairperson. The leader and the panel would then be expected to perform all their appropriate duties described previously for the panel and the forum.

Colloquium

A colloquium is a form of public discussion in which a group of three to six persons discusses a problem among themselves and with the audience under the leadership of a chairperson or moderator. The colloquium, or colloquy, as a form of public discussion is essentially a hybrid in which the panel and forum are combined. The members of the group are experts on the problem or topic under discussion, and their views may be quite divergent. Sometimes, representatives of the audience may sit with the experts in front of the audience to participate in the forum portion of the discussion (Harnack, Fest, and Jones, 1977), but it is essential that the primary members of the panel have expertise relevant to the problem under consideration.

The purpose of a colloquium is to identify, develop, and work toward the solution(s) of a problem and related subproblems within the problem-solving format for the benefit of the participating audience. Accordingly, a colloquy is a public discussion conducted for the benefit of the audience, in which the audience shares in the deliberations on the problem and its solution(s).

The colloquium has two levels of purpose that are similar to those identified previously for a panel. At one level, the experts on the panel for the colloquium attempt to solve the problem by following the problem-solving format. At another level of purpose, the panel has the objective of informing the audience and stimulating the audience to participate in the problem-solving process—or, at least, to make an effort toward the solution of the problem and its interrelated subproblems.

Because the colloquium is a combination of the panel and the forum, it possesses a number of characteristics we have discussed previously. Panel members would undoubtedly wish to proceed through the pre-planning phases detailed above to help ensure an effective outcome for the colloquium (see p. 219). The chairperson opens the discussion, calms the audience, makes a few comments about the occasion, announces and introduces the topic or problem, introduces the panel, and gets the problem-solving discussion under way.

You will find at this point in the colloquium that there is a departure from the procedures typically employed in the "pure" panel discussion. When either the chairperson or the panel members determine that some matter is deterring the pursuit of a satisfactory solution to the problem or subproblems, the audience is invited to participate by asking questions or making remarks. For example, as a chairperson you might observe that two panel members disagree on a matter; that a salient issue, subproblem, or solution is being omitted or ignored in the discussion; or that a questionable point is not being challenged. At this point, you would shift from the panel discussion to the forum discussion until the matter was settled. Then you would shift back to the panel discussion until the next opportunity occurred for the audience's participation. This process would continue until the discussion was concluded, either by the time limit or arrival at an agreed-upon solution to the problem and interrelated subproblems.

You might have surmised from our brief description of the colloquium that there are no set speeches and, as in the panel discussion, this is so. Individuals, either on the panel or in the audience, do not speak in any set order. Interaction among panelists, and between panelists and the audience, is informal. At a colloquium you would expect substantial give-and-take and interruptions under the flexible guidance of the chairperson. The systems analysis must be ongoing.

However, a skillful leader alone is not enough to ensure the effective operation of a colloquy. Panelists must also assist the chairperson in performing his or her responsibilities. As Wagner and Arnold have observed so well: "Panel members must be almost as active as the chairman in encouraging, controlling, interpreting, and synthesizing audience contributions and their own. In effect, panelists must function as expert discussion participants within the panel itself and, with the chairperson, become a team of forum leaders during the intervals of audience participation" (1965, p. 185). Moreover, the chairperson and the panelists must perform all these functions while still following the systematic inquiry explicit in the problem-solving format.

The environment, an external variable, can contribute significantly to the outcome of the event. The leader and members of the panel are, ideally, seated on a platform at the front of the room. Seating should be arranged so that the panel members can see one another, the chairperson, and the audience. Of course, it is also important that everyone be able to hear what is being said. Panelists as well as members of the audience should speak loudly enough to be heard by all in the room.

While the length of time may not be a constraint for some small group discussions, it is an important matter for public discussions. Usually an hour and a half is a reasonable time limit for a colloquium. Some colloquies may run slightly longer or shorter, depending on the audience's interest in the topic and its commitment to becoming involved in the deliberations.

PRINCIPLES

1. The colloquium is a form of public discussion in which a group of three to six experts, selected for their divergent views, discuss a problem following the problem-solving format in front of an audience under a chairperson's leadership.

2. The purpose of the colloquium is to identify, develop, and work toward the solution(s) of a problem and related subproblems for the benefit of the participating audience.

3. You should plan for the colloquium by following the two-phase planning operations described previously for the panel (see p. 219).

4. The principles for the problem-solving format and its related informal style of interaction as listed in the earlier chapter on problem solving should be followed.

5. The environmental conditions should be such that the discussion group of the colloquy is on a platform, can see and hear one another easily, and the discussion group can be seen and heard by the audience/participants.

plans made for the symposium at this meeting typically are not as involved or complete as those plans made for panel discussions. Nevertheless, a planning session helps to ensure that the symposium will accomplish its purpose. The participating speakers determine in advance how the topic or problem will be divided. The problem may be divided by such means as divergent positions relevant to the problem, particular interests of individuals concerning the problem, or significant probable solutions for the problem. However, all aspects or phases of the divided topics should relate directly to the single problem under examination. The specific order in which speakers will make their presentations may also be determined at the planning session.

In addition, the speakers generally will agree in advance on the time to be allocated for each speech. Typically, the time periods are divided equally among speakers, usually ranging from a little less than ten minutes to not more than twenty minutes per speaker. Of course, the amount of time per speaker will depend on the number of speeches to be given and the time available for the symposium. When the symposium is planned as a separate event, it should usually not run longer than an hour and fifteen minutes. We mentioned earlier that plans frequently are made for a panel discussion, forum discussion, or a combination of the two to follow a symposium. When a symposium is to be used in combination with another type of public discussion, the symposium itself should run for less than an hour, with not more than a total of an hour and forty-five minutes devoted to the combined forms of public discussion.

After the planning meeting, each speaker prepares his or her speech following the general procedures taught in public speaking classes. Between the initial planning session and the symposium, substantial individual work is required by speakers to develop and practice effective speeches. While it is important that the speakers for a symposium be knowledgeable concerning their subject matter, it is equally important that they be competent speakers. You have undoubtedly had the opportunity to hear a speech given by an outstanding expert that was presented very poorly (e.g., many of the lectures presented in your college classes). If the audience is to become and remain involved in the speeches given at a symposium, then the criterion of the speaker's competence must be considered when selecting participants for the symposium. Failure to attend adequately to the criterion of speaker competency has resulted in some disastrous symposia.

The speeches for a symposium are presented from a stage, a raised platform, or the floor level in the front of a room. As with other forms of public discussion, it is important that the speakers be heard and seen by all members of the audience. Before and after speaking, the speakers sit on chairs in the front of the room. Sometimes they sit behind a table, but this may not be necessary if the symposium is to be presented as a separate event. What is important is that the seated participants can be seen by the audience; this is particularly important when a panel or panel-forum discussion is to follow the symposium. Of course, a speaker usually stands behind a lectern, rostrum, or a table to deliver his or her speech.

As with other forms of public discussion, the chairperson is responsible for getting the symposium started and making sure that it moves along smoothly. The chairperson's first task is to bring the audience under control by quieting them with a few comments. He or she next begins the introductory remarks which probably would include commenting on the occasion, announcing the topic or problem, stressing the problem's importance for the audience, and stating how the problem is to be divided among the speakers. Then each speaker is introduced in succession, and the respective speeches are presented. If a panel discussion, forum discussion, or a combination of the two is scheduled after the symposium, the chairperson follows the procedures outlined above for these forms of public discussion.

PRINCIPLES

1. The symposium is a form of public discussion in which a series of brief speeches (usually made by two to six speakers), on different aspects of a specified problem, is presented uninterrupted to an audience.
2. The purpose of the symposium is to present information to an audience.
3. Persons knowledgeable about the topic and skilled in public speaking should present the speeches.
4. The symposium should be combined with the forum for better audience involvement.
5. A planning session prior to the symposium is used to determine how the speakers will divide the topic, choose the specific order in which the speakers will speak, and determine the time to be allocated to each speech.
6. Speakers should prepare and practice their speeches thoroughly.
7. When scheduled separately, the symposium should run no longer than an hour and fifteen minutes and not longer than an hour and forty-five minutes when it is combined with another form of public discussion.
8. The speakers and chairperson should be on a platform, if possible, and they should be seen and heard by one another and by the audience.
9. A chairperson should quiet the audience, make introductory remarks, stress the importance of the topic and occasion, state how the topic has been divided by the speakers, introduce the speakers, and provide a brief summary at the conclusion of the meeting. (If a forum or a panel discussion is planned in conjunction with the symposium, the principles stated previously for these forms of public discussion should be followed.)

Now, let us consider an example of a symposium. In our discussions of the forum and the colloquium, we provided an example of how each could be used by a task force of student publications, on which you might serve as a member. We will continue to use this example here and assume that you are still a member of this task force. Also, we will assume that the group has deliberated several months since holding the forum and the colloquium to provide the campus community with access and input into the task force. The task force has now arrived at consensus on the tentative recommendations to be made concerning student publications to the president of the university.

In order to inform the campus community about the tentative recommendations, to get feedback on possible problems relevant to them, and to ensure that no worthy suggestion has been overlooked, the task force might now schedule a symposium-forum discussion prior to submitting the final recommendations to the president. The topic-problem for the symposium-forum might be stated as follows: What Should Be the Policy Concerning Student Publications at the University?

The task force's chairperson might serve as the moderator for the

FIGURE 11.4   The Symposium

symposium-forum, performing the responsibilities identified earlier. Each member of the task force might speak briefly at the symposium on a particular aspect of student publications and the tentative recommendations related thereto. For example, one member may speak on the role of student publications in meeting students' needs, another on the range of student publications needed to meet these needs, still another on financial support for student publications, and so on. After all speeches are concluded the chairperson would be expected to present a summary and then begin the forum discussion, following the procedures discussed previously. Of course, it would be possible for the task force to have scheduled only a symposium in this case, but the advantages of doing so are obviously limited. Generally, symposia are scheduled in conjunction with at least a forum.

PRIVATE DISCUSSIONS

In the following sections we will examine forms of *private discussions*. Unlike the public forms of discussion, private discussions are not held before an audience, nor do they involve participation by nonmembers. To that extent, private discussions are similar to both the informative and problem-solving discussions examined in earlier chapters. However, the private discussions considered in the following sections are special types of discussions which differ in specific format and purpose from the informative and problem-solving discussions. The private discussions we will examine are sensitivity training groups, role-playing groups, and buzz sessions.

Sensitivity Training Groups

While several different labels have been given to this special type of group discussion (e.g., encounter group, confrontation group, T-group, and sensitivity group), we will use the term *sensitivity training group*. Whatever the label, this special type of private group discussion is characterized by participants who come together, usually under the direction of a leader or trainer, to grow and develop intrapersonal and interpersonal effectiveness through a group experience (Egan, 1970).

As you might guess, the goals of sensitivity training groups differ from most other types of groups we have examined. Although members of sensitivity groups vary in what they expect to gain from the experience, a few consistent purposes emerge. DuBrin (1981) suggests that these purposes include the following:

- Make participants more sensitive to how they are perceived by others and how their behavior affects others.
- Acquire knowledge about the processes that help and hinder group functioning.

- Help participants become more aware of their own feelings and how these feelings influence behavior.
- Help participants, in general, achieve greater self-understanding, including insight into their conflicts, feelings, defenses, and impact on others.
- Develop specific behavioral skills such as improved listening ability, praising and criticizing others, and communicating with body language.[3]

These goals are clearly different from those of most other groups we have discussed. People often infer that the goals of sensitivity training groups are therapeutic in nature. While there is some truth to this, there are several distinctions between sensitivity training groups and therapy groups. The members of sensitivity training groups usually are "normal" individuals such as students, managers, social workers, members of the clergy, and others who desire to improve their communication and relations with others. Therapy groups, on the other hand, are composed of individuals who need help in coping with various emotional problems. The members of sensitivity training groups are motivated to improve their sensitivity and social skills, whereas members of therapy groups seek relief from anxiety and distress. Sensitivity training groups also differ from therapy groups in size, direction, physical setting, and leadership functions.

Although there are some distinctions among various types of sensitivity training groups, there are some common characteristics which most types share. In almost every instance the group is small (from eight to eighteen members), relatively unstructured, and chooses its own goals. The leader's responsibility is to facilitate group members' expression of feelings and thoughts. The primary task of most sensitivity training groups involves the interaction among group members. However, some kinds of interaction are regarded as more relevant to the group, such as conversations about the interaction and relationships of group members.

Unlike most other groups, sensitivity groups do not have an agenda; they proceed in a largely undirected, almost rambling manner. Sensitivity groups tend to experience periods of confusion, disorganization, frustration, and conflict. Lundgren and Knight (1978) suggest that the following sequence of stages is characteristic of most training groups.

Stage 1: The Initial Encounter. In this initial stage of development, group norms and goals are unclear. Group members generally have little knowledge about one another's expectations and tend to feel insecure.

---

[3]From A. J. DuBrin, *Human Relations: A Job Oriented Approach*, 2nd ed., 1981, p. 246. Reprinted with permission of Reston Publishing Co., a Prentice-Hall Co., 11480 Sunset Hills Road, Reston, VA 22090.

FIGURE 11.5 Sensitivity Training Group

Stage 2: Intermember Conflict and Confrontation of the Trainer. Group members begin to express themselves, but much of the interaction is aggressive and hostile. The group tends to subdivide into competing subgroups: one subgroup desires more directive leadership while the other subgroup resists the efforts for a dominant leadership role.

Stage 3: Group Solidarity. In this stage there usually is a reduction of conflict. Group members relax their efforts to pressure the trainer into a more directive leadership role and begin to accept greater responsibility for decision making.

Stage 4: Exchange of Interpersonal Feedback. The group becomes unified by strong but flexible norms. Group members begin to discover things about themselves and others through open and honest feedback.

Stage 5: Termination. During this last stage group members discuss concern about separation. Members generally express positive feelings toward each other and toward the trainer.

While it is not difficult to describe the purpose, function, and various stages of typical sensitivity training groups, there is some validity to the position that a person must actually participate in a sensitivity group before a

Before moving on to another type of private discussion, we will make a few additional comments about sensitivity training groups. Participants in sensitivity training groups often can experience great personal satisfaction and reward. However, some people may respond quite differently to the experience. It is not uncommon for certain types of people to become very uptight in sensitivity groups, and in some cases even experience serious psychological harm. Moreover, the growing popularity of sensitivity groups has made sensitivity training a surprisingly lucrative trade for charlatans and quacks who lack the professional skill and training necessary to run such groups. As a result, there are some guidelines you should follow when choosing a sensitivity training group.

1. You should not engage in any sensitivity training group unless it is run by an experienced, qualified trainer.
2. You should avoid, or scrutinize closely, sensitivity training groups that are advertised in newspapers and magazines.
3. You should avoid participation in sensitivity training groups if you are overly high-strung and sensitive to criticism.
4. You should not engage in a sensitivity training group unless you really want to. Do not let social pressure from peers or others influence your decision.
5. You should not engage in sensitivity training with close friends or family.

Role Playing

Role playing is a procedure in which group members are assigned roles relevant to a particular problem under study and then are placed in situations where they *act out*, in an impromptu fashion, the implications of the situation (Bormann, 1969). For example, a group of students discussing problems of handicapped students might employ role-playing techniques by assigning members of the group to play the part of blind persons in various campus oriented situations. The experience gained through role playing might provide group members with a fresh, personal perspective on the problems handicapped students encounter.

Role-playing techniques for group discussion often are considered public discussions. However, we have considered role playing as a type of private discussion because the effects of role playing focus most on the actors (i.e., group members) and less on the observers. For example, considerable research on attitude change suggests that as a result of role playing, subjects (i.e., actors) in experiments have changed their attitudes about such issues as minority groups (Culbertson, 1957), alcohol (Harvey and Beverly, 1961), measures to protect one's health (Janis and Mann, 1965), and capital punishment (Wallace, 1966). The technique of role playing is also used widely in business and industry for training in supervision, interviewing, and improving industrial relations. The general purpose of role playing is actor oriented. Chase has said, "It [role playing] is a way to develop imagination, tolerance, and the power to see yourself from the outside and other people from the inside, and so a way to reduce conflict and further agreement" (1951, p. 99).

Although role playing is actor oriented, it does enhance group goals as well as personal, actor-related goals. As for personal goals, role playing helps us (1) learn new roles, (2) become more aware of our own roles, and (3) understand others' point(s) of view more clearly.

Role playing enhances group related goals because it gets all members involved in problem solving and can help the group pretest ideas and solutions that may be important later.

Like sensitivity training, role playing is difficult to understand clearly without the benefit of actually experiencing the procedure. However, unlike sensitivity training, role-playing techniques follow a more structured sequence of steps which are more easily applied in group discussion by persons lacking in therapeutic training. Keltner (1957) suggests several steps in the development of successful group role-playing techniques. A systems analysis of communication channels and interpersonal attraction may help your group make decisions about role playing.

The first step is to *find the problem*. For example, suppose a group of students is discussing problems of racial discrimination on campus and one group member asks, "What do we mean by racial discrimination?" Suppose after much talk the group is still at a loss to agree on those situations which clearly illustrate racial discrimination. At this point the group has a clear problem. Keltner suggests that the following principles be applied in finding a problem for group role playing:

1. Give the group a chance to explore several kinds of problems.
2. Do not pick the first one that comes along without hearing others.
3. Watch the group to determine which of the problems described seems to have the greatest degree of interest and personal association to the individuals in the group.
4. If there seems to be a choice between several problems, ask the group to decide on the problem (Keltner, 1957, p. 264).[5]

The second step in using group role playing is to *work out the plot and the characters*. The plot should not be so detailed as to limit the actors' freedom of expression, but it should be specific enough to provide a setting in

[5]From John W. Keltner, *Group Discussion Processes*. New York: Longmans, Green and Company, 1957, pp. 264–266. Reprinted by permission.

FIGURE 11.6   Role Playing

236

which the role playing is to occur. The characters should be described in terms of the relevant aspects of their background and personality and their relationship to other characters. For example, our student group on racial discrimination might use the following plot/character description for a role-playing event:

> Joe, Tom, and Andy have been assigned as roommates by the campus dormitory director. Tom and Andy are white. Joe is black. Although they have been roommates for only two weeks, there have been constant arguments about their respective duties, such as housecleaning and cooking. Joe contends that Tom and Andy constantly side together on the arguments, which puts him at a disadvantage. The three men are now in the director's office discussing the problem with him.

After the plot and the characters are determined, group members should be assigned to their roles. This step can sometimes be difficult. Keltner (1957) suggests the following guidelines in assigning group members to roles:

> 1. Do not select members at random.
> 2. Avoid selecting persons too deeply involved in the particular problem to be objective about it.
> 3. Do not force a role on a person if he does not want to play it.
> 4. Maintain a free and easy atmosphere so that the members will not feel ill at ease in playing their roles (Keltner, 1957, p. 266).

The next step is to *instruct the nonplayers of the group*. Since it may be difficult to involve all of the group members in each role-playing situation, it is a good idea to use nonplayers as observers. Nonplayers might be asked to take note of such things as the players' handling of the problem and the important points relevant to the group goal.

Once this is done, the group is ready to begin the *actual playing of the scene*. It is sometimes helpful for players to use props such as desks, chairs, and other objects to lend more realism to the scene. The group leader should note the action very carefully and not let it continue too long. It is difficult to set a definite time limit, but the play should be stopped when it reaches a significant or critical point. If the play is allowed to continue beyond the critical point, players and observers tend to lose interest and the role playing begins to lose its effect.

The next step is to *discuss the scene*. The discussion should focus on several questions: What happened in the scene? Did the characters play their roles convincingly? Was the scene realistic? What important points are illustrated? Sometimes the discussion results in additional questions, controversy, and differing opinions among group members. When this occurs, it is often beneficial to replay the scene, using either the same players or different group members. If a replay of the scene is necessary, it is usually a good idea to have a final discussion to resolve any additional questions the group members may have.

While group role-playing techniques may be very beneficial, you should realize that role playing can have limitations and problems if it is not conducted properly. You should consider the following points before using group role-playing techniques (Keltner, 1957):

1. Since role playing requires imaginative, creative people to work properly, you should not attempt to use role-playing techniques in groups lacking in this talent.
2. The problems and situations to which role playing is applied should be realistic, practical, and detailed enough for clear issues to arise.
3. Role playing should involve the entire group as much as possible. You should avoid using the same group members as players without giving others an opportunity to role play. Also, nonplayers should be used as observers.
4. It is wise to avoid using role-playing techniques until group members have become acquainted with each other. Otherwise, group members may become known in terms of their roles rather than how they really are.
5. Sometimes players get carried away with their roles and "ham up" their portrayal. When this happens, the real issues tend to become clouded and role playing loses its effectiveness.

Buzz Sessions

The buzz session is a technique often used to maximize the number of people involved in group discussion. Usually a larger group is broken up into smaller subgroups consisting of about six members each. Each subgroup is then given a specific aspect of the problem to discuss within some specified period of time (usually five or ten minutes). After the buzz sessions, a representative from each subgroup then reports back to the large group.

Buzz sessions often are considered a type of public discussion designed to achieve audience participation, but other forms of discussion would appear more appropriate for generating audience involvement (e.g., the forum and colloquium). We consider the buzz session a private discussion because it essentially takes place within private conference.

Buzz sessions usually work well when they are preceded by some stimulus event such as a speech, film, or case study. The purposes of the buzz sessions are to maximize group participation and examine more closely specific aspects of some problem arising from the major stimulus event. Since most buzz sessions last only five to ten minutes, it is important that the question for discussion be very specific; otherwise, it is difficult for the buzz sessions to accomplish anything meaningful. The reports which buzz group representatives make to the large group also should be kept brief. Unless the representatives' reports are limited, time usually runs out before all the buzz groups have had a chance to report.

PRINCIPLES

1. A buzz session is a technique for maximizing participation when a larger group is broken down into groups with three to six members.
2. The reporter for a group in a buzz session should obtain feedback from the group to ensure that he or she accurately reflects the views of the group; if necessary, the reporter should take notes so that important points are not omitted in the *brief* report to the larger group.
3. When appropriate, a film, lecture, case study, or some other type of stimulus should be employed prior to the buzz session.
4. Instructions given to the audience and tasks or questions for discussion should be clear to all participants prior to breaking into buzz groups.
5. The task or questions for discussion should be limited to something the small groups can do meaningfully within the allotted time period.

FIGURE 11.7   Buzz Sessions

Buzz groups may be used for a variety of purposes. For example, consider a group of students in a film course who have been given the assignment of critiquing a student-made film. The group might employ the buzz session technique by forming several subgroups to discuss specific aspects of the film. One buzz group may be given the task of discussing the filmmaker's use of lighting, another group may focus on camera technique, another on the film's sound. Or each buzz group could be assigned to discuss the same aspect of the film. In either case, after five or ten minutes of discussion, a representative from each buzz group would then report to the entire group.

SUMMARY

In this chapter we examined several special forms of small group communication. We placed the special forms into two categories: public and private discussions. Public discussions include forms of discussion which take place before an audience or in some way engage participation from persons who are not members of the group. On the other hand, private discussions include those forms of small group communication which are not conducted before an audience or do not involve participation on the part of nonmembers.

Under the category of public discussions we examined the form, purposes, and characteristics of the forum, panel, colloquium, and symposium. The forms of private discussion examined were sensitivity training groups, role playing, and buzz sessions.

While it is unlikely that you will engage in all of these special forms of group discussion, it is probable that sometime in the next few years you will have occasion to participate in one or more of the special forms discussed in the chapter.

IDEAS FOR DISCUSSION

1. What are the distinguishing characteristics of the forum, panel, colloquium, and symposium? Which of these forms of public discussion are most and least formal? Which involve the audience the most and least?

2. What are the similar characteristics of the forum, panel, colloquium, and symposium?

3. What are some specific events in which you think it might be appropriate to use a forum, panel, colloquium, or symposium separately? What are some situations in which you think it might be appropriate to use certain combinations of these forms of public discussion? Why did you make these choices for your selected situations?

4. In what specific ways do you think students might benefit from participating in a sensitivity training group? Do you think these benefits could be achieved through participation in other special forms of discussion?

5. In what ways do role playing and sensitivity training appear similar? In what ways are they different?

6. What are some ways you think students may benefit from role-playing techniques? Provide some examples of specific problems where role-playing techniques can be applied. Do you think other special forms of discussion could be used to accomplish the same goals?

7. What are some specific situations in which the buzz session would be a useful form of group discussion? What particular characteristics of the situations led you to your decision?

SUGGESTED PROJECTS AND ACTIVITIES

1. Plan a real forum, panel, colloquium, or symposium in which you would like to participate. Start with the specification of the topic or problem and list every step you should execute, including principles to follow while the public discussion is in operation.

2. Select and observe a public discussion. Identify the type of discussion the group represents and write a brief paper analyzing the discussion according to principles in your text.

3. Obtain a written transcript or tape recording of an actual sensitivity training group session. Examine the group interaction carefully and determine if the group reached the various stages discussed in the chapter. Point out the specific examples of group interaction which led you to believe the group had reached each of the four stages.

4. Use the suggested steps for developing group role playing by selecting a case study from a source of your choosing and setting up a role-playing event with your group, and by developing your own case study or plot and using group members to act out the various roles. Did you see any differences in role playing between the two?

5. Select a person whom you know to have negative attitudes about a particular issue (e.g., legalization of abortions). Ask the person to role play with one or more other persons in a situation where he or she is playing a role which requires attitudes opposite from the person's real attitudes (e.g., to play the part of a person seeking an abortion). Be sure to make the situation as realistic as possible. After the role-playing event, attempt to assess the person's attitudes about the issue and the role that was played. Was there any change in the person's attitude? Why do you think the person changed or did not change?

REFERENCES

Auer, J. J., and H. L. Ewbank. *Handbook for discussion leaders.* New York: Harper & Row, Pub., 1954.

Bormann, E. G. *Discussion and group methods.* New York: Harper & Row, Pub., 1969.

Chase, S. *Roads to agreement.* New York: Harper & Row, Pub., 1951.

Culbertson, F. Modification of an emotionally held attitude through role playing. *Journal of abnormal and social psychology*, 1957, 54, 230–233.

DuBrin, A. J. *Human relations: a job-oriented approach*, 2nd ed. Reston, Va.: Reston, 1981.

EGAN, G. *Encounter: group processes for interpersonal growth.* Belmont, Calif.: Brooks/Cole, 1970.

GIBB, J. R. Defensive communication. In R. S. Cathcart and L. A. Samovar, eds. *Small group communication: a reader,* 3rd ed. Dubuque, Iowa: Wm. C. Brown, 1979, 374–380.

GULLEY, H. E. *Discussion, conference, and group process.* New York: Holt, Rinehart & Winston, 1968.

HARNACK, R. V., and T. B. FEST. *Group discussion theory and technique,* 2nd ed. Englewood Cliffs, N.J.: Prentice-Hall, 1977.

HARVEY, O., and G. BEVERLY. Some personality correlates of concept change through role playing. *Journal of abnormal and social psychology,* 1961, *63,* 125–130.

JANIS, I., and L. MANN. Effectiveness of emotional role playing in modifying smoking habits and attitudes. *Journal of experimental research on personality,* 1965, *1,* 84–90.

KELTNER, J. W. *Group discussion processes.* New York: Longmans, Green and Company, 1957.

LUNDGREN, D. C., and D. J. KNIGHT. Sequential stages of development in sensitivity training groups. *Journal of applied behavioral science,* 1978, *14,* 204–222.

ROGERS, C. R. The process of the basic encounter group. In J. F. T. Bugental, ed. *Challenges of humanistic psychology.* New York: McGraw-Hill, 1967.

SATTLER, W. M., and N. E. MILLER. *Discussion and conference.* Englewood Cliffs, N.J.: Prentice-Hall, 1968.

UTTERBACK, W. E. *Group thinking and conference leadership.* New York: Holt, Rinehart & Winston, 1964.

WAGNER, R. H., and C. C. ARNOLD. *Handbook of group discussion,* 2nd ed. Boston: Houghton Mifflin Co., 1965.

WALLACE, J. Role reward and dissonance reduction. *Journal of personality and social psychology,* 1966, *3,* 305–312.

SUGGESTED READINGS

APPLEBAUM, R. L., E. M. BODAKEN, K. K. SERENO, and K. W. E. ANATOL. *The process of group communication.* Chicago: Science Research Associates, 1974.

Chapter 10, "Methods of Discussion," provides definitions and procedures of several types of discussion, including panel, forum, etc. Chapter 11, "Small Group Techniques," presents techniques used to assist group interaction and group understanding of roles such as brainstorming and role playing.

GIBB, J. R. *Trust: a new view of personal and organizational development.* Los Angeles: The Guild of Tutors Press, 1978.

This book discusses the importance of trust to the effectiveness of all social systems. Chapter 1, "Trusting Me, You, and the Process," provides excellent material on the importance of trust and introduces TORI (Trust Level) Theory. In subsequent chapters TORI Theory is applied to various types of groups and organizations.

GOLEMBIEWSKI, R. T., and A. BLUMBERG, eds. *Sensitivity training and the laboratory approach: readings about concept and applications,* 3rd ed. Itasca, Ill.: F. E. Peacock, 1977.

This text investigates the spectrum of sensitivity training. The T-group is presented as a medium to improve personal growth and interpersonal relationships.

HUGHEY, J. D., and A. W. JOHNSON. *Speech communication: foundations and challenges.* New York: Macmillan, 1975.

Unit 9, "Private Discussion," presents definitions, types of leadership, and types of decision making needed for private discussion. The unit includes exercises to assist in planning, demonstrating, and evaluating the discussion. Unit 12, "Public Discussion," provides definitions, methods, and planning for public discussion such as panel/forum and symposium/forum.

Appendix

A needs assessment is a systematic procedure for determining the needs of a group at a given point in time and with regard to a particular matter salient to the group. A needs assessment in small groups is the procedure employed to identify discrepancies between the ideal status and present status from which prioritized needs are inferred (Dodl et al., 1974; Toomb et al., 1975). The minimum, but essential, steps for a needs assessment for the small group are shown in Figure A.1, sequentially arranged by elements or components in the system for determining a group's needs.

However, before examining the diagram, let's consider why this procedure is important in today's world. First, the needs assessment procedure helps individuals and groups to look systematically at the difference between where they are or where they want to be. Frequently, we are caught up in doing the same thing again too often, we get stale, we stop dreaming, and we even stop thinking about the future. At the same time, we sometimes get bored and even disgusted with our current style of life or job.

Groups have these same problems, particularly groups meeting over many years. The needs assessment procedures described here are useful for getting a fresh perspective on what we *really* want to do, on what our needs *really* are. Lest you think these procedures aren't useful or relevant to the real world, you should know that many industrial organizations employ these procedures or a variant of them in looking at their needs. Needs assessments are frequently required as part of federal and state grants for funds to improve communities, schools, transportation systems, and the like. Clearly, needs assessment is likely to play a substantial role in the small groups you

Conducting a Needs Assessment for Small Groups

encounter in life—personally, in community groups, and in your occupation. Now study the model in Figure A.1 and then read the following procedures for conducting a needs assessment.

1a.   Individuals within the group may have different perceptions of an unharmónious or problem situation which exists and which might or will have consequences for the group. Some imbalance, inequity, uneasiness, potential problem, or the like usually emerges in the perceptual field of one or more members as a stimulus for initiating a needs assessment for the group. It is important to get the impressions of the individual members concerning each other's perceptions of the *present status* of the matter(s) under consideration. Perceived current status of the matter under examination is determined by such considerations as perceived present philosophy, policy, goals, criteria employed, procedures currently in operation, decision points, style of decision making, responsibilities, and roles of person involved. Only by so doing can the group really understand the perceptions of others in the group. These perceptions of the present status for each individual concerning the matter(s) under consideration are listed as the product or outcome of component 1a.

1b.   This component is similar to 1a, except that the focus is on determining the perceived ideal status for each individual member, rather than the perceived present status. If a set of goals exists relevant to the matter under consideration, each member will want to examine them to ascertain if they are acceptable outcomes for his or her perceived ideal status. Any means or measures used to evaluate the stated goals are other sources to stimulate descriptions of the ideal outcomes. Still other sources to stimulate thinking about the ideal status for a given situation include: rationale for current goals, procedures for developing and charging current goals, ranking of current goals by priority of importance, persons involved in making and achieving goals, criteria for an ideal status, time involved to achieve an ideal status, persons influenced by ideal status, and roles and responsibilities of persons operating in an ideal status. The arrows going between 1a and 1b are there to indicate the interactive nature between these elements. The product or final outcome for this component is a description of each group member's perceived ideal status.

2a and 2b.   These elements are considered together here because of the similar processes involved. While we discuss elements 2a and 2b together here, each should be done separately. Of course, there will be some overlapping considerations between the two elements, as indicated by the double arrows between them. In Chapter 4 we discussed the importance of consensus to groups and strategies for reaching consensus or agreement. It is enough here to note that the group must now begin to compare and contrast their

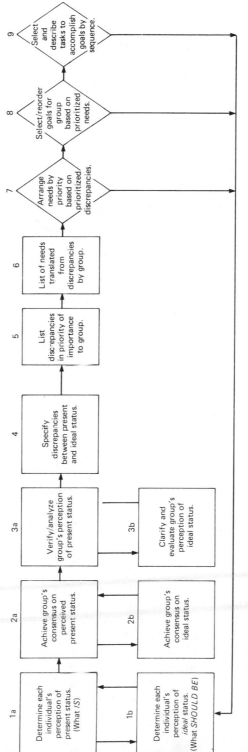

FIGURE A.1 Conducting a Needs Assessment for a Small Group

individual perceptions regarding present and ideal status on the particular matter. This procedure of comparing and contrasting should begin first by isolating items of agreement. Then, the perceptual items of disagreement should be located and arranged in priority of importance to the group. Going from the highest item of priority to the lowest, the group should resolve perceptual disagreements and arrive at consensus on them. The final product for each of the elements independently is a statement of the group's consensus concerning the (2a) perceived present status and (2b) perceived ideal status for the matter(s) being considered.

3a. Given the group's consensus statement on perceptions of the present status, 2a, it is now time to verify the accuracy of those perceptions in this element. All available evidence, using verifiable evidence where possible, should be collected concerning each aspect listed in the group's consensus statement of perceived status. The information required is of the sort listed earlier for components 1a and 1b, except that this time the information should be evidential in nature and have been verified or tested against reality. The task here is to determine if what the group perceives to be so is in fact supported by evidence in the real world. This verified evidence should then be summarized item by item to determine differences between the evidential findings and the group's perceptions of the present status. This process will frequently result in some modification of the group's perceived status concerning a matter, because the group usually sees the wisdom of resolving such observed differences between its perception and observed evidence. Also note there is interaction between what goes on in elements 3a and 3b, indicating the input and output between these procedures. The product of this component is a statement or revised statement by the group of the perceived present status relevant to the matter in question, with verified evidence used to support each aspect of the present status identified.

3b. Using the group's consensus statement on perceptions of the ideal status, the group now attempts to clarify and evaluate these perceptions. Based on input from element 3a, changes might be necessary and/or new or different thoughts might emerge in 3b that would change the outcome for element 3a. So there is a kind of symbiotic relationship between these two elements. However, in this element the first task is to evaluate the previously formulated ideal status by using criteria developed by the group. Of course, the statement resulting from the completion of element 3a should also provide some evidential basis for considering the group's previous consensus on the ideal status. Sometimes the group will only need to refine and formalize perceptions of the ideal status. Other times the group will be required to reconceptualize the entire nature of the ideal status, based on new information assimilated in element 3a or irreconcilable differences found between the ideal and present status, or other ideational difficulties. The final product for this component should be a description of the perceived ideal status organized into a series of steps required to facilitate its achievement.

4.   Based on the two statements developed for elements 3a and 3b, the group now identifies the perceived discrepancies between the perceived present and perceived ideal statuses. Initial discussion of the feasibility of resolving discrepancies should also begin, with a view toward reconciling differences where appropriate and possible. Groups are usually well advised to specify criteria they deem appropriate to identify a discrepancy between perceived present and ideal status. An effective means to examine possible discrepancies systematically is to list each problem, condition, procedure, etc.; next the perceived present status; then the perceived ideal status; and finally, the discrepancy, if any, between the two. Some groups find it easiest simply to list this information horizontally across a page. The final product for this element is a listing of the discrepancies by the group, hopefully through consensus, of the perceived discrepancies between perceived present and perceived ideal status.

5.   Once specified, the perceived discrepancies are classified by the group according to importance. Using either a three- or five-point scale, each member rates and ranks each discrepancy by *importance to the group*. Next the individual ratings and rankings are summarized and presented to the group for final consideration. Criteria for determining importance to the group may or may not be developed for these deliberations. For example, suppose your student health center did not dispense birth control pills on request to women over eighteen years of age. Upon student demand, the Woman's Affairs Council of student government reviewed this policy and decided that the ideal condition would be for women over age eighteen to receive birth control pills on request. In this example, the highest priority for a discrepancy was that birth control pills were not being dispensed on request at the health center for adults when they should have been. Based on consensus or the best agreement possible, the group lists the perceived discrepancies between the perceived present and ideal status in priority of importance to the group. This statement is the final product for element 5 of the model.

6.   With the list of prioritized discrepancies the group has the task of translating the discrepancies into needs. The perceived discrepancy relevant to the dispensing of birth control pills in the health center discussed above might be translated into the following statement of need: Policies and procedures should be implemented to permit persons over eighteen years of age to receive birth control pills on request at the health center. This is a simple step, but careful wording of the needs to reflect the interests and intents of the

Achievement goal: The major outcome or product that the group intends to produce or seeks to achieve.

Active listening: Listening with the total self—including attitudes, beliefs, feelings, and intuitions.

Agenda: Step-by-step plan to be followed by a group or meeting.

Antagonistic goal: Goals that are not to the best interest of all the group members' goals.

Assembly effect: Occurs when the group is able to achieve something which could not have been achieved by any member alone or by a combination of individuals' efforts.

Buzz session: Technique used to maximize the number of people involved in group discussion.

Closed-minded: Strong adherence to views that will prevent undertaking or listening to anything that is different, innovative, or new.

Closed system: One which is isolated from its environment; it does not exchange energy, matter, or information with elements outside the system.

Cohesiveness: Complex of forces which bind members of a group to each other and to the group as a whole.

Colloquium: Form of public discussion in which a group of three to six experts, selected for their divergent views, discuss a problem following the problem-solving format in front of an audience under a chairperson's leadership.

Communication channel: Type of communication interaction between two individuals.

Communication net: Communication interaction patterns in a group, whether it be two persons, three persons, etc.

Communicative act: A transmission of information, consisting of discriminative stimuli, from a source to a recipient.

Glossary

Competitive situation: One in which the achievement of an individual member's goal is possible only when other members do not achieve their goals.

Conscious personal goal: An awareness of the goal to satisfy a need.

Cooperative situation: One in which the achievement of an individual member's goal is contingent upon other members achieving their goals.

Decision making: Process of selecting among several alternatives.

Deductive reasoning: Begins with a general observation and leads to a specific conclusion.

Designated leader: Person who is assigned the primary responsibility for guiding a discussion.

Diffusion: The process of transmitting information to other people.

Directive feedback: Involves a value judgment of the speaker's message.

Discussion attitude: An individual's mental predisposition toward the topic, group members, and self.

Environment: The total external conditions and factors which surround us daily and are capable of influencing us as individuals.

Equifinality: The process whereby a system may reach its final state (equilibrium) from different initial conditions and in different ways.

Evidence: Facts and perceptions to be used to prove a point in determining problems and developing solutions.

Feedback: Message transmitted to indicate some level of understanding and/or agreement to a stimulus or verbal message from another.

Forum: Form of public discussion in which the full audience examines a topic or problem by giving impromptu speeches, taking issue with what has been said, asking and answering questions, and responding to comments under a chairperson's leadership.

Goal: The objective or end result that a group or an individual seeks to achieve.

Group: Three or more individuals collectively characterized as sharing reasonably similar attitudes, beliefs, values, and norms; these persons possess defined relationships to one another so that each participant's behavior has consequences for the other members of the group.

Group goal: The reason for the group's existence; the object or end result that a group seeks to achieve.

Heterophily: The extent to which people who interact are different with respect to attributes, beliefs, values, attitudes, social status, etc.

Homophily: The degree to which people who interact are similar in attributes, beliefs, values, attitudes, social status, etc.

Individual: A single person functioning in a reasonably isolated setting.

Inductive reasoning: Proceeds from a number of specific statements to a general conclusion.

Information: Knowledge about objects and events and about the relationships between objects and events.

Interpersonal conflict: The disagreement that most people call a "personality clash."

Interrole conflict: Results when individuals simultaneously occupy two roles which have incompatible role expectations.

Intrarole conflict: Exists when one or more groups of relevant others hold contradictory expectation for the same role.

Leaderless small group: All members of a group share the leadership function.

Leadership: Influential behavior, voluntarily accepted by group members, which moves a group toward its recognized goal, and/or maintains the group.

Leadershipless small group: No member provides actions which move the group toward its goal.

Listening: The selective process of attending to, hearing, understanding, and remembering aural (and at times visual) symbols.

Masking: Displaying a facial expression that is different from inward beliefs or feelings.

Motivation: Force that impels or repels an individual toward or from people or conditions of the group.

Need: A perceived discrepancy between perception of the present status and perception of an ideal status.

Nondirective feedback: An attempt by the listener to replicate the message.

Nonverbal communication: All communication forms other than the written or spoken word which impart meaning to an individual or group.

Open-minded: Objective reflection on the ideas presented by others.

Open system: One which interacts with the environment.

Panel: Public discussion in which a group of four to eight experts discuss a problem following the problem-solving format in front of an audience under a chairperson's leadership.

Passive listening: Absorbing the message without critically evaluating it or trying to understand or remember it.

Perception: An awareness or process of becoming aware of objects, events, conditions, and relations that are internal or external to a person, as a result of sensory stimulation.

Perception field: Composed of all those stimuli that are discriminated collectively at a given time and determines what is perceived, not what is there to perceive.

Personal goal: An objective or end result that an individual attempts to achieve.

Personal space: Thought of as an expanding and contracting bubble of air which surrounds a person. (Invasion of personal space may result in withdrawal.)

Presence of others: Unleashes social contingencies and constraints that are not always present when an individual works alone.

Principle of least group size: Group just large enough to include individuals with all the relevant skills to solve the problem, yet small enough to provide opportunities for individual participation.

Private discussions: Discussions not held before an audience; they do not involve participation by nonmembers.

Problem: A question proposed for solution or consideration implying certain obstacles which must be overcome.

Procedural conflict: Disagreement about the procedures to be followed in accomplishing the group goal.

Process: The dynamics of small group communication, or the changing nature of the individual and intragroup interactions.

Proposition: A statement advocating a particular plan or point of view.

Public discussions: Discussions held before an audience that often encourage participation from the audience members.

Purpose: That which makes a goal attractive; the objective or end result that a group or an individual seeks to achieve.

Reasoning: Used to demonstrate how the evidence proves a particular point.

Role: Set of behaviors that are expected of and/or displayed by the individual who occupies a particular position in a group's structure.

Role influence: Influence of one individual over another by power, authority, or persuasion.

Role playing: Procedure in which group members are assigned roles relevant to a particular problem under study and then are placed in situations where they act out, in an impromptu fashion, the implications of the situation.

Role skills: Characteristics that enable an individual to enact a role effectively.

Selective attention: The tendency to focus attention only on information that is consistent with personal attitudes, beliefs, and values.

Selective exposure: The tendency to avoid information which is felt to be potentially nonrewarding and/or inconsistency producing.

Selective perception: The tendency to perceive what is wanted or expected and to interpret the information in a manner consistent with expectations.

Selective retention: The tendency to forget information that is nonrewarding or inconsistent.

Self-concept: A person's attitude about or view of self.

Sensitivity training group: Special type of private discussion which is characterized by participants who come together, usually under the direction of a leader or trainer, to grow and develop intrapersonal and interpersonal effectiveness through a group experience.

Serious listening: Listening to analyze the evidence or ideas of others and making critical judgments about the validity and/or quality of the material presented.

Small group: A collection of individuals, from three to fifteen in number, who meet in face-to-face interaction over a period of time—generally with an assigned or assumed leader—who possess at least one common characteristic, and who meet with a purpose in mind.

Small group communication: Process of verbal and nonverbal face-to-face interaction in a small group.

Social listening: Employed in informal small group settings, and usually associated with interpersonal conversations and entertainment.

Solution getting: Process of discovering possible solutions to a particular problem.

Stereotypes: Categories individuals are placed in by first impressions and snap judgments from past experience; impressions quickly formed from physical appearance or small details of clothing.

Subgoals: Implied in the main goal or explicitly stated as subordinate goals by the group after the formulation of the main achievement goal.

System: A complex of interacting elements.

Systematic: Step-by-step plan for approaching problems in small group discussion.

Systems analysis: Suggests that one consider information about each element and the interrelationships among the elements to understand and make predictions about the system as a whole.

Task: An act, or its result, that a small group is required to perform, either by itself or with someone else; tasks are performed to accomplish goals.

Task conflict: Disagreement about the substance of the discussion.

Territory: Area over which ownership is felt. (Invasion of territory may result in aggressive behavior.)

Unconscious personal goal: A goal a person pursues without much awareness that he or she seeks it.